A prominent scholar of the Renaissance, Valery Rees is a senior member of the Language Department of the School of Economic Science in London. Among her published works are two essay collections she co-edited, *Marsilio Ficino: His Theology, His Philosophy, His Legacy* (2002) and *Laus Platonici Philosophi* (2011). She has appeared several times on BBC Radio 4's flagship programme *In Our Time* with Melvyn Bragg.

'Valery Rees's *From Gabriel to Lucifer* is a terrific read. An absorbing account of angels weaving across world history, ancient and modern. She finds comparisons and connections in civilizations which appear to be quite different, and presents what could seem mere antique speculations in a fresh and most thoughtful way. She gives us visions of worlds in which angels played their part as much as we reckon that particles do today. She brings to life an aspect of our past often forgotten or dismissed but compellingly relevant to the world view of their time.'

Melvyn Bragg

'Whether as mediators between the divine and human, or involved in the complex intertwining of good and evil, angels form a central part of human culture. In her fascinating book, *From Gabriel to Lucifer*, Valery Rees offers her readers a tantalising glimpse of the multi-faceted role angels have played in religion and history. She thereby helps restore to a more prominent position this much-neglected feature of human experience.'

Christopher Rowland
Dean Ireland's Professor of the Exegesis of Holy Scripture, University of Oxford, and author of *Blake and the Bible*

'Our fascination with angels and the angelic seems to go from strength to strength, and in her readable new book Valery Rees provides a lively and engaging account of why that is. Thoughtful and intelligent throughout, *From Gabriel to Lucifer* is a thorough and thought-provoking guide to the role of angels in many of the world's religions and cultures.'

Oliver Leaman
Professor of Philosophy and Zantker Professor of Judaic Studies, University of Kentucky

'This work of deep learning traces the idea of angelic beings through the history of the religions of the Book, and the cultures from which they emerged. Speculations so widespread and of such duration and elaboration plainly represent some general need or intuition; the book is an angel in itself, bringing us a message about human attempts to imagine and comprehend the mysterious universe we live in.'

Jill Paton Walsh
CBE, author of *Knowledge of Angels*
(shortlisted for the Booker Prize, 1994)

FROM GABRIEL TO LUCIFER

A CULTURAL HISTORY OF ANGELS

VALERY REES

I.B. TAURIS
LONDON · NEW YORK

Paperback edition published in 2016 by
I.B. Tauris & Co. Ltd
London • New York
www.ibtauris.com

Hardback edition first published in 2013 by
I.B. Tauris & Co. Ltd

References to websites were correct at the time of writing.

ISBN: 978 1 78453 431 8
eISBN: 978 0 85773 285 9

A full CIP record for this book is available from the British Library
A full CIP record is available from the Library of Congress

Library of Congress Catalog Card Number: available

Typeset by Free Range Book Design & Production Limited
Printed and bound in Sweden by ScandBook AB

TABLE OF CONTENTS

LIST OF ILLUSTRATIONS

Figure 1. Gilded altar angel by Jacques Bernus. One of a pair on the high altar of the Cathedral of Saint Siffrein, Carpentras, *c.*1700. Photograph courtesy of Chris Rees.

Figures 2–21 appear in the Plate Section

Figure 2. Winged figure of *Ma'at*, Egyptian Spirit of Truth, ink on paper, Naomi Spiers.

Figure 3. Zoroastrian winged *Fravashi*, ink on paper, Naomi Spiers.

Figure 4. Islamic angel, after illustrations in illuminated manuscripts of Al-Qazwīnī (Persian physician and astronomer, 1203–83). Ink on paper, Naomi Spiers.

Figure 5. Stained glass window by Edward Burne-Jones, made in the William Morris studio, 1878, for St Martin's Church, Brampton, Cumbria. By kind permission of the Rector and Parish of St Martin's. Photograph courtesy of Chris Rees.

Figure 6. Demon created by magic lantern. Giovanni Fontana, *Bellicorum instrumentorum liber*, *c.*1420. Bayerische Staatsbibliothek München, Cod. icon. 242, fol. 70r.

Figure 7. Paul Klee, *Angelus Novus*, 1920. Indian ink, coloured chalk and brown wash on paper, 318 x 242 mm. The Israel Museum, Jerusalem.

Carole and Ronald Lauder, New York. Reproduction by The Bridgeman Art Library.

Figure 8. *Hospitality of Abraham* by Andrei Rublev, sometimes known as *The Holy Trinity,* 1425–27, tempera on wood. State Tretyakov Gallery, Moscow. The Bridgeman Art Library.

Figure 9. Fra Angelico, *Annunciation* (*c.*1445), fresco. Museo di San Marco, Florence. The Bridgeman Art Library.

Figure 10. *Nike.* Gold earrings made either in Bolsena or Taranto, fourth–third century BCE. British Museum. Photograph courtesy of Anna R. Raia, the VRoma Project (www.vroma.org).

Figure 11. *Archangel Israfil 'Lord of the Horn'*, detached manuscript folio from *Aja'ib al-Makhluqat* (Wonders of Creation) by Al-Qazwīnī; early fifteenth century, opaque watercolour, ink and gold on paper (32.7 x 22.4 cm). Freer Gallery of Art, Smithsonian Institution, Washington, D.C.: Purchase, F1954.51, with kind permission.

Figure 12. *Annunciation*, from MS 101, *The Wolsey Epistle Lectionary*, from Christ Church, Oxford, folio 13 verso, with kind permission of The Governing Body of Christ Church, Oxford.

Figure 13. Colossal statue of a winged lion from the North-West Palace of Ashurnasirpal II, Neo-Assyrian, Nimrud (Iraq), ninth century BCE. © Trustees of the British Museum.

Figure 14. *Relief from an Altar*, by Benedetto da Rovezzano (1474–1554). Florence, marble, 1507–12. National Gallery of Art, Washington, D.C. Photograph courtesy of Chris Rees.

Figure 15. *Levites at the Temple*, accompanied in prayer by seraphic beings, papercut by Naomi Spiers, with kind permission of the artist.

Figure 16. Scorpion men encountered by Gilgamesh, guarding the Mountains of Meshu. From an Assyrian engraving, drawn by M. Faucher-Gudin, in G. Maspéro, *History of Egypt, Chaldea, Syria, Babylonia, and*

ACKNOWLEDGEMENTS

I am indebted to many people for their encouragement, suggestions, forbearance and practical help throughout the writing of this book. I would like to offer particular thanks:

To Charlie Taylor of the BBC and Melvyn Bragg for welcoming the idea of angels as a topic for Radio 4's *In Our Time*; to Alex Wright of I.B. Tauris for inviting me to turn the ideas raised there into a book; to Sonja Guentner who appeared at the crucial moment (as angels do), to Naomi Spiers, who has been a constant presence from afar, to Dr Cristina Neagu for inspiration and help with pictures, and to Toinette Lippe for wise advice throughout.

To the Trustees and staff of many libraries for access to their magnificent collections, but especially the British Library, Cambridge University Library, Christ Church, Oxford, the University Library at Claremont, California, the Freer and Sackler Galleries of the Smithsonian Institution, Washington, D.C. and to Professor Jonathan Steinberg for introducing me to the papers of Henry Latham in the Jerwood Library of Trinity Hall, Cambridge.

Among those who offered their own angel stories and their enthusiasm, to Majoie Rampersand, Jane Fetherston, Shlomo Fischl, Donna de Marta and Annette Currington. Verena and the late Robert Watson expounded mysteries of icon paintings; Eileen and Michael Posnick discussed 'the thirteen-petalled rose' of Kabbalah; Dr Maude van Haelen introduced me to George Benigno's angel treatise and Dr Edina Eszenyi brought angel researchers together at Leeds Medieval Congress in 2009. Antoinette Keulen and Professor Otto van Eikema Hommes added more tales, and offered a perfect refuge for writing at their home in Provence.

Rabbi Yuval Keren has been ready with constant help throughout. Together we presented two Angel sessions at the Limmud Conference in December 2010, and his knowledge of sources has been invaluable. Rabbi Naftali Brawer's short course on Angels and Demons at the London School of Jewish Studies in 2011 provided rich and stimulating discussions, and I thank Professor Moshe Idel, Professor Emeritus of the Hebrew University of Jerusalem, for guiding me to material I would not otherwise have found. For discussions on Arabic material I thank Amir Zahedi, Dr Masoome Soleymani and Professor Charles Burnett.

To all, named and unnamed, my warmest thanks. The greatest debt of gratitude is to my ever patient husband, for constant encouragement, wise comment, assiduous reading of several versions and for taking endless angel photographs. Lastly to my children and grandchildren whose constant visits were never interruptions but continual reminders of the immediacy of angelic presence in our lives.

INTRODUCTION

In our increasingly secular age, when the presence of angelic beings seems remote and unreal, angel imagery still holds an immense power of attraction. Books on angels have begun to proliferate and are no longer confined to the shelf of religious books, or theology, but in many bookshops now warrant a shelf of their own. This is curious, but perhaps parallels events over 400 years ago when the Reformed churches threw out imagery, rituals and superstitious practices, yet somehow angels managed to escape being banned. Clearly, people are fond of angels and they continue to be a source of inspiration and consolation.

But this book is offered in a spirit of enquiry: what did people understand by angels in times past, and what can they mean to us today? It is called *From Gabriel to Lucifer* in recognition of the fact that Gabriel is the first angel most people recognize, and Lucifer is the angel who disturbs us most. Gabriel is the only angel named in the Hebrew Bible. In the New Testament he appears to Zacharias, and his part in the story of Christ's nativity is familiar to all – or was until very recent times. For Muslims, Gabriel is Muhammad's instructor in the writing of the Qur'an. Lucifer is less familiar, though as 'light-bearer' he shares his name with the morning star, bearer of first light to the earth; yet he fell from his high estate and took on powers of darkness. Thus to many people Lucifer is synonymous with Satan.

These two angelic beings mark two poles of our enquiry, but it will range beyond both. We shall enquire into the earliest beginnings of angel lore, long before the three great religions of the book (Judaism, Christianity and Islam), and we will glimpse beyond their sphere in the modern world too. Many questions will be addressed, including the most basic ones: Did angels really exist? Do they still exist now?

What are they? What might they look like? How many different kinds
are there? Are they male or female? Can human beings become
angels? Were angels once human beings? These questions underlie the
themes of this book and will therefore be approached from different
angles in different chapters rather than in a single chronological
sweep. But within each theme there may also be a chronological story.
While each theme can be studied alone, it also stands inextricably
in relation to the rest. Some overlap is therefore unavoidable. I have
indicated this by adding references to other chapters, rather than by
repetition. These cross-references do not imply a need to jump about,
but merely indicate how one part may relate to another and be more
fully explored in a different way.

No prior knowledge is needed to follow the exploration presented
here – though, as in all such enquiries, any knowledge brought to
bear will enrich and shape the questions one can ask of the material
presented. My own journey with this topic began from a very small
and specific question, but my eyes were soon opened to an immensely
rich treasury of stories, allusions, imagery and insights in the literature
of all ages. In religious art, angels are ubiquitous. They may be loving
and protective, fierce and defensive, mysterious or reassuring. Angels
are with us even at the trivial level: we have angel-fish and angel
sharks; there are culinary angels, from angelica to angel cake and even
'angels on horseback'.[1] More seriously, we recognize as angels both
heavenly beings and human beings whose kindly intervention helps or
protects us.

Not surprisingly, there is some doubt as to what we mean by
'angels', and whether we should 'believe' in them or not. But belief is
not essential, and my aim is not to convince or persuade. In fact, it
may be better to approach the whole enquiry with an open mind. Even
if a rational discussion of angels may seem to some a contradictory
proposal, there is a level at which they may be the legitimate subject of
rational enquiry, especially in respect of their historic presence in our
own culture and those of our neighbours. At the same time, we are
bound to encounter ideas that take us into the realm of imagination
and memory, of inspiration and transcendence. The Greeks called this
the 'irrational', but irrational does not necessarily mean 'wrong'.

The task of understanding this vast topic can, of course, never be
complete. There will always be room for further discussion, discovery

and interpretation. I hope at least that the following pages will give a sense of the wonder and glory conveyed by the writings about angels that we are heir to, without any suggestion that we should abandon our reasoning faculty or our intelligence in approaching it.

Figure 1. Gilded altar angel by Jacques Bernus. One of a pair on the high altar of the Cathedral of Saint Siffrein, Carpentras, *c.*1700.

Chapter 1

ANGELS – UNIVERSAL AND ARCHETYPAL

What is an angel? According to its name, an angel is a messenger. The English word 'angel' derives directly from the Greek word $\alpha\gamma\gamma\varepsilon\lambda o\varsigma$ (*angelos*), and represents an earlier Hebrew word מלאך (*mal'akh*) whose meaning also centres on the role of messenger or minister. For those interested in etymology, the lexicon provides a three-letter root form for *mal'akh*, namely *l-a-kh*, with a core meaning cognate with an Arabic counterpart word for 'to send'.[1]

In many of the most familiar stories angels do indeed bear messages. They announce news of forthcoming births: to Abraham, to Samson's father, Manoah, and to John the Baptist's father, Zacharias; they give messages for action to Hagar, to Elijah, to David. The angel Gabriel announces the birth of Christ to Mary and, as Jibra'il, conveys the entire text of the Qur'an to the Prophet Muhammad. In all these cases, they are bringing messages from the divine world to men and women in the everyday human world. Angels also act as messengers from the human world to the divine. It is said that 'the soul speaks to the angel, the angel to the cherub, the cherub to God'.[2] This presumably is also a function of the angels to be found on altars in many a Catholic church in southern Europe (see Figure 1).

In other stories, angels prevent actions, as in the case of Balaam and his ass, or even of Socrates, if we can include his *daimon* as a kind of angel.[3] Angels protect, guard, and sing praise, sounding the music of the spheres, or playing on harps and lyres. All these aspects will be the subject of chapters to come, but at the outset it is good to acknowledge that angels belong equally to all three 'religions of the book', that is to Judaism, Christianity and Islam. They also belong to other less familiar cultures, to the Sumerians and Akkadians, the Assyrians and

Babylonians, to the Persians, Egyptians and Greeks, and possibly
farther afield too, to the Hindu Vedas, where they appear in the form
of Gandharvas. They can even be related to certain messenger spirits of
shamanism as found both among the ancient Altaic tribes of Asia and
the indigenous people of the Americas.

It would be tempting to reach for a universal definition that could
apply across all these cultural settings. This was certainly an aim of
some of the great ethnographers of the nineteenth and twentieth
centuries, seeking to identify archetypal symbols and images that
speak to deep psychological patternings within the human soul, found
universally across cultures. Carl Jung developed the idea of 'archetypes'
as organizing principles within the collective unconscious, and many
interpreters of myth and symbol have applied his theories fruitfully to
their fields. For nearly 2,000 years before Jung, one way of thinking about
'angel' was indeed as a kind of universal higher mind (see Chapter 2).
Yet if we wish to consider the idea of angel as a psychological archetype
we must first decide whether we are considering a simple messenger,
a protector, a concept of goodness, a motivating idea, or a soul free
from bodily form. For angels fulfil all these roles. So we shall proceed
by considering a selection of examples of angels across the centuries,
celebrating their diversity, and exploring the many different strains of
rich tradition on which we can draw.

What we can say at the outset is that angels cover quite a large
class of beings; they are generally unseen as they proceed about their
business, but are able to become visible when necessary. They thus
belong most of the time to the world of unseen forces. They carry out
their tasks according to the will of God rather than their own will. In
fact, in most traditions they are considered not to have any will of their
own, and hence to be incapable of the kind of rational choice, devotion,
sacrifice or compassion to which humans may aspire. They are not
necessarily, therefore, any higher than humans – just different. And yet,
according to legend, they had enough free will that some could choose
to rebel.

Angels in early times are male, and are generally (but not always)
represented as winged. During the Middle Ages there was much
discussion about whether they had bodies at all. If they did, of what
were these bodies made? According to some, their bodies were formed
of fire and ice. The apparent contradiction of these materials thus set

angels apart as defying the laws of physics. We recently saw just such an admixture of fire and ice in clouds of volcanic ash, though without it appearing to generate any new clouds of angels![4] According to others, their bodies were of 'subtle substance', suggesting something other than normal matter, and, if this was the case, did they actually occupy space? If so, did they occupy a particular place singly, one at a time, or could many of them crowd together and, as the saying goes, 'dance on the head of a very fine needle without jostling one another'? This question has often been considered as the quintessence of pointless discussion ascribed to scholastic theologians of the thirteenth and fourteenth centuries. In fact, it seems instead to have been thought up by the satirical writer François Rabelais in France (*Pantagruel*, 1532), picked up by the philosopher Ralph Cudworth in the seventeenth century, and then repeated by Isaac D'Israeli in his *Curiosities of Literature*, of 1791. Thomas Aquinas (1225–74), an original scholastic, asks much more reasonably, 'Whether a multiplicity of angels can co-exist in the same place?'[5] If they need space, it would indicate some degree of materiality to their existence. If they need no space, then they would have even greater freedom of access to exert their influence upon human beings, with good angels prompting towards good action and evil demons urging towards the bad. Five hundred years later, Emanuel Swedenborg (1688–1772), a respected scientist and devout Christian, sagely observed that evil demons may also urge us towards good things, but of a purely passing nature. This therefore distracts us from higher aims. We each have, he taught, at least two angels and two spirits accompanying us. Claiming to have conversed freely with them himself, he felt that establishing a channel of communication with them was vital.[6] In fact, many have thought that angels interact with human beings either one at a time, or in such pairs.

To get a sense of how our ideas of angels have been formed, I shall examine a series of biblical texts that will serve as a kind of introduction and basis for comparison with other ideas considered in later chapters. The majority of these texts will be from the Jewish scriptures, the 'Old Testament', simply because these so strongly set the pattern for later developments. But there is a vast literature from later periods that is also important.

The first angelic being to be mentioned in the Bible is a cherub (Genesis 3:24).[7] After Adam and Eve have been expelled from the

Garden of Eden, we are told that God 'placed at the east of the garden of Eden Cherubim[s] and a flaming sword which turned every way, to keep the way of the tree of life'. Cherubim are clearly guardians or protectors. Figures of two cherubim with wings outstretched were also made for the Ark of the Covenant to guard it (Exodus 25:18), and since no instructions were given to the craftsman, Bezalel, about their appearance, it was clearly assumed that he (and everyone else) knew what they looked like. For us, however, it is puzzling unless we realize that the origin of the cherubim is to be found in the winged protective figures of ancient Mesopotamia. This will be discussed in Chapter 5. Cherubim flank the mercy seat, the throne of God's presence (Exodus 25:18 and 37:8), and in David's song of deliverance from King Saul (II Samuel 22:11, repeated in Psalm 18:10), the Lord 'rode upon a cherub and did fly: and he was seen upon the wings of the wind'.[8]

The puzzle is compounded for those who think of cherubim (the plural of cherub) in terms of chubby infants with wings and smiling faces found in European art from the Renaissance onwards. Also called *putti*, their very name suggests a human origin; from the Latin *putus*, 'boy', though it is thought that they were inspired by the *spiritelli* of Greek antiquity. These originally denoted the soul of the recently deceased. They were popular on ancient sarcophagi in second-century Rome, and are seen again in tombstone decorations from the sixteenth century onwards, following the revival of interest in classical art, while their painted cousins adorn many an allegorical scene, denoting the presence of *genii* (guiding spirits) or other sprightly powers.

The next kind of angelic beings in the Bible make their appearance almost unnoticed by some, in two short verses at the beginning of Genesis 6:

> And it came to pass, when men began to multiply on the face of the earth, and daughters were born unto them that the sons of God saw the daughters of men that they were fair, and they took them wives, whomsoever they chose.

Eliezer the Great, a rabbi of the first century CE, asserted that the 'sons of God' were angels who fell from heaven. This story marks the moment when a limit is set to the life of mankind, a span of 120 years. We are then mysteriously told that 'the Nephilim were in the earth in those days'. Much has been built on this line, as will be seen in Chapter 11. For now, we need only note that the children of those 'sons of God'⁹ and 'daughters of men' were in some way very special: they were the 'mighty men that were of old, the men of renown' (Genesis 6:4). According to tradition, however, this should not be read positively. The great medieval commentator Rashi[10] (1040–1105) tells us that the Nephilim were so named because they 'fell' (*naphal*) and caused the world to fall. Their children, he says, were 'mighty' in respect of their rebellion, while 'men of renown' means men who brought desolation on the world.

Messenger angels make their first biblical entrance at the door of Abraham's tent in Genesis 18, yet this too is a mysterious entry. Verse 1 tells us that 'the Lord appeared unto him' as he sat in the tent door in the heat of the day. But what he saw, when he lifted his eyes, was 'three men'. He ran to meet them, and welcomed them in, preparing the finest food for them. Furthermore, unlike some angels we learn of later, they ate the food he prepared. Then they asked where Sarah was, and one of the angels delivers the message that Sarah would give birth to a son a year hence. Sarah overhears this, hiding behind the tent door, and thinks the idea hilarious, given her advanced age and that of her husband. Then it is God who speaks, not any angel (but perhaps God is one of three men/angels?), asking Abraham, 'Is anything too hard for the Lord?' He repeats the message about the coming child, and Sarah is so embarrassed that she denies laughing, but God says 'Nay, but thou didst laugh'. The angels then continue their journey, for they have a message also to deliver to Abraham's nephew Lot, and Abraham goes with them – but he is clearly still in company and conversation with God.

The scene that follows is the occasion for Abraham's great argument with God, pleading with him for the lives of the people of Sodom and Gomorrah. By the beginning of Genesis 19, the angels are at the gates of Sodom. It is the turn of Lot to receive them hospitably, and they try to protect him from the disaster that is about to unfold. But now there are only two of them.

In this story we are hard pressed to tell whether all three are really angels, or just human messengers. Rashi solves the problem neatly by saying that God sent three angels to appear as humans. His authority, the Talmud tractate *Bava Metzia*, even names them as Michael, Raphael and Gabriel. Or is it two messengers (who at Genesis 19:10 are again called 'men') and the Almighty himself in person? At all events, the three visitors have surely come as messengers, in that they have not just one message to deliver, but two: one for Abraham, and one for Lot. *Bava Metzia* finds a third 'message' in the healing of Abraham, which is Raphael's task – arguing that any angel can only perform one mission – and this also explains why only two proceed to Sodom.[11]

Even though they do not have wings and are called men, tradition clearly records the three as angels. In the Eastern Orthodox Church they became a traditional subject for icon painting, as a representation of the Trinity (see Andrei Rublev in Chapter 4), and there they do have wings, in spite of the text clearly calling them men.

The child that was promised to Sarah (Genesis 18:10) is duly born, and named Isaac (which means 'laughter'), but further angelic interventions are required to ensure that he grows up to fulfil his destiny. His mother, Sarah, becomes worried for the future on account of the behaviour of Ishmael, the son that Hagar, her Egyptian servant, had already borne to Abraham. She prevails upon Abraham to turn Hagar and Ishmael out of the house. In Genesis 21:17, 'the angel of the Lord', whom one might think to be a superior kind of angel, is sent to give succour to Hagar as she wanders in the desert. Once again, when Abraham is tested at Mount Moriah (Genesis 22: the 'binding of Isaac'), it is 'the angel of the Lord' who calls to him out of heaven and stays his hand from slaying his son.

In Genesis 24:7 and 24:40, God sends an angel to accompany Eliezer on his journey to find a wife for Isaac. Angels appear to Isaac's son Jacob when he falls asleep by the wayside at Luz. He dreams of angels going up and down upon a ladder that stretched from earth to heaven (Genesis 28:11-12). Many commentators have noted that the 'ascending' comes first, before 'descending': these are angels who walk upon the earth, and only then go up to heaven. In a book whose every word and phrase is laden with meaning, this is of course significant.

We mostly think of God as somewhere at the top of the ladder: 'the Lord stood above it' (King James Version and derivatives). Yet that phrase can also be construed as 'the Lord stood beside him' (Jewish Publication Society and derivatives).[12] One could argue that God, being everywhere, is both at the head of the ladder and at its foot at one and the same time. But if God was already at the foot of the ladder, where were the angels going? And why do they need a ladder at all when they have wings? In fact, is it even a ladder? The Hebrew word *sulom* occurs nowhere else. It could therefore indicate something more like a slope or a Mesopotamian Ziggurat.[13] These ancient structures were also considered to be gateways to heaven. The possibilities for interpretation of Jacob's dream are endless, but he is clearly struck by the holiness of the place and by the angels' movements.

The experience of this dream vision transforms Jacob. No longer 'the deceiver', he becomes dedicated to serving God, and enters into a covenant with Him. He also calls the place Beth-el, because it is 'the house of God, and the gate of heaven' (Genesis 28:17, 19). In Genesis 31:11, the 'angel of God' speaks to Jacob, to resolve an impasse with his treacherous father-in-law, Laban. Once again, this is in a dream, so shifting identities should not surprise us: when this angel speaks, he says 'I am the God of Bethel, where you anointed the pillar, and vowed a vow unto me.'

Jacob's famous encounter with an angel who would not reveal his name (Genesis 32:24-32) is discussed in detail in Chapter 10. But with a degree of mystification we are now recognizing as usual, we should already note that this angel will be described in the text only as a 'man'. However, on his deathbed (Genesis 48:16) Jacob speaks of him as the angel who redeemed him, and invokes that angel's blessings on his grandsons, Ephraim and Manasseh. Moreover, the larger episode in which that encounter is set begins with angels: Jacob leaves Laban who pursues him to Gilead, after which, 'Jacob went on his way, and the angels of God met him' (Genesis 32:1-2). He recognized them as 'God's host'[14] and already understood the life-changing nature of his journey even before his night-time encounter.

The 'angel of the Lord' appears again in Exodus 3:2, this time to Moses, manifesting in a flame of fire in the burning bush. Yet when the voice speaks from the bush to Moses, as before, it is not the angel, but God himself. There are clearly ambiguities in what we might understand by 'angel', in particular, 'the angel of the Lord'.

The same 'angel of the Lord' (or another?) served as a guide to the children of Israel in the wilderness (Exodus 23:20-23, and mentioned three times again thereafter); elsewhere it is none other than God himself who goes before them as a pillar of cloud by day and a pillar of fire by night (Exodus 13:21). These contradictions are the very stuff of textual exploration. We could get frustrated by them, and many no doubt do, but it is far more fruitful to see them as inviting further examination.[15]

The next two appearances of angels are unquestionably messengers. Balaam and his ass encounter a fierce angel, sent to prevent Balaam from uttering the powerful curse upon the Israelites that he had been commissioned to do by the Moabite king, Balak (Numbers 22:22-35). Again, at Bochim, an angel of the Lord causes the Israelites to repent (Judges 2:1-4). But the angel who appears to Gideon (Judges 6:12-24) to persuade him to take on the task of delivering the people from the Midianites, performs his sign with fire, and then vanishes, being replaced by the voice of the Almighty. The angel, on the other hand, who appears to Manoah's wife, to announce that she will no longer be barren, has all the appearance of an ordinary man, albeit a 'man of God' (Judges 13:2-23). He tells her to abstain from wine and unclean things (suggesting perhaps that she had not been living a blameless life). Manoah feels he needs to know much more, and the angel duly comes to her again in the field, and even waits while she runs to fetch her husband. Like Jacob's angel, he will not give his name, nor will he eat the food they offer him. In fact, it is only when they offer the food to the Lord that they realize they have been visited by an angel:

> For it came to pass when the flame went up toward heaven from
> off the altar, that the angel of the Lord ascended in the flame
> of the altar. And Manoah and his wife looked on it, and fell on
> their faces to the ground.
>
> (Judges 13:20)

It was only when he failed to reappear that Manoah, a simple soul, knew for sure he was an angel – yet even then he says to his wife, 'We shall surely die, because we have seen God.'

From all these passages we begin to get a sense of angels as messengers who metamorphose sometimes between their own identity and that of him whom they serve. To this we may add several instances of angels in the book of Psalms, who offer guardianship and protection of the individual, which will also be discussed in Chapter 10.

The later prophetic visions of angels shift into an entirely different register. King David saw a vision of an angel standing between earth and heaven, with a drawn sword in his hand (I Chronicles 21:16). The Prophets Isaiah and Ezekiel both had visions of angels that were of immense influence throughout following ages.

Isaiah lived in the eighth century BCE. In fact, his vision of angels can be historically dated to the 730s BCE. Scholars are agreed that the second half of the biblical book ascribed to Isaiah dates from the time of the Babylonian exile nearly two centuries later, but the part with which we are concerned belongs to the eighth century, when Tiglath-Pileser III was a mighty king in Assyria, Egypt was somewhat in eclipse under its twenty-third dynasty and the epics of Homer were being composed in Greece. Isaiah's vision is the first to take us right into the realm of the angels:

> In the year that King Uzzi'ah died I saw the Lord sitting upon a throne, high and lifted up; and his train filled the temple. Above him stood the seraphim; each had six wings: with two he covered his face, and with two he covered his feet, and with two he flew. And one called to another and said: 'Holy, holy, holy is the Lord of hosts; the whole earth is full of his glory.' And the foundations of the thresholds shook at the voice of him who called, and the house was filled with smoke.
>
> And I said: 'Woe is me! For I am lost; for I am a man of unclean lips, and I dwell in the midst of a people of unclean lips; for my eyes have seen the King, the Lord of hosts!' Then flew one of the seraphim to me, having in his hand a burning coal which he had taken with tongs from the altar. And he touched my mouth, and said: 'Behold, this has touched your lips; your guilt is taken away, and your sin forgiven.' And I heard the voice of the Lord saying, 'Whom shall I send, and who will go for us?' Then I said, 'Here am I! Send me.'
>
> (Isaiah 6:1-11)[16]

Isaiah's vision starts from the highest: he sees the Lord upon a throne. In his train are all the ministering angels, specifically the seraphim. These are six-winged creatures, who use their wings for flight but also for modesty, and protection. Close as they are to God, they must protect their own eyes from the direct sight of his glory, and they cover their bodies for modesty: rabbinic interpretations suggest either that the word 'feet' is used as a euphemism for their private parts – though arguably angels have no sexuality and therefore nothing to hide. Alternatively, according to one *midrash*,[17] they cover their feet because, as in Ezekiel's later description, their feet are 'straight' and 'like the sole of a calf's foot'. By association, this would be a reminder of Israel's sin of the golden calf, so they discreetly cover them!

These winged creatures clearly have the hands of a man, and manipulate the coals from the altar to good effect, achieving what would not be possible with mere human hands, for the fire that purifies here does not scorch or burn them. More importantly, these seraphim seem to be wholly engaged in a communal act of praising the holiness of God and his world-filling glory.

The winged creatures of Isaiah are very different from those of the other great visionary, Ezekiel. Ezekiel was a member of the dynastic family of priests, and was amongst those carried off into captivity by Nebuchadnezzar, from Jerusalem to Babylon in 597 BCE. One day, five years into the experience of exile, he was on the bank of the river Chebar or Kevar when the heavens opened, and he saw a vision, related in the book of Ezekiel, chs 1–2. He describes the experience as 'the hand of the Lord' being upon him.

> And I looked and behold, a storm wind came out of the north, a
> great cloud, and a fire flaring up, and a brightness was about it,
> and out of the midst of it, as it were the colour of electrum.
>
> (Ezekiel 1:4)[18]

Also out of the fire appeared four living creatures, which appeared to have the likeness of a man.

> And every one had four faces, and every one had four wings.
> And their feet were straight feet; and the sole of their feet was
> like the sole of a calf's foot: and they sparkled like the colour of
> burnished brass. And they had the hands of a man under their
> wings on their four sides … they turned not when they went.
>
> (Ezekiel 1:6-9)

The description of these living beings with outstretched wings is precise, and bears comparison with those winged beings who appear on gateways in Assyrian and Babylonian architecture – the original cherubim (see Chapter 5) – and in the temple of Solomon. After these 'living beings', he saw 'wheels, yet the wheels seemed also to have life, and the 'spirit of the living creature was in the wheels' which were emerald[19] in colour, and moved wherever the spirit was minded to go. Over these beings was a firmament of ice; the noise of all the wings was like the noise of great waters, of a tumult, of an army. But then the creatures stood still and let down their wings. Above them was the firmament, and above that, a sapphire throne,[20] and more fire, electrum and rainbow brilliance. All these things are described in terms of 'appearance' and 'likeness' rather than actual fact. Above everything else, 'was the appearance of the likeness of the glory of the Lord'. After he has seen this, Ezekiel hears a voice, and a conversation follows, instructing him how to lead the people through the most testing of times, and a curious incident of being required to eat a parchment scroll (Ezekiel 2:9–3:3).

Even leaving aside the strange figure of the 'appearance of a man' seated upon the throne with whom this conversation takes place, and who seems to represent God rather than an angel, none of the beings of Ezekiel's vision fit easily with our idea of angels, and indeed he never calls them angels. Nevertheless they come to be classed among the angels by later writers, because they are among those powerful agents of God's bidding whose influence can be felt.

The message that Ezekiel needs to hear is spoken to him by 'the voice of one that spoke'. The text does not say 'the voice of the Lord', nor does it say it was of any of the 'living creatures' already mentioned. In fact, biblical scholars have remarked on the reticence of this verse compared with the great detail of all that precedes it. Because the voice addresses him as 'son of man', we deduce that in spite of his transcendent vision, Ezekiel remains a human being, just like ourselves. His vision, which came to be known as 'The Chariot' (*Merkavah*) inspired centuries of endeavour by mystics to follow him into the divine realm, and it will be further discussed in Chapter 7.

The vision of Isaiah also formed a focus for speculation among the mystics. Studied in conjunction with the Chariot, it too gave rise to a collection of interpretative texts known as *Heikhalot* literature, meaning descriptions of the halls or palaces of the upper world. These generally discern seven firmaments of heaven, filled with the angelic hosts. Rivers and bridges connect the palaces. Knowledge of secret seals is required by the soul who wishes to cross these and many dangers are met upon the way.

There are also books of mystical import among the *Apocrypha* and *Pseudepigrapha*. The Greek word *apocrypha* simply means 'hidden', and refers to that group of books which remained associated with the Bible but not fully accepted into it for liturgical use. The contents of the Apocrypha vary according to different traditions. Thus, for example, there were books included in the Greek Septuagint and the Latin Vulgate that were excluded from the Jewish and Protestant canons of the Old Testament. How and when the canon was set in each tradition is a complex matter and still subject to scholarly debate. Pseudepigrapha are writings attributed to a figure from the past, even though they were written long after. Amongst these is the *Book of Enoch*, which exists in three quite different forms.[21] Attributed to Enoch, grandfather of Noah, but actually written in stages between the third and first centuries BCE, this book was accepted as canonical by the Ethiopian Orthodox church, but not by others. Further important writings on angels include the *Book of Jubilees*, which claims to present further knowledge revealed secretly to Moses by the angels while he was on Mount Sinai, and the *Ascension of Isaiah*, from the first or second century of the Christian era. Some of these are described as 'apocalyptic', as they contain revelations of times to come. Further apocalyptic writings and Gnostic texts add to our fund of sources on these matters, some long known, others discovered more recently at Nag Hammadi (a Gnostic library, discovered in 1945) and Qumran (the Dead Sea Scrolls, found between 1947 and 1956 but still being assessed and interpreted). Among the latter are the *Songs of the Sabbath Sacrifice*, describing the angelic liturgy of worship around the throne of God in the heavenly realm. All these works will contribute to the themes of later chapters.

Returning now to the later books in the Bible, the vision of the Prophet Zechariah, occurred towards the end of the Babylonian captivity, in 520–518 BCE.[22] Angels intervene with the Lord to plead for Jerusalem to be spared and restored (Zechariah 1:7-17) and, as in many apocalyptic stories, they explain to the prophet what he is seeing.

In Ecclesiastes, at least one angel is involved in judgement: 'Suffer not thy mouth to cause thy flesh to sin; neither say thou before the angel, that it [was] an error' (Ecclesiastes 5:6). King David was likened to such an angel: 'for as an angel of God, so [is] my lord the king to discern good and bad' (II Samuel 14:17). Angels can also bring death and destruction. An angel is entrusted with slaying 185,000 Assyrians (II Kings 19:35) and the sword of the angel that David saw is plague or pestilence, sent by God to punish the people (I Chronicles 21:12-27). Three days of this punishment is presented as the alternative to three months of war, or three years of famine. David chose direct punishment in the knowledge that divine judgement is accompanied by divine mercy.

In the story of the exodus of the Jews from Egypt, it is sometimes said that the angel of death passed over during the night and slew all the Egyptian firstborn. But the text itself is quite clear that it was God himself and not an angel who slew the firstborn (Exodus 12:12, 23 and 29; 13:15) and rabbinic commentary, incorporated in the Passover *Haggadah* stresses that.[23] So angels are not always required to play the part of agents of destruction. Even when they are, they are not supposed to take sides: when the Red Sea closed over the Egyptian pursuers and the Israelites were saved, God rebukes the angels for celebrating their escape: 'How can you sing when my creatures are drowning?' (*Exodus Rabbah* 23:7).

In the New Testament we find angels of every hue. In the Gospels, we have the archangel (Gabriel) of annunciation (Luke 1:26-38),[24] the angel who appeared to the shepherds (Luke 2:9), the angel who troubled the waters (John 5:4), the angel who descended from heaven in a great earthquake and opened the sepulchre where Jesus was buried (Matthew 28:2) and we learn that there are angels in heaven representing every child (Matthew 18:10). In the Book of Acts, we find the angel who opened the prison not just once (Acts 5:19) but twice (Acts 12:5-9) – though Peter seems not to have been sure if it was real or a dream; the angel of death strikes Herod dead (Acts 12:23) and we learn that the Pharisees and the Sadducees differed in their views about angels (Acts 23:8). On several occasions angels speak, though how they speak would become a subject for much later discussion.[25] An angel supported Paul in Corinth (Acts 18:9) and at the shipwreck in Malta (Acts 27:23). Paul also warns that Satan can transform himself into an angel of light (2 Corinthians 11:14). The Book of Revelation is positively crammed with angels, acting as messengers, guides, keepers of knowledge, keepers of the seals, winged hosts and participants in the last judgement. The angel who instructs John (Revelation 1:13-15) has eyes 'as a flame of fire' and feet of brass, reminiscent of Ezekiel's angels, while others have six wings and cry 'Holy, holy, holy' like those of Isaiah (Revelation 4:8). Satan himself appears as an angel in 2 Corinthians 11:14 as already noted and in Revelation 12:7-9 has his own troops of angels against whom Michael leads the fight. Finally, at the end of days, the angel will blow 'the last trump' (Revelation 9:14 and I Corinthians 15:52).

These, then, are the biblical angels, who loom large in our idea of angels to this day because they have been the basis for images in art across the world. They multiply their presence at Christmas time in children's nativity plays and on Christmas cards, where musician angels seem to have special appeal. The Christian angels had their origin in Jewish and non-Jewish sources. They also have their direct counterparts in Islam.

The Archangel Jibra'il reveals the Qur'an to Muhammad in much the same way as angels reveal knowledge to Enoch or St John the Divine. According to the Hadith (the body of traditions related to Muhammad that form a supplement to the Qur'an) the Archangel Israfil will sound the trumpet on the Day of Judgement and at the first blast everything will be destroyed (referring to Qur'an sura 69:13-14 and 80:33-37); a second blast will announce the resurrection. This alludes to sura 36:51, and may surely be compared to the last trump of I Corinthians 15:52, I Thessalonians 4:16 or the blowing of the *shofar* (ram's horn) for repentance in Judaism. Recording angels are mentioned in the Qur'an at sura 82:11, charged with writing down the good and evil deeds of each human being. Messenger angels are sent to assist humans in sura 13:10-14. The angel Mikha'il is only mentioned once by name, in sura 2:98, but occurs several times in the Hadith, where he is known for his mercy, and is charged with the care of plants and rain, and with nourishing mankind. Mikha'il was one of the three angels sent to Abraham when Sarah laughed (sura 11:69-77). It is recorded that he never laughs. In the biblical version, we saw that those angels were indistinguishable from men, and they ate the food Abraham placed before them. In the Qur'an, however, Abraham notices that the angels do not eat, which immediately rouses his suspicion and fear, so they announce themselves and their mission. The angel of death is also present in the Qur'an, in sura 32:11. Jibra'il may be likened to Gabriel, Mikha'il to Michael, and Israfil to Raphael. In spite of some differences, which will be observed in their due place, much of what can be said of angels applies to all three 'religions of the book'.

Having briefly surveyed angels of scripture, what can we derive from them in terms of the archetypes mentioned at the outset? What does it mean to be a messenger? Or a guardian or protector? Or an agent of destruction or salvation? Do the angels of scripture bear any similarity to comparable figures from other cultures beyond our own?

The Taino people of the Caribbean used to travel in the world of spirits on a wooden throne. It is described as

> a stool of great power, a strange and exotic ceremonial seat
> carved into the shape of an otherworldly being, half-human,
> half-animal, which would take its owners travelling between
> worlds, and gave them the power of prophecy.[26]

The spirit embodied in this seat is perhaps akin to depictions of cherub thrones in the ancient Near East. However it is thought that the rituals associated with its use most likely involved a change in the state of consciousness of the user. Rituals in South America today make use of the psychoactive Amazonian potion *ayahuasca*, which allows the user to see things that are beyond normal perception. Shamanic rites the world over make use of various leaves and plants to induce trance states, and bring about contact with the gods or the spirit world.

Does this then apply to visions of angels in traditions nearer to home? Medieval mystics certainly engaged in fasting and other techniques which, intentionally or otherwise, enhanced sensitivity and perception, resulting sometimes in visions of angels or the blessed Virgin.[27] There have also been a few scholarly voices asserting that certain biblical texts are indicative of hallucinogen use.[28] Whether or not such theories can ever be proven, it would be wrong to consider visions as 'disturbances', or solely the product of mind-altering techniques, for the interpretation of what is seen in a vision belongs also to the creative imagination. This perhaps is why the angels and spirits are so perennial a theme in both religious and secular art.

In Egyptian iconography there are winged figures of Isis shown resting over the heart of the deceased on coffin cases, as a reminder of how Isis restored life to her dead brother Osiris with a beating of her wings. Even more remarkable in our context are the figures of the human soul represented as birds with a human head. If proper funeral rites were followed, these winged figures would be able to fly back and forth from the tomb freely, giving the soul of the deceased an afterlife between earth and heaven, which would imply a mingling with gods and angels. There is also a winged figure, *Ma'at*, who represents the spirit of Truth and the principle of harmony or order (see Figure 2). From her, aspirants seek true knowledge and an understanding of justice. She has the status of a goddess – a shining one – and she possesses knowledge of good and evil, and knowledge of law, both the moral law that should bind mankind and the laws of nature. Our Judaeo-Christian-Islamic angels are also resplendent figures, shining with radiance. They too have knowledge of good and evil, and of truth. *Ma'at* also has knowledge of the courses of stars, a gift with which the 'watchers' of the *Book of Jubilees* were also endowed. Just as angels record a person's deeds for final judgement, so is *Ma'at* involved in judging the dead. Her feather is placed in the balance against the hearts of the dead: according to how they weigh against it, their fate in the afterlife is decided.

In Sumeria, Akkadia and the later Mesopotamian kingdoms of Assyria and Babylon, winged figures conveyed strength and protection. They guarded access to holy places and royal treasures. Besides the large winged figures already mentioned (in connection with Ezekiel's vision, but see also Chapter 5), many small figurines and amulets survive of a winged figure called Pazuzu, associated with the power of storms and wind. Pazuzu was invoked as a protector against famine and plague. He is usually depicted with a man's body, a lion-like face, bird-feet and two pairs of feathered wings.

The Hindu tradition also has winged beings who act as intermediaries. In the earliest texts, such as the Rig Veda, there was only one Gandharva, guardian deity of the Moon, and knower of the secrets of heaven.[29] By the time of the great epic poems, Gandharvas became spirits of nature, generally male, who can fly through the air and serve as celestial musicians.[30] They also are connected with ecstatic states of mind, and they regulate the courses of the stars. It is said that they issued forth from the creator, 'imbibing melody and drinking of the goddess of speech'.[31] Among their female counterparts are Apsarasas, embodiments of loveliness.[32] These are sometimes called water-nymphs or water-sprites, since they dwell in cloud-vapour. Their beauty is irresistible and it is sometimes said they are sent to earth to distract sages from an asceticism so powerful it might win them victory over the gods. Yakshas, sometimes called 'mysterious persons', are considered to be tutelary spirits.

In ancient Greece there are plenty of winged figures among the gods, spirits and *daemons*. Hermes is a winged messenger-god, presiding over many things from eloquence to trade and trickery. Zeus himself occasionally dons wings, as when he chose to ride upon eagle's wings to carry off the young Ganymede to be his cupbearer.[33] Why an eagle? Perhaps because it was traditionally honoured for its nobility, its ability to gaze at the sun with unblinking eyes, and its capacity to fly higher than other birds, swooping directly down for its prey.

Greek deities later became wholly identified with their nearest Roman equivalents, so that Mercury and Jupiter may be considered essentially as Hermes and Zeus. Likewise, Juno, or Hera, wife of Jupiter-Zeus. In addition to her gorgeous peacock, she had a winged messenger attending on her. This was the iridescent goddess Iris, personification of the rainbow. Every star was also believed by the Greeks to have its own chain of daemons.

For Zoroastrians the winged figure of the *Fravashi*, represented as a pair of wings with a central disc, often with a superimposed human figure, is both guardian angel through life and spiritual model (see Figure 3). *Fravashis* represent divine energy, and are charged with preserving order in the creation, but each one also has a relationship with a human soul, presenting by example an ideal towards which that soul may strive and with which it may ultimately, in death, unite. This may not be a very ancient Zoroastrian belief (it is thought to have been a nineteenth century adaptation), but it does reflect the universal appeal of guardian angel figures. In the place of archangels, Zoroastrians have seven immortal Amesha Spentas (beneficent immortals), providing inexhaustible funds of intelligence, light, devotion, good health and other such imperishable qualities.

The same qualities have also been represented among our more familiar angels: they tell people what they need to know, they convey illumination, promote tasks that would otherwise be left undone and prevent mishap; they ensure that justice is done, they defend and protect – and they accomplish all this by powers that seem to elude all earthly explanation. In this sense we can consider angels as archetypal models of knowledge, power and protection.

But what does it mean to be a messenger, or a protector? Simple observation tells us that even in the human realm, to be an effective messenger one must first truly hear the message. This means that the mind must be clear of other competing thoughts at the moment that the message is entrusted. It must then be carried faithfully to its destination, without diminution or embellishment and be delivered in an appropriate way, at an appropriate time. To be able to judge what is appropriate requires a continuation of that calm, unruffled state of clear perception in which the message was initially received, so as to see and assess every nuance of the recipient's frame of mind. For who ever heard of an angel delivering a message that was not heeded? We may therefore infer that angels have a steadiness and clarity of mind that enables them to carry out their appointed task. Were this not so, angelic communications might be as apt to go wrong as human ones, and we would be surrounded by lost and discarded messages, angelic communiqués that we have chosen to ignore.

Secondly, to be a protector or a guardian, also requires a wide and alert view. The ability to perceive the slightest change, to detect motion so small it has hardly yet happened in order to guide one's charge past any hazard, or to summon sufficient power to defeat an adversary, these too are qualities which require a steadiness of vision, a comprehensive gaze, nerves of steel, adamantine courage, and yet a loving heart. This kind of guardianship is indeed angelic, though not entirely unknown within the human realm. Moreover, when a person is rescued from danger, illness or distress, a human agent of rescue is apt to be regarded as an angel, even by those who might normally regard themselves as total non-believers. This lends weight to the idea that angels may be true archetypes in the Jungian sense, that is, pervasive symbols in the collective unconscious. If so, from Gabriel to Lucifer, they would be symbols of calm clarity of mind, to which may be added the imprint of divinity, justice and companionship. These qualities, which can manifest in humans or angels, will form a foundation as we follow the angels more closely through questions of location, character and history.

Chapter 2

FILLING THE SPACE
BETWEEN EARTH AND HEAVEN

> A man is to know and understand, that all from the Earth to
> the Firmament is full (and no place is empty) of Troops, of
> spirits, together with their Chieftains all of which have their
> Residence and Fly up and down in the Air; some of them incite
> to peace, others to War; some to Goodness, and Life, others to
> Wickedness and Death.
>
> (George Hamond, *A Modest Enquiry*)[1]

Since angels may be messengers, guardians, protectors, and agents of
salvation or destruction, it is no wonder that they seem to be everywhere.
But how do they fit into the greater picture, into the cosmos as a
whole?

When God is referred to as the Lord of Hosts, it is easy to imagine
him surrounded by troops of angels. Some theologians have suggested
that the title 'Lord of Hosts' referred originally to an early Semitic moon
god, with the hosts being the stars that fill the clear night skies. Others
have taken these heavenly hosts as indications of a shift from polytheistic
to monotheistic thinking in early times. All the ancient sources seem to
agree about the ubiquity of their presence. As Milton described it,

> About his chariot numberless were poured
> Cherub and Seraph, Potentates and Thrones,
> And Virtues, wingèd Spirits, and chariots winged
> From the armoury of God, where stand of old
> Myriads, between two brazen mountains lodged

Against a solemn day, harnessed at hand,
Celestial equipage;

(*Paradise Lost*, VII, 197–203)[2]

The space between earth and heaven is filled with armies of angels ready
to act. Whether these troops are military hosts, ministering angels, or
massed choirs has varied from time to time and place to place. But
according to most ancient sources the angels are innumerable, so that
even each blade of grass on earth has an angel dedicated to making it
grow.[3]

Angels in the Judaean Desert

For the community of Qumran, living in the Judaean desert during the
late second-temple era, from the mid-second century BCE to the first
century CE, the activity of the angels mirrored that of the community of
the faithful on earth. Among the Dead Sea Scrolls, special prominence is
given to angels in the *Songs of the Sabbath Sacrifice*, and in the *War Scroll*,
describing a 40-year conflict between the sons of light and the sons of
darkness during which heavenly reinforcements in the form of angels
and demons intervene on both sides.[4] To the writers of the Qumran
scrolls, heaven and earth were a unity. Conflict on earth necessarily
involved conflict in heaven. Likewise the ritual cycles of the Temple on
earth, if maintained with due order and observance, would perfectly
mirror the cyclical movements of the heavenly bodies, with angels
providing a supernal priesthood. Observing the calendar was therefore
vital, but it became a political issue. After conquering Jerusalem in 167
BCE, Antiochus IV Epiphanes imposed on the country a lunar calendar
system. The priests saw this as a violation of traditions established in
the natural laws of astronomy and a solar calendar, so a new priesthood
was appointed in their place.[5] If the *Songs of the Sabbath Sacrifice* are, as
some think, associated with the old priesthood, it is no wonder that a
heavenly temple, replete with angels, and fixed upon a system of weeks
and sevens, plays such an important part in the ceremonials and liturgy.
The beleaguered priests of the old school would have had every reason
to call upon heavenly assistance in their fight against imposed religious
change. Separated from the sacrificial cult in Jerusalem, either through

banishment or because they now considered it impure, separated also from the material support of temple tithes and offerings, the desert community at Qumran developed a means of participating in the sacrificial cult of the heavenly temple itself. Whether or not the *Songs of the Sabbath Sacrifice* are the work of Zadokite priests, and controversy remains active on this point,[6] what the songs themselves communicate, in their numinous, poetic way, is the experience of the heavenly temple, with its gates, portals, vestibules and architectural features based on descriptions in the book of Ezekiel 40–48, as well as a strong sense of communion with the angels.[7] This probably constituted a new departure, perhaps one that led to the idea of joining with the angels in their praises of God at the high point of the Sabbath service, that was adopted into mainstream Judaism and Christianity. The Jewish *Kedusha* prayer as we currently know it and its later Christian equivalent, the *Trisagion*, probably date from late Tannaitic times, around the end of the second century CE, a little after the active period of the Qumran community. Its origins remain somewhat obscure but its significance will be discussed in Chapter 6.[8]

The *Songs of the Sabbath Sacrifice* do not suggest actual words for the angels' praises, yet they are known as the 'Angelic Liturgy'. In fact, there is some question as to whether the angels make a sound at all. Despite descriptions elsewhere of the rushing of wings, the roar of water, and loud cries of praise, when we look for what words might be used, we find a contradiction:

> The Cherubim fall before him and rise. As they rise, the sound of divine stillness is heard, and there is the tumult of jubilation as their wings lift up, the sound of divine stillness. The image of the chariot throne do they bless … [And the splendour of] the luminous firmament do they sing. …
>
> There is a still sound of blessing in the tumult of their movement. And they praise his holiness as they return on their paths. As they rise, they rise marvellously, and when they settle, they [stand] still. The sound of glad rejoicing falls silent, and there is a stillness of divine blessing in all the camps of the godlike beings.
>
> (*Songs of the Sabbath Sacrifice*, 4Q405)[9]

Though the Hebrew uses the word *kol* (a voice), the sound is one of silence.

For the human participants, there are cycles of hymns for each of the 13 Sabbaths of each quarter of the year, designed to induce a progressive experience of purification and participation. Praises are sung, and God's majesty is extolled until the whole structure of the temple, heavenly and earthly together, will ring with praise. Calendrical prescriptions are important and the number seven recurs with insistent frequency, as the number of holiness, the number of angelic priesthoods, the number of known planets, of days in the process of creation, and is also the midpoint in counting to thirteen, for the weeks of each quarter.[10] The following passage is from the song for the seventh Sabbath, midpoint of the quarterly solar cycle; it falls on the sixteenth day of a 30-day month, and is thus at the midpoint of a lunar cycle too:

> Praise the God of the lofty heights,
> O you lofty ones among all the *elim* of knowledge.
> Let the holiest of the godlike ones
> Sanctify the King of glory who sanctifies by holiness all His holy ones.
>
> O you chiefs of the praises of all the godlike beings,
> Praise the splendidly praiseworthy God.
> For in the splendour of praise is the glory of His realm.
> From it come the praises of all the godlike ones
> Together with the splendour of all His majesty.
>
> And exalt his exaltedness to exalted heaven,
> You most godlike ones of the lofty *elim*,
> And exalt His glorious divinity above all the lofty heights.
> For He is God of gods, of all the chiefs of the heights of heaven
> And King of kings of all the eternal councils.
>
> By the intention of His knowledge,
> At the words of His mouth
> Come into being all the lofty angels;
> At the utterance of His lips all the eternal spirits;

By the intention of His knowledge all His creatures in their
undertakings.

(*Songs of the Sabbath Sacrifice*, hymn 4Q403, vv. 30-35)[11]

Recitation of these songs has an effect on the singers that has been
likened to a communal mystical experience, but it also invokes the *elim*
to perform their natural functions. Who are the *elim*? In the singular, *el* is
a name of God, associated with his might and power. More generally it
can denote a heavenly being. In the plural form, *elim*, it may mean mighty
men, heroes, or the gods of the other nations. But in the Qumran texts
it is used for angels more frequently than the word for angel (*mal'akh*)
used elsewhere.[12]

It may be difficult for us to think ourselves into the minds of a
desert community seeking in heaven for the temple it had lost on earth.
It is certainly difficult to understand exactly what is meant by some of
the hymn's expressions. But clearly heavenly beings full of knowledge
and with free access to the throne of God seem to have been present to
the writers of Qumran. We can only speculate whether, like some later
mystics, they aspired to join the angelic ranks themselves.[13]

Gnostic Angels

More familiar to many people today, at least by reputation, are Gnostic
texts from a similar period. Many of these, too, were chance finds in
the desert, where climatic conditions favour preservation. Substantial
finds were made in Oxyrynchus, from 1896, and at Nag Hammadi in
1945, both in Upper Egypt. Blending ancient mythology with biblical
texts, sometimes in variants that were later rejected, the Gnostic writers
introduce angels in some new guises.

In a text called *On the Origin of the World*[14] we find squabbling
broods of heavenly beings, vying to out-create each other. Sabaoth,
the son of the chief creator, Yaldabaoth, turned against his father and
mother, who were 'darkness' and 'the abyss', and he turned against his
sister, who 'moves to and fro over the water' (cf. the spirit of God, as in
Genesis 1:2) and he worshipped Faith, mother of wisdom. Faith (*Pistis*)
seems to have had ownership of the archangels: she sent seven of them
to snatch Sabaoth up to the seventh heaven, from the sixth, his own

abode, and they became his servants. Three more were sent to establish
the kingdom for him, so that he might prevail over chaos. Faith then
sends her daughter Zoë ('life' but also called Sophia, 'wisdom') to teach
him about the eighth heaven, while he builds for himself a palace and
throne in the seventh. The throne is a chariot throne, complete with
cherubim – but, in an extravagant elaboration of biblical texts, it has 64
of them. From these 64 plus the seven archangels and himself are born
the 72 gods of the nations. Sabaoth also created 'other dragon-shaped
angels called seraphim' who set about glorifying him constantly.

He then proceeds to create an angelic assembly of 'thousands,
myriads without number', just like the original assembly in the eighth
heaven, home of the stars. With lyre, harps and trumpets seven virgins
praise and glorify him. A firstborn, called Israel, and Jesus Christ are
beside him, while Sophia continues whispering in his ear all the secrets
of the eighth heaven. However it seems that he overreached himself in
his glory, because Yaldabaoth fought back, and created death, setting
it up in the sixth heaven and breeding from it androgynous children:
envy, wrath, weeping, sighing, mourning, lamenting and groaning, seven
children in their male aspect, and wrath, grief, lust, sighing, cursing,
bitterness and quarrelsomeness in their female aspect. They then
interbred and produced more. A great number of strange happenings
ensue, some dark, some contradictory, most in half-parallel with biblical
tales. An unusual detail is the appearance of the phoenix. Not just the
single phoenix of classical mythology, but three: the first is spiritual and
immortal; the second lives for a thousand years, belonging to the world
of soul or mind; of the third we are told 'it is written in the Holy Book
that it is consumed'. Which 'holy book' is not known – the Bible as we
know it has no phoenix – but 'consumed' is traditional: after a great
many years the phoenix, bird of paradise with gorgeous iridescent wings,
burns itself to ashes on a funeral pyre of twigs ignited by the sun, but
emerges from the ashes renewed, to live again.[15] More importantly, the
phoenix in this Gnostic text is described as 'a witness for the angels', and
features in a weird variant of the expulsion from Eden story, watching
over the jealous minor gods who dealt unjustly with Adam and Eve.

In another Gnostic text, *The Secret Revelation of John* (first or
second century CE), angels participate with Yaldabaoth in the creation
of Adam.[16] Each one has a different task and they are listed by name.
The first seven, called 'powers' (that is, goodness, forethought, divinity,

lordship, kingdom, jealousy and understanding), create the 'psychic body'. The network of limbs, organs, flesh, bones, teeth, veins and arteries are created by 74 named angels, who create one part each. Seven further angels or gods preside over the labour – among them Sabaoth, Cain and Abel – then the limbs are activated by 30 more angels, under seven overseers led by Michael and Uriel (and therefore perhaps all archangels). Five more angels preside over the senses, perception, imagination, arrangement and impulse to action. Notably few of the angel names in this text end in the familiar suffix '-el', which denotes connection to God. Presumably they have come from a different tradition. Besides angels, four demons are allotted to the body: heat, cold, wetness and dryness. These demons have matter as their mother, and further demons preside over the arrangement of matter, as well as pleasure, desire, grief and fear. From them come a whole host of further demons – until in the end the number of angels and demons together is 365, all collaborating to complete the body and mind of man.[17] More angels govern the remaining passions, but instead of naming these, the text refers the reader to 'the Book of Zoroaster', which, alas, cannot be identified.

As in the previous text (*On the Origin of the World*), Yaldabaoth is a thing of darkness. At one point he is even identified with Samael, the devil.[18] Yet he can create realms of luminous fire, and then, mating with mindlessness, he embarks on the creation of angels to fill the seven heavens and the five depths of the abyss. He creates man (Adam) 'so that this human image may give us light'. Humans now must guard themselves against the angels of misery and the demons of chaos or they will end up in 'the place where the angels of misery go, where there is no repentance'; but the soul that avoids their influence will find eternal rest. The creation of Eve, her seduction by Yaldabaoth, and the angels who descend to mate with the daughters of men are all woven into the story.

Much of the content of these Gnostic texts is profoundly puzzling, even disturbing. It is almost with relief that we find in the *Testimony of Truth* a simple list of questions:

What is the light? And what is the darkness? Who is the one that has created? And who is God? and who are the angels? and what is soul? And what is spirit? And where is the voice and

who is the one who speaks? And who is the one who hears? ...
And why are some lame and some blind? ... and some rich and
some poor? ...[19]

Hardly less strange are Gnostic works that have come down to us in an
edited or censored form such as the *Book of Baruch* ascribed to Justin,
preserved in the *Refutation of All Heresies* of the Christian theologian
Hippolytus of Rome (170–235 CE).[20] In it we find a curious array of
'prime angels' who have their birth from the union of God and Earth,
named here as Elohim and Edem. Edem is seen as evil, or at least half
evil – though she elicits our sympathy when she finds herself deserted
by her beloved but foolish Elohim. Although he is supposed to be the
creator god, he is only secondary, being sent from the Good, who is
supreme. It becomes clear as the tale unfolds that the writer is trying to
combine Jewish, Christian and Greek mythology: he brings in Moses,
Jesus and Herakles as characters, and he identifies the Plotinian idea of
pleroma, the fullness of Good, with Priapus, the Graeco-Roman god of
fertility.

  Through the union of Elohim and Edem, which seems to have been
a one-time event, two sets of twelve angels are born. The first twelve
follow their father, and include Michael and Gabriel, but also Baruch,
Amen and Esaddaeus. The other names are lost. The maternal angels are
Babel, Achamoth, Naas, Bel, Belias, Satan, Sael, Adonaios, Kauithan,
Pharaoth, Karkamenos and Lathen. The third angel in each band has
special significance, being identified allegorically with the two great trees
of the Garden of Eden. Baruch, whose name means 'blessed', is the tree
of life, and Naas, whose name equates with *naḥash* (serpent), is the tree
of the knowledge of good and evil. These two angels lead their respective
teams, good and evil. The maternal angels govern the cosmos, moving in
a circular chorus at fixed intervals and periods. They do not always rule
well: where their greed reigns, famine and disease follow. The paternal
angels seem to remain more detached from matter.

  Elohim, meanwhile, creates mankind, in whom his spirit is
imprisoned. But he ascends to the upper border of heaven and sees a
light stronger than any he has created. Realizing he is not 'the lord',
as he had thought, he is allowed to pass through the gate and to be
with the Good where he 'saw what eye has not seen nor ear heard and
what has not arisen in the human heart'. He is invited to sit down at

the Good's right hand and to stay. In shame, he wants to destroy the cosmos he had made, just because it imprisons spirit, but the Good bids him stay, and leave the creation to Edem. It cannot be evil if it came ultimately from the Good. When Elohim passes through the gate to the Good, it is without his angels. Edem still has her angels, who help her adorn herself to attract Elohim to return. As revenge for being abandoned, she sends Naas to torture the spirit of Elohim that is in human beings. Elohim sends Baruch to bring them relief, though Naas continues to plague them.

These various tales offer extravagant variations on the Bible as we know it, grappling with questions of good, evil, life, punishment and death, through mythology. Edward Gibbon famously described the doctrines of the Gnostics as 'vain science ... sublime but obscure', yet despite much criticism and a generally heretical status the Gnostic texts have enjoyed various revivals. Part of their appeal lies in the insight they give into the early years of Christianity, but part is undoubtedly the intrinsic appeal of the idea that transcendental realities may be directly apprehended through mystical texts, imaginative mythology or spiritual practices. Whoever receives gnosis may travel freely between earth and heaven, either with the angels, or as an angel.

For a more rational thinker of that era, Philo of Alexandria (20 BCE–50 CE), the space between heaven and earth was filled with spirits. Philo bridges the gap between Judaism and Christianity in that he was writing from the heart of Judaism but was later read mainly by Christian readers. He explains that what the Greeks call demons (*daimons*), the Jews call angels,

> souls, that is, which fly and hover in the air. And let no one suppose that what is here said is a myth. For the universe must needs be filled through and through with life, and each of its primary and elementary divisions contains the forms of life which are akin and suited to it. The earth has the creatures of the land, the sea and rivers those that live in water, fire the fire-born, which are said to be found especially in Macedonia, and heaven has the stars. For the stars are souls divine, and without blemish throughout, and therefore as each of them is mind in its purest form, they move in the line most akin to mind – the circle. And so the other element, the air, must needs be filled

with living beings, though indeed they are invisible to us, since even the air itself is not visible to our senses.

(Philo, *On the Giants*, 6-8, tr. F. H. Colson)[21]

Neoplatonic Daemons

One of the great questions theologians face in any religion that conceives of God as supreme, unique and ever unchanging is how such a God can relate to a creation which is in constant flux and motion. Or, as ancient philosophers formulated the question, how does the One relate to the many? One approach would be to regard the creator as remote and distant from creation. In such a view, angels flying back and forth carry news of the created world to the creator, and also carry messages or instructions from God to man. At times this view has prevailed. But another fruitful approach has been to consider divine powers as pouring out of the Supreme Being and into the created world, by a series of emanations. In this view, knowledge, light and power are imparted by means of a flow from the source to created beings in a series. Those nearest the source will naturally receive more of the light, more of the power, more of the knowledge. The angels, being nearer to God than mankind, receive proportionately stronger infusions. Human beings receive a smaller portion of knowledge, light, and power than the angels, but more than the animal world, and animals receive more than plants, rocks, and so on. We might consider it as a descending scale of consciousness.

This kind of view was especially developed by Neoplatonic schools of philosophy, and was also embraced into the religious philosophy of Judaism, Christianity and Islam. Its roots are already present in Plato, or arguably even before, in Parmenides of Elea, in the early fifth century BCE, who had an important influence on Plato.[22] It was developed in a systematic way by Plotinus (203–262 CE), who speaks of three great levels of being: the One stands supreme at the apex of creation; from it there flows *nous* or the divine mind, pouring out by emanation to form a world of pure intelligence. *Nous*, like its source, is universal and transcendent. From here, again by emanation, comes soul, both a universal 'world soul' and individual souls. The world of the senses represents a step beyond these three levels or *hypostases* and plain matter is regarded as utterly lifeless and inert, since at every step the shadow of the original light gets dimmer.

It is in a way surprising that so many religious thinkers were able to adopt Neoplatonic emanationist ideas, since the principal idea might be thought to argue with religious doctrines of creation. However biblical exegesis can be highly creative, and arguments are found to include this view within an interpretation of the traditional story where God first speaks, and light appears. Certainly the opening of St John's gospel supports an emanationist view, with the Word as the originating power.

An important feature of the process of emanation by which divine mind and soul are formed is that it is matched by a process of return. The *nous* or divine mind, through contemplation of the One, can merge again in the One. Even a human soul which has been formed by the emanation of divine substance from the divine mind into the particularity of a human being can merge again in that divine mind, through contemplation.[23]

In the fifth century, this emanationist system was considerably filled out by Proclus (410–485 CE), the last great philosopher of the Platonic Academy of Athens. According to his understanding, everything in the cosmos was arranged according to great chains of emanation from the One, under nine orders of gods, some above the cosmos, some within it, and some participating both above and within the cosmos. Within each order are found several gods, often in triads, and under each, in a chain of being, are ranged the creatures special to them that partake in some measure of the same qualities. Prominent among these are whole hosts of *daemons*, who carry out their bidding, but also whole sections of the physical creation. Thus, for example, under the Sun are solar daemons; among its animals are the lion, the cockerel, the swan and the scarab beetle; its flowers include heliotrope. Gold, chrysolite and carbuncle are its metal and stones; frankincense, myrrh, cinnamon, saffron and spikenard all convey its influence, as does yellow honey, and people who have golden, curly hair. Likewise, under Jupiter (Zeus) are silver, sapphire, topaz, wine, and Jovian daemons.[24]

Each power in the godly realm has its own cohort of daemons, as well as creatures and substances under its influence. These 'daemons' are not the same as our general understanding of 'demons', (who will be discussed in Chapter 3), though the two words are obviously related.

The daemons[25] are rather to be considered as angelic powers, doing the things that angels do, though some of them undoubtedly cause trouble and behave more like demons.

It was this kind of daemon that Shakespeare sought to represent with his spirit Ariel in *The Tempest*. In this case, he is a spirit who has successfully been bound to serve a human master, and what enabled this binding is Prospero's knowledge of natural and supernatural science of just the kind implied in the writings of Proclus. Ariel's arrival at the beginning of the second scene tells us first of his service:

> All hail, great master! grave sir, hail! I come
> To answer thy best pleasure; be't to fly,
> To swim, to dive into the fire, to ride
> On the curl'd clouds; to thy strong bidding
> task Ariel and all his quality.

He then reports on all that he has accomplished:

> I boarded the king's ship; now on the beak,
> Now in the waist, the deck, in every cabin,
> I flam'd amazement: sometime I'd divide,
> And burn in many places; on the topmast,
> The yards and bowsprit, would I flame distinctly,
> Then meet and join. Jove's lightnings, the precursors
> O' the dreadful thunder-claps, more momentary
> And sight-outrunning were not; the fire and cracks
> Of sulphurous roaring the most mighty Neptune
> Seem to besiege and make his bold waves tremble,
> Yea, his dread trident shake.
>
> (*The Tempest*, Act I, scene 2)

From the point of view of the passengers, he was indeed a demon: they leapt into the foaming brine, and Ferdinand cries out, 'Hell is empty, And all the devils are here.' But from Prospero's point of view, Ariel is a ministering spirit, and Miranda a 'cherubin'.[26] While scholars still argue over his sources, there had been a revival of Neoplatonic ideas, especially through the translations of Marsilio Ficino of Florence (1433–99) whose work was widely read.[27]

Besides some works of Proclus, Ficino translated two treatises specifically on daemons, one by Porphyry, a student of Plotinus, writing in the third century CE, and one by Michael Psellus, a Byzantine scholar of the eleventh century. Porphyry had attempted to clarify exactly what these daemons were and did. He describes them as

> a host of invisible beings, which Plato, without making any distinction, called dæmons. People have given some of them names, and they receive from everyone honours equal to the gods, together with forms of worship. Others have no name at all in most places, but acquire a name and cult ... in villages and some cities.[28]

Plato had discussed daemons in *Cratylus*, interpreting their name from *daēmon* as 'knowing or wise'. He located them on earth, as the remnant of a golden race now lost from earthly life but with a continuing presence as 'beneficent averters of evil and guardians of men' (*Cratylus*, 397, quoting Hesiod, *Works and Days*, 120 ff.) and they assist in the government of the world (*Statesman*, 271). In the *Symposium*, Plato describes love as a daemon, meaning a great spirit, intermediate between the gods and men, carrying messages in both directions (*Symposium*, 202). In *Timaeus*, 41-42, the work of creation is carried out in its detail by a whole host of gods and children of gods (or younger gods), whose task it is to blend the physical elements of earth, air, water and fire as bodies for the divinely created soul. Socrates had a daemon who prevented him from doing wrong, and every individual is said to have their own personal daemon (*Phaedo*, 107-8, 113). These daemons and indeed the lesser gods came to be regarded in late antiquity as angels.

Whether angels should be worshipped would become a question theologians discussed, and generally answered with a resounding 'no', though among certain sects including the Gnostics, and in the Catholic Church to this day, prayers are made to angels. A hint within the poetry of John Donne (d. 1631) suggests that this was also common practice at one time in the Church of England, despite the strictures of theologians:

> So in a voice, so in a shapeless flame
> Angels affect us oft, and worshipp'd be.
>
> (Donne, *Air and Angels*)

Among Jews, too, despite prohibition of angel-worship, a popular Sabbath hymn greets the angels, and in its third stanza seeks a blessing from them.[29] Many Jews through the centuries have declined to recite this verse, considering it a form of inappropriate worship (despite Jacob's example in Genesis 32:26). Rabbi David ibn abi Zimra in the sixteenth century was asked whether one might offer incense to demons who were the causative agents of illness – not in order to worship them, but to force them to desist from harm. He spends a long time discussing the matter before concluding it is not advisable, especially as anyone offering incense in order to attract demons is liable to a death penalty from the authorities of the state. However, one may use invocations of 'holy names' for, he says, 'what difference is there between consulting demons or angels?'[30]

Worship of daemons in the classical world was, however, acceptable and Porphyry lays out exactly what kind of offerings are appropriate for which kinds of spirits. Offerings of fruit and flowers are to be preferred, as smoking meats may attract evil kinds of demon. In fact, the evil demons often obtain food by deceit, fattening themselves upon burnt offerings intended for the gods. It is not clear whether the good daemons actually eat to nourish their spirit-body, or whether, in fact, it is they who nourish others by what flows from them.[31] If they do eat, they would be breaking the mould of angelic abstinence, for, with the exception of Abraham's three visitors, angels do not usually eat or drink. It is, however, clear that the evil daemons eat and that they can do harm if they are angered by being neglected. The good daemons can do good for those who offer supplication and prayer. What distinguishes the good from the bad seems to be self-control:

> All dæmons are souls emanating from the universal soul. They
> administer large parts of the regions below the moon. They also
> have spirit, that is, an insubstantial body. The dæmons which
> have greatest control over their own body are good and do good,
> while those which have least control of their body are evil and
> do evil.
>
> (Porphyry, *On Abstinence*, II, 38)

Neither kind of daemon has a physical body, but they are liable to disturbances in their spirit-bodies.[32] The daemons which do not have control of their own spirit-bodies and therefore get carried away by wrath and lust, deserve the name 'demons'. The daemon-souls which master their own spirit-bodies do so by the use of reason. They are the ones who have charge of the creation. They are described as if they are at once nature-gods and angels,

> whether they have charge over certain animals or particular crops, or over conditions conducive to the well-being of these, such as showers, temperate winds, clear skies, moderation of the seasons, and everything else that contributes to all these. Again, in the world of men, the good dæmons preside over the arts, musical training, medicine, gymnastics, and similar disciplines …
>
> Among these good dæmons are to be numbered 'the transmitters' as Plato calls them, who, convey and announce the concerns of men to the gods and divine matters to men. They convey our prayers to the gods as if to judges, they also bring down to us their commands and guidance together with prophecy.
>
> (Porphyry, *On Abstinence*, II, 38, citing Plato, *Symposium* 202E)

Not having a physical body, daemons are not perceptible to our senses, though they may from time to time assume a variety of shapes and forms. There is even a hint that their spirit-body may partake to some extent in corporeality. Certainly bad daemons live nearer to earth, and devise all sorts of tricks and ambushes for us, while good daemons live higher in the heavens. Good and bad daemons together form a continuous presence, as Philo had already indicated, filling up the space between earth and heaven.[33]

Porphyry summarized and clarified the views of Plato and of Plotinus but his main aim was to defeat the rising power of Christian opposition to Greek philosophy in his own day. This explains why his works were for so long treated with suspicion in the Christian West. Yet on the subject of daemons he was very close to the views of Origen, an early father of the Christian Church, and a slightly older fellow-student of Plotinus.[34] Origen additionally suggests that all souls must have been created equal, but tiring of their happiness, they fell from their exalted state, finding their own levels as angels, stars, men or demons.[35]

Through all these writers of antiquity we can see the enduring primacy of the 'One' and its connection with the kaleidoscopic 'many'. These ideas had their roots in Parmenides and Plato, they were applied to the God of the Jews by Philo, and they flowered in Plotinus,[36] where Origen, Porphyry and later Proclus provided further elaborations and ensured their wide currency in late antiquity.

In Egypt, the same ideas are reflected in the writings associated with the legendary Hermes Trismegistus. These are Greek texts written in Egypt around 200 CE, blending ancient wisdom from Greek and Hebrew sources with Egyptian elements.[37] In the dialogues known as the *Corpus Hermeticum*, we learn that the Sun holds a special place in maintaining the distribution of daemonic powers through the heavens:

> Every kind of creature is sustained and nourished by the Sun. As the spiritual world embraces the physical and fills it out with every different kind of form, so the Sun also embraces everything in the cosmos, raising up and strengthening all generations. And when they are spent and ebbing away he receives them back.
>
> The choir of spirits, or rather choirs, are placed under the command of the Sun; 'choirs' because there are many different kinds of powers. They are set in formation under the stars, and are equal in number to them. Thus arrayed they serve each of the stars.
>
> (*Corpus Hermeticum*, XVI, 12-13, tr. Salaman et al.)

We learned from Porphyry that these spirits or daemons can be good or bad in their activities, but Hermes tells us they can also be mixed. It is the daemons collectively as a body who are given authority over the earth, and over all kinds of turbulence there, both public and individual. 'For they shape our souls after themselves and arouse them by residing in our sinews, in our marrow, veins and arteries, and even in our brain, penetrating as deep as our very entrails' (*Corpus Hermeticum*, XVI, 14). They are set as attendants to each star, and seem to take possession of us at birth, agitating the soul and producing our destiny – yet the rational part of the human soul is not bound by their activities.

Because the soul need not be bound by this intermediary layer of daemons, Iamblichus of Chalcis, writing in the third century on *The*

Mysteries of Egypt, felt that it was possible to reach beyond them, and call upon higher powers, be they gods, angels, archangels or heroes. He recommends both prayer and sacrifice in order to draw upon the wisdom and knowledge of these higher powers, as a kind of empowerment or acquisition of creative force. Divine inspiration may come through dreams or through absorption or possession. The limitations of the human condition can be transcended by seeking out divine light and, through careful preparation and devoted practice, one can exchange one's limited life for the life divine:

> For the human race is feeble and puny, it sees but a little
> ahead, and is endowed with a congenital futility. But there is
> one remedy for its inherent straying, confusion and unstable
> changing, and this is, if it participate so far as possible in some
> portion of the divine light.[38]

It was not so much a question of drawing down higher powers into oneself by some kind of unholy force – as critics of such rites implied (and Iamblichus's teacher Porphyry was a strong critic) – but of allowing one's invocations to rise and attach themselves to higher beings by a process of assimilation. The emphasis was thus firmly on purification of body and mind, as it had been for Porphyry, but with the added dimension of seeking absorption in 'the divine fire which shines universally on its own initiative, self-summoned and self-energising' (*On the Mysteries,* IV, 3). Such absorption is possible because the individual parts of the universe, although they are distinct, strive towards each other by virtue of the fact that the universe is a single living being (IV.12). The space between earth and heaven thus becomes bridgeable at every level, in leaps small or large.

What Proclus later elaborated in this view was the mechanism by which the soul can exert its rational powers to transcend bodily attachments and rise through the layers between earth and heaven. Just as all things are ranged under the stars in a series of downward emanations and influences, so too can any created and animate being exercise the power of 'reversion', of rising back into its own 'cause' – which is whatever stands above it in the process of outward flow. Just as there is an outward flow into creation, so is there also a flow of return. All that exists proceeds from a single first cause, which is the Good.

What is nearer the Good is greater in power. What is further away is nevertheless capable of 'reverting' towards its cause by virtue of that within it which is still incorporeal in its nature.[39]

All these Neoplatonic ideas are relevant to our enquiry for two reasons. Firstly, they show how beliefs about daemons in pagan antiquity shared many features that were also enshrined within Judaism, Christianity and later Islam. Especially they shared the sense of a cosmos operating under the authority of a supreme divine power but guided and shaped in its workings through the agency of a whole host of unseen forces which these religions would describe as angels and demons.

Secondly, they remind us that countless generations have had a well-developed sense of the space between heaven and earth being alive with such powers. Such beliefs are, of course, also found in many more traditions, from the Indian sub-continent to the American Indians and beyond. For example, the dakinis of Tibetan Buddhism seem to bear a particularly close relation to the daemons of Iamblichus and Proclus. But for now we shall stay within the rich unfolding tapestry that forms our Western tradition, to trace the further development of some powerful views.

Here we must follow two paths, one following Greek philosophy as it continued among the Arabic-speaking nations of the Near East, North Africa and Spain, and the other among Greek-speaking Christians of Byzantium. The two paths ultimately lead to the same result, namely a wider knowledge and understanding of the heavens, but they differ slightly in character and development, with the Arabs particularly contributing to advances in astronomy.

Taking the Arabic path first, the outstanding exponent of angelic cosmology is the Persian scholar Ibn Sina (980–1037), known for centuries in the West as Avicenna, and appreciated for his medical and philosophical teachings. Avicenna's medical *Canon* was well received in Italy, with the founding of the medical school of Salerno,[40] but his philosophy was also warmly received in Muslim-Jewish-Christian Spain, from where it soon spread across Europe.[41]

Many of Avicenna's views were based on those of Al-Farabi (872–951), who spent most of his life in the Abbasid capital of Baghdad. According to Al-Farabi and Avicenna, the creation of the world begins from a First Cause or Intellect. Through contemplation of its own existence, it gives rise to a Second Intellect. Contemplating its emanation from God, the

Second Intellect gives rise to a First Spirit, which animates the Sphere of Spheres, which is the universe. By its own contemplation it gives rise to matter, which fills the universe and forms the first heaven, the sphere of the planets. It has also set in motion a continuing unstoppable flow, giving rise to all the rest: the higher heavenly hierarchy of the cherubim, and a lower heavenly hierarchy which Avicenna populates with Angels of Magnificence, animating the heavens. These angels have no instruments of sense, but they do have imagination, therefore they can desire a return to their source. Their quest for return is what causes eternal movement in heaven, and their power of imagination directly inspires prophetic vision among men.

The remaining heavens are then divided into seven, each ruled by an Intellect that creates its own angel, associated with one of the seven planetary spheres: Saturn, Jupiter, Mars, the Sun, Venus, Mercury and the Moon (the standard Ptolemaic division of the heavens which assumes as a given the earth's centrality to the system.[42] This system prevailed until questioned by Copernicus and Galileo). The Angel Gabriel, who has especial significance for mankind in both Christianity and Islam, is the one associated with the Moon, and is hence nearest to the earth. Later, these angels created by the Intellects would come to be identified with the Intellects themselves. As such, they move the spheres, and each angel sounds its note as it does so, producing the heavenly harmony, the music of the spheres.[43]

Below the level of the Ninth Intellect, that is below the Moon – the 'sublunary world' of the poets – is our own worldly domain, which is so far removed from First Intellect that the next step of emanation explodes into fragments. So no further heaven is created, but human souls, and they are endowed with those very organs of sense perception that the higher angels lack. But they are correspondingly weak in rational intellect, imagination and ability to illuminate others. For their potential, so limited in these regards, to come to anything, they rely upon illumination by 'Angel'. This is the tenth angel, a sort of universal angelic mind, rather like Plotinus's *nous*. In the Renaissance, Ficino would come to think in these terms too, reviving Angel as a singular concept, alongside angels as we normally regard them.

According to Al-Farabi and Avicenna, those who are most fully illuminated are the prophets, who have rational intellect, imagination, vision, and ability to inspire others. Prophets may additionally be illuminated by planetary angels (e.g. Gabriel). Some people receive from the tenth 'Angel' enough light to write, teach, pass laws and contribute to the welfare of society. Others receive only enough to take care of themselves, and some unfortunate souls not even that. But this tenth angel becomes for Avicenna the giver to each soul of a share in the collective consciousness, which confers likewise a share in immortality. For Avicenna, the final stage of human life is reunion with Angel.[44]

The Celestial Hierarchy

Turning to the Christians of Byzantium, a work of immense significance for all later discussion of angels was written by Dionysius, a Christian Neoplatonist, who flourished between 485 and 528 in Syria. Dionysius enjoyed a special status in the Christian world as he was thought, from indications in his writings, to have been the Athenian judge converted by St Paul on the Areopagus (Acts 17:34). His true identity was not known for a thousand years.[45]

Dionysius points out first the mystical and symbolic nature of the heavenly intelligences, which he calls the concealment of the divine ray in a variety of sacred veils. Angels do not have the numerous feet and faces the biblical prophets describe; they do not have eagles' beaks or feathered wings, nor must we allow ourselves to picture flaming wheels in the skies, thrones or the like. The divine intelligences are formless. They are so simple that we cannot know or contemplate them. Any description we find in scripture is only to aid us by simile.

So, if angels are not golden, gleaming men in lustrous clothes, what are they? He tries to answer this by focusing on hierarchy, by which he means a perfect arrangement. The orders of angels represent levels of understanding, purification and illumination by which the work of God is carried out. God is the source of continuous and perfect illumination. Those best fitted to receive the divine light in its fullness are those who are fully engaged in contemplation. They then joyfully pass it on, spreading their overflowing light to the next most able to receive. All heavenly beings are called 'angels', at one level of speech, and they engage in bringing about the divine will in various ways. But there are also different ranks of angelic beings, arranged according to their capacity to conform to the divine, and to enter into communion with the light coming from God, and in this sense, those simply called 'angels' are the lowest rank.

Dionysius sets out a system which he claims to have taken from a certain Hierotheus, his teacher, but whose identity or even existence has never been established. The heavenly beings are divided into three groups of three orders, their names taken from various parts of the scriptures.[46] The first group consists of seraphim, cherubim and Thrones. Being grouped directly around God they receive the 'primal perfections'. The name 'seraph' designates a perennial circling around the divine, a penetrating warmth and an overflowing heat from movement that never falters, stamping its own image on others and uplifting them too. The seraphim can hold unveiled and undiminished the light they receive, and they can push away every obscuring shadow. The cherubim have the power to know and contemplate divine splendour, and to share the gifts this brings as an outpouring of wisdom. The Thrones are completely intent on remaining in the presence of the most high, and are ever open to welcome God. These three ranks are eternally self-moved and undiminished. They are filled with love and with a triply luminous contemplation of the source of all beauty. They are specially gifted to be as alike to God as it is possible to be. Among them are the ones who constantly proclaim 'Blessed be the glory of the Lord from his place' (Ezekiel 3:12) while others thunder out 'Holy, holy, holy is the Lord of hosts. The whole earth is full of his glory' (Isaiah 6:3; Revelation 4:8).

The middle hierarchy consists of Dominions, Powers and Authorities (sometimes translated as Dominations, Virtues and Powers). The Dominions are unfettered by any earthly tendencies or tyrannical harshness; the Powers connect with the source of all power, displaying unswerving courage; the Authorities indicate the ordered nature of celestial authority. As a group these three orders of the second rank receive their enlightenment through the beings of the first rank. The third hierarchy consists of Principalities, Archangels and Angels.

Each rank is attuned to the powers of the level above itself, and acts as a transmitter, so that it is able to lift up those of the level beneath them towards the power they have themselves received. They do this by engaging in the threefold activity of purification, illumination and perfection. This, in essence, is the arrangement described in *The Celestial Hierarchy* of Dionysius.[47]

Dionysius's classification was adopted almost universally in the centuries that followed, apart from minor variations on nomenclature and order.[48] Gregory the Great placed principalities in the second hierarchy, and virtues in the third. Thomas Aquinas discussed the differences in detail in his *Summa Theologiae* (Part I, question 108) but concludes they are of little significance and reflect only slight differences of emphasis. Dante (1265–1321) prefers the ordering of Dionysius, but calls the second hierarchy dominations, virtues and powers. In one of the final cantos of the *Divine Comedy,* he sees a fiery point of light, and nine radiant circles of love turning around it, singing choir on choir. These comprise the whole angelic brotherhood and Beatrice explains them (canto 28 of *Paradiso*).[49] The arrangement of angels was considered worthy of inclusion in the highest poetic reaches.

A useful way of thinking about the nine orders and their functions is to recognize the lowest level, ordinary angels, as guardians of persons, bearers of divine messages to individuals, and of human messages back to the divine. Archangels, in this system, are the protectors of nations, and carry messages of great importance. Principalities are the regulators of human government, having to do with empires and the like. The Powers incorporate the image of divine power and majesty, and combat darkness and disease. The Virtues are an image of divine strength and fortitude, giving us signs and directions, and inspiring endurance. Dominations are the image of divine dominion. For the Thrones we should read steadfastness and execution of judgement. The cherubim are the image of divine wisdom, and the seraphim the image of divine love.[50]

These ideas, expressed by Dionysius and echoed later by Dante, are essentially Greek and Neoplatonic in their origin, but they enjoyed a continuing presence in the medieval West. Many great theologians from the ninth to the thirteenth centuries wrote commentaries on Dionysius including John Scotus Eriugena, Hugh of St Victor, Robert Grosseteste, Albert the Great, Bonaventure and Thomas Aquinas. Many other Neoplatonic works did not enjoy such good fortune, though some knowledge of their content was preserved through summaries, for example, in Cicero, a great admirer of Plato, through the Church Fathers, such as St Augustine and Eusebius, and in an Arabic work known as *The Theology of Aristotle*, which was in fact based on Plotinus, *Enneads*, IV-VI.[51] Hermes survived in part (the *Asclepius* and some other fragments) and Proclus lived on in the Latin translation of William of Moerbeke (*c.*1215–86) and in the Arabic *Book of Causes*, mistakenly attributed to Aristotle.

In spite of being partly cut off from the classical past, ideas about angels were developed to new levels of intricacy during the Middle Ages, in what was truly the age of angelology, and this will be the subject of Chapter 3. But while we are discussing the space between earth and heaven we cannot pass so swiftly over Dante's travels through this realm in his *Divine Comedy*.[52] To the theology of Dionysius and Aquinas, Dante adds a series of connections between the angelic hierarchy, the planetary heavens, and human virtues. Dante's scheme for the heavens follows the standard Ptolemaic system based on a series of spheres, each one embraced within its greater neighbour and sharing the imprint of the divine (a useful analogy is a nested set of Russian dolls, but in this case they are simple spheres, each full of light). Closest to earth is the Moon, realm of the ordinary angels. Next comes Mercury, associated with the Archangels; Venus is linked with the Principalities, the Sun with Powers, Mars with Virtues, Jupiter with Dominations and Saturn with Thrones. These were all the planets then known. Lovers of astrology may wish to reflect on what this signifies in terms of qualities, but the picture does not end here. Above the planetary heavens, the cherubim are linked to the constellations of the zodiac and the fixed stars (for the planets are 'wanderers'); the seraphim are in the realm of Dante's crystalline heaven, which is filled with the presence of the Prime Mover, the creative aspect of God which sets all other things in motion. Above and beyond all of these is the Empyrean, beyond movement and even the source of movement. This is the highest or furthest heaven, where Dante locates the snow-white rose of Paradise, the light of all lights, representing God.

In another set of cross-linkages – and his wonderfully complex poem abounds with hidden links and references – Dante connects the angelic hierarchy to the four so-called cardinal virtues, those derived from Platonic philosophy and ancient wisdom literature. He joins Angels and Virtues with fortitude, Archangels and Dominations with justice, Principalities and Thrones with temperance and Powers with prudence. The three Christian virtues of faith, hope and love, are reserved for the eighth heaven of the fixed stars, the home of the cherubim.

After Dante's time, the rediscovery of Greek sources gathered pace, and their translation from Greek to Latin in the fifteenth century was of profound significance. The writings of Dionysius were among the first to enjoy a revival. A new translation was made in the 1430s by Ambrogio Traversari, head of the Calmaldolese monastery in Florence. This circulated widely in manuscript and was printed in 1498. Another printed edition followed in 1502–3, in three large folio volumes, containing various Latin versions of Dionysius and a selection of commentaries. Among these were Marsilio Ficino's translation of the *Mystical Theology* and *Divine Names* from 1491 and 1492, first published in Venice in 1496.

Ficino's Angels

Ficino played a vital role in bringing together Greek philosophy and religious devotion, into a Christian form of Platonism. We know far more about him than the earlier figures we have discussed. Chiefly renowned as a translator and interpreter he wrote prolifically, developing many ideas of his own. His early training in Aristotelian philosophy and medicine, his love of music and poetry, his interest in science and astronomy, his astute observation of public life and genuine love of people all combined to give his rendering of the ancient texts particular power. He became a priest in 1474, and later a canon of the cathedral, but he is mainly known to posterity for bringing Platonic teachings to life and for changing ideas about love, both human and divine.[53]

Ficino was deeply influenced by Dionysius, especially since, like everyone else at the time, he believed him to have been the personal pupil of St Paul, who had himself been 'snatched up into the third heaven', and was therefore uniquely placed to understand angels. Ficino's last work, a commentary on St Paul's Epistles, reflects a life-long interest in the heavenly realms and mankind's connection to them. The realm of angels, in his view, is not beyond our reach:

> Letting go of bodily sense and feeling, as earth, disregarding
> active reason as being a first heaven, not giving too much
> importance to natural reason as a second heaven, we should,
> under Paul's guidance, use all our powers to lift ourselves up to

mind which contemplates the divine, like a third heaven in us and an angelic stature.[54]

In undertaking this spiritual endeavour we can rely upon the three gifts of which St Paul spoke, namely, faith, hope and love:

> but chiefly love, towering over all knowledge and uniting us with the order of the seraphs. Here finally a triple heaven will face us. For in seraphic love that ineffable warmth of the Holy Spirit will be kindled in us. In this life-giving warmth, the light and wisdom of the divine word will at once shine out.[55]

Where there are no clouds to impede it, that divine light which is ever present holds the angels in a state of constant turning around God, in love. Their eyes are constantly upon him, and the light works upon them to illuminate and to attract in similarly constant fashion. In us, the effect of this light is limited, partly by clouds, internal and external, but mainly because our minds are designed to look both ways: we look towards heavenly things with one part of our being, and towards earthly things with another. It is only our love of sensory things that prevents us from turning fully into angels, and the fact that we move towards and away from the light over time, at will.[56] Human souls therefore differ from angels only in the fact that angels are uninterruptedly illumined by God, while souls receive the same light, but only inconstantly.

Like Avicenna, Ficino sometimes speaks of Angel in the singular, as a metaphysical layer of being. When he does so, he is speaking of universal intelligence. In the *Platonic Theology* (1482), he explains how the creation we see around us has come into being through successive layers of emanation, from God (or the One), through Angel or 'angelic mind', then Soul (including human souls), Quality and Body. The human soul is the middle term in this progression, and therefore, in a manner of speaking, looks both ways. It stands on a horizon. It is rational and reflects the divine light; it has much of the angelic about it. Then there are also aspects of the soul that generate physical desires and powerful emotions. These are called the irrational soul, and he equates them with what he calls 'quality'. Finally there is the body, which has demands of its own, and is a faint reflection of the light: a shadow of a shadow.[57]

Angel spoken of in this way is motionless. (It would therefore have no need of wings!) But movement can come from stillness: the continuous and orderly, multifarious movements of the heavenly bodies are brought about by 'mind' without form or body. Linking the arguments of Avicenna to Aristotle's eleventh book of *Metaphysics*, it is angels, now in the plural, who move the heavenly spheres, acting on behalf of the one unmoved mover.[58] Ficino also takes up ideas on how angels move from another work of Dionysius, *On Divine Names*, and reintroduces these into the tradition. An angel has three kinds of movement: circular, straight and spiral. They move in a circle while focused on the illumining power issuing from their source; they move in a straight line when they come to offer guidance to other creatures; their spiral motion results from a combination of the two.[59]

Ficino also speaks about angels in a more conventional sense, such as the angels of the *Sanctus* or the guardian angels of the Psalms. He invokes angels at the beginning of certain sermons (perhaps those he conducted in the Camaldolese church of Santa Maria degli Angeli in Florence).[60] In another work, *On the Christian Religion* (1476), he describes the angelic hierarchy, following Dionysius and Dante, at least to start with. Looked at from the point of view of earth, which consists of elemental matter, there are seven planetary heavens, an eighth distinguished by its brightness and radiance, leading to the ninth, the Crystalline heaven, and beyond that the Empyrean, full of light, and still.[61] Its stillness makes it suited to the stability and light of the Trinity. The single essence of God is 'drawn down' first into the ternary number of the Trinity. The Trinity is then itself drawn down into the three hierarchies of three orders each, with each hierarchy relating specially to one person of the Trinity. The nine heavenly spheres of astronomy provide the locations in which the nine orders of angels circulate. But multiplicity begins to establish itself:

> Each order, as some theologians reckon, contains many legions. Each legion, they think, consists of six thousand six hundred and sixty-six individual spirits, and there are as many legions in each individual order as there are individual spirits in a legion.
>
> (Ficino, *On the Christian Religion*, 14)

A quick calculation shows that this would make for some 44,435,556 spirit-beings per order – that is, 399,920,004 daemons or angels in all. But Ficino backs away from putting a definite number to them, agreeing with Dionysius that it surpasses the capacity of human reckoning. Elsewhere he says that there are as many stars in heaven as there are legions of daemons, and each of those legions contains as many daemons as there are stars in the sky.[62]

In Dionysius, the hierarchies show a progressive diminution, each acting as interpreter and mediator of divine enlightenment for the next rank, but each passing on slightly less than the one before. Ficino's decision to link the three hierarchies more closely with the three Persons of the Trinity reduces this sense of diminution:

> In the first hierarchy the Seraphim contemplate the Father in Himself, the Cherubim contemplate the Father as begetting the Son, and the Thrones contemplate the Father with the Son as bringing forth the Spirit.
>
> In the second hierarchy the Dominions contemplate the Son in Himself, the Virtues the Son emanating from the Father, and the Powers contemplate the Son with the Father bringing forth the Spirit.
>
> In the third hierarchy the Principalities contemplate the Spirit in Itself, the Archangels the Spirit coming from the Father and the Son, and the Angels the Spirit depending upon the Son and the Father.
>
> (Ficino, *On the Christian Religion*, 14)[63]

Each sees the Trinity as a whole, but in its own way, without depending on the rank above. But when it comes to activities, the gradient of rank is restored: the seraphim, cherubim and Thrones are engaged in gazing upon divine providence and goodness while the other six orders 'descend to its works':

> The Dominions, like architects, instruct the others in what they should do. The Virtues carry out their commands, they move the heavens, and as the instruments of God hasten to perform his miracles. The Powers ward off whatever might seem able to disturb the order of divine government.

The rest descend more to human affairs. The Principalities
look after state matters, nations, rulers, public officials. The
Archangels lead the divine worship for everyone and are present
at sacred occasions. The Angels order lesser matters, each one
standing as guardian, one for every person.

(Ficino, *On the Christian Religion*, 14)

The real surprise occurs when Ficino declares that human souls are also
distributed into nine orders, and are capable of rising up to the order
and spirit of their choice, or indeed of tumbling downwards, according
to how they have lived their lives.

It is clear that heaven and earth, angels and mankind form one single
continuum, and both angels and mankind occupy a condition of being
a 'mean', in that they join two different states by participating in both.[64]
Because of the nature of the rational soul, we as humans can live at the
level of angel, or at the level of a beast, according to our actions and our
will. In fact, the options are wider still, because the soul can 'strive to
become all things', emphasizing the fluidity of the whole system:

It lives the life of a plant insofar as it indulges the body by
fattening it up; the life of the beast insofar as it flatters the
senses; the life of man insofar as it calls upon reason to handle
human affairs; the life of the heroes insofar as it investigates
things in nature; the life of the demons insofar as it contemplates
mathematics; the life of the angels insofar as it inquires into the
mysteries divine; and the life of God insofar as it does all things
for God's sake.

(Ficino, *Platonic Theology*, 14.3.2)

The association of demons with mathematics seems strange, but he
probably means the principles of scientific thinking, so his demons,
or daemons, are of no small stature. The angels are associated with a
higher kind of understanding, here called mysteries. Elsewhere, they
represent love. Essentially love and understanding are inseparable, being
both aspects of divine light, which illumines and also warms. In fact,
the whole creation is seen as an expression of the outward flow and the
subsequent return of divine light and love. Angels and humans differ
only in their capacity to transmit or reflect this.

Three times we have noted how little humans differ from angels, and Ficino does eventually ask why angel and soul are not equal in perfection, since both depend on God without an intermediary (*Platonic Theology*, 5.13.11). The answer is that they are produced under different 'ideas', and the idea of angel is 'loftier' than that of soul. A further difference is the time of their creation. Although human souls have a degree of immortality, they 'have not existed through all time like the angels, who emerged in the natural order from the very beginning of things before the circling of the heavens', that is, before time (*Platonic Theology*, 18.2.3). Souls are created daily within time, and are subject to mutability. Angels were created before time and are devoid of matter. This is stressed in an essay prompted by closer study of Dionysius: it is angelic light that is spoken into existence on the first day of creation, while the light of the sun appears only on the fourth day.[65] He also suggests that we simply raise our eyes to the clear night sky if we wish to understand angelic divinities:

> When you wish to affirm the presence of a multitude of angelic minds in the heavens above, which like lights, succeed each other in their proper order and are all placed in relation to the one God, father of lights, of what use to you will be the circumlocutions of long investigations? I beseech you, turn your eyes towards heaven … that heaven made by God in the most perfect and manifest order for the very purpose of making all this evident.
>
> (Ficino, *On the Sun*, ch. 2)

The Sun is the symbol of God, but the stars make visible the presence of invisible angelic powers.

The daemons who throng the region between heaven and earth in Neoplatonic thought figure frequently in Ficino's writings. He often considers them to be guardian angels, or innate guiding spirits. In contrast with the general thinking that one guardian angel is created for each soul,[66] Ficino asserts that several good daemons can be watching over an individual, exerting their influence 'by an easy and hidden persuasion'.[67] Similarly, he often claims that two individuals can share one guiding spirit in common. This helps to account for a sense of common purpose where two men are, so to speak, 'born under the same star', for stars are the governors of daemons. However in such passages, Ficino himself never uses the word 'angel' (*angelus*), only *daemon* or *genius*.

Again thinking Neoplatonically, in Ficino's work the nine orders of angels occasionally transform themselves into the nine celestial Muses, since they are 'divinities distributed through the nine spheres of the universe ... hidden from our view, dedicated by degrees, to single stars'. Acknowledging the importance of this tradition, he tells us that these are what Proclus calls angels and Iamblichus mainly calls archangels and principalities.[68]

Ficino's thinking about angels, whether personal angels or ontological, metaphysical Angel, draws heavily upon non-Christian sources and Christian ones. But all the threads are aligned in a single direction: for Ficino, the realm between earth and heaven is the realm of the angels, a region of universal higher mind, to which individual minds have access in varying degrees. It is a realm where knowledge is held, knowledge of things beyond the world of the senses. It is also full of light and love. Ficino's angelic world can hardly be called a 'collective unconscious', to use the Jungian term, as it is full of consciousness and light.[69] Similarly we can hardly dismiss it as being 'just' a matter of psychology, in the sense of being a projection of our inner neuroses. It does, however, present an early form of 'psychology' in its original sense of being concerned with the *psyche*, the mind or soul.

Angels and Humans

If angels fill the heavens, and the space between earth and heaven, what more can be said about their relationship with humankind? Who else, besides Ficino, believed that this space was accessible to humankind? The Metaphysical poet Thomas Traherne (1637–74) felt a personal connection with the angelic world through memories of earliest childhood.[70] He reminds us that in infancy we are still close to that light, and see things almost with angels' eyes.

> All appeared new, and strange at first, inexpressibly rare and
> delightful and beautiful. I was a little stranger, which at my
> entrance into the world was saluted and surrounded with

innumerable joys. My knowledge was Divine. I knew by intuition those things which since my Apostasy, I collected again by the highest reason. My very ignorance was advantageous. I seemed as one brought into the Estate of Innocence. All things were spotless and pure and glorious: yea, and infinitely mine, and joyful and precious ...

The corn was orient and immortal wheat, which never should be reaped, nor was ever sown. I thought it had stood from everlasting to everlasting. The dust and stones of the street were as precious as gold: the gates were at first the end of the world. The green trees when I saw them first through one of the gates transported and ravished me, their sweetness and unusual beauty made my heart to leap, and almost mad with ecstasy, they were such strange and wonderful things: The Men! O what venerable and reverend creatures did the aged seem! Immortal Cherubims! And young men glittering and sparkling Angels, and maids strange seraphic pieces of life and beauty! Boys and girls tumbling in the street, and playing, were moving jewels.

(Thomas Traherne, *Third Century of Meditations*, 2-3)

For Traherne, our highest aspiration is to return to that state. He bids us pray earnestly for that pure apprehension and divine light, 'for they will make you angelical, and wholly celestial', dwelling in a state of constant eternity. One poem begins with a startling memory, 'How like an Angel came I down!' and in three stanzas of sparkling clarity, he carries us back to a time of purity, when his senses were bright, his mind attuned to the presence of the creator, and he himself walked on earth but had not yet lost his heavenly connection.[71] The American Transcendentalist, Bronson Alcott (1799–1888), used Traherne's line as his title when recording conversations with children on the Gospels, and on angels.[72]

One consequence of the Neoplatonic, emanationist view of angels is that it tends to confirm the idea that angels are above humankind. As one late Talmudic source puts it,

Everything in the world exists in a hierarchy: the heaven is above the earth, the stars are above the heaven ... man is above the beast since he has knowledge; the ministering angels are above humans.

(*Avot de Rabbi Natan*, B, 43:7)

Another related consequence is the assumption that light and love are progressively diluted, until only a very diminished light reaches the dense matter of plant life, rocks and stones. Thus reflections of the divine in the material world are undervalued. Against such a tendency, we have seen Ficino and Traherne speak out, as did William Blake (1757–1827) who reminded us 'to see a World in a grain of sand, And a Heaven in a wild flower' (*Auguries of Innocence*).

In recent decades, a question that has exercised theologians is how humans and angels relate to one another in the Bible. According to traditional thinking, man is below the angels because he has to eat, drink, multiply, sleep and die. Angels do not (late Talmudic *Avot de Rabbi Natan*). Christian doctrine agrees, seeing angels as spiritual beings without bodily needs. Yet recent work focuses on overlap between men and angels in ancient texts, and speculates on whether Christ had an angel's form.[73] According to Psalm 8 mankind is 'a little lower than the angels' yet occupies God's attention and is 'crowned with glory and honour'. Some Hebrew commentators point out that it means 'scarcely' lower than the angels, that the crowning is with a soul and splendour, implying that, at least potentially, man may therefore attain superiority over the angels.[74] The Babylonian Talmud states unequivocally that the righteous are higher than the ministering angels.[75] Luke 20:36 points out that in the resurrection the righteous become 'equal to the angels', having left behind bodies, gender and death. The distinguished commentator and former Chief Rabbi of the United Hebrew Congregations, Rabbi Dr J. H. Hertz asserted not so long ago that 'Angels are held by the Jewish Mystics to be inferior to man in the scale of spiritual existence; because man is no mere "messenger" but is endowed with free-will.'[76]

One writer even suggests that humans can create angels: in *The Thirteen Petalled Rose*, Adin Steinsaltz defines angels as occupants of the world of 'formation' rather than 'action', and each angel is the embodiment of a single emotion or impulse. Human beings differ from angels not by having a body (because for him the human being is in any case defined by 'soul') but by being complex, rather than single, and operating in the world of place, time and self. However, when a person acts with purity of intent, the action transcends its physical place, time and individual connection and rises into the angel world: an angel is created.[77]

An early statement of the special role of human beings in linking the heavenly and earthly worlds is attributed to the second-century Jewish sage, Simeon ben Halafta, recorded in a compilation, *Midrash Leviticus Rabbah*, dating from the fifth century. Although this passage makes no specific mention of angels, it balances human and heavenly powers in a typical kind of argumentation from early rabbinic Judaism:

> Great is peace, for when the Holy One, blessed be He, created
> His universe, He made peace between the upper and the lower
> [parts of the creation]. On the first day He created part of the
> upper regions and the lower ones, as it says, 'In the beginning
> God created the heavens and the earth' (Genesis 1:1). On
> the second day He created some of the upper portions of
> the universe, as it is written, 'And God said: Let there be a
> firmament' (1:6). On the third day He created some of the
> lower created things, 'Let the waters under the heaven be
> gathered together … Let the earth put forth grass,' etc. (1:9 ff.).
> On the fourth day [He created] some of the upper objects, 'Let
> there be lights in the firmament of the heavens' (1:14). On the
> fifth day He created some of the lower objects, as it is said,
> 'And God said: Let the waters swarm with swarms of living
> creatures' (1:20). On the sixth day, when He came to create
> man, He said: 'If I create man as one of the upper elements
> of the universe, the upper elements will outnumber the lower
> by one created object, and if I create him as one of the lower
> created objects, the lower will outnumber the upper by one
> created object.' What did He do? He created man as of the
> upper as well as of the lower beings.
>
> (*Midrash Leviticus Rabbah*, 9:9)

This special intermediate role was accepted in principle by the early Church Fathers, though in general the lower and upper worlds were kept apart, except for visiting angels performing specific functions, and guardian angels presenting us with good (or bad) opportunities on a more regular basis. Angels had been waiting since the expulsion from

Eden (which was 'caused by their own jealousy') to welcome humanity
back into their ranks, and when this happened it would restore the broken
unity and relieve them of the burdens of their ministry. But for the time
being, the arrival of humankind among the angels was envisioned only
upon death and resurrection.[78] Occasional appearances by angels in our
world occurred at moments of special significance, either in the lives
of individuals or publicly, as in Pavia on Easter Sunday, 970, enabling
the Emperor, Otto I, to reverse a decision without losing face.[79] But,
in general, the ability of angels to take visible form in our world was
doubted.

A major distinguishing mark of angels became their lack of free will.
It was through the exercise of free will in the form of rebellion that Satan
had lost his status as an angel. Ever since that event, the majority of
Christian writers have assumed that angels do not have free will, but are
simply bound to obey divine commands. Only fallen angels and humans
have free will. Perhaps this is why so many modern writers have found
the character of Satan and the fallen angels so very much more attractive
than the obedient angelic hosts. Human beings, although apparently
'held back' by being imprisoned in a physical body, have the innate
capacity to desire both good and evil. We therefore enjoy a situation
that is in crucial ways more interesting than that of the angels. We face
challenges, we can surmount obstacles of an inward and an outward
kind, we have potential for development and change that angels do
not have. This is poignantly illustrated in Wim Wenders's film, *Wings
of Desire*, where the angel willingly exchanges his angelic life of steady
contentment and compassion for the vagaries of exaltation and passion
experienced by humans. Even in Dante's *Paradiso*, where angels abound,
and their entire hierarchy is celebrated in glory, the significance of the
story is the human desire to know God.[80] Likewise the focus of Milton's
great angelic drama, *Paradise Lost*, is humankind.

But if angels cannot become human, can humans become angels? It
is intriguing to note that the word used in the Bible for human work or
occupations, *mal'akha*, comes from the same root as the word for angel,
mal'akh.[81] Swedenborg was convinced that he had kept company with
them, seeing and hearing 'the most amazing things in the other life'
where the angels had protected him there against a host of swarming
evil spirits.[82] But his experiences in the spirit world are not the same
as becoming an angel. We still must ask, is there a ladder of ascent,

and does it lead to man's transformation into an angel? Do the loved ones we have lost take up residence among the stars, and continue to move among us as angels? A young child bereaved of a parent may find deep consolation in such an idea, but with our adult minds we are not so certain. Yet Enoch was taken up into heaven and became the angel Metatron, Elijah became the angel Sandalphon, and Moses too was taken up. But is it limited to these three? Ficino seems to point to a fluidity of existence, and a second-century inscription of the teachings of the Oracle of Apollo at Claros proudly proclaims that we, humankind, are 'a portion of God: his angels'.[83] To answer questions such as these, we need to clarify our view of what angels are, and follow a few of the many writers who have considered them in depth.

Chapter 3

ANGELS AND DEMONS

Our ideas about angels and demons have their roots partly in the literature of the three Abrahamic religions, and partly in that of the classical world. Recently, there has been a great interest in inner angels and demons. For example, the evolutionary psychologist Steven Pinker plots a historic decline of our demons of violence and a corresponding rise of what he calls 'the better angels of our nature'.[1] This internalization of angels and demons as purely psychological forms has become a valid discourse, and 'facing one's demons' is always a useful step. But here we shall be principally concerned with angels and demons as understood theologically. Any idea that demons have no part to play in a book on angels has already been countered by the overlap we have noted, arising from the fact that there are good demons (and daemons) as well as bad. But in this chapter we shall attempt to segregate them, and deal first with the study of angels (though that is never entirely demon-free) from the medieval period up to recent times; then we shall briefly consider demons.

In medieval villages and towns, people were surrounded by numerous reminders of the presence of angels in the community, not just in art, but by references and allusions in daily life. One example is the Angelus: this sweet-sounding bell announced the end of the working day for farming communities as monks gathered to recite the Angelus prayer commemorating the annunciation to Mary by the Angel Gabriel, and the triple sounding of a triple stroke perhaps called to mind the ninefold hierarchy of angels.[2]

In the age of Enlightenment, many thought that the time had come to sweep away beliefs about heavenly hierarchies and angelic interventions as mere superstition. After Descartes, angels had no place in a mechanistic universe. However, angels were not so easily discarded! They lived on, vigorously, in art, in hymns and prayer, in the world of imaginative thinking, and in popular affection. One major reason for this is not hard to see. What the ancients called the divine mind and the realm of the gods has not disappeared so much as been renamed, and addressed in a new way. It is still the world of the soul, of archetypal images, of dreams and the unconscious, and of the inner workings of the mind, but it has become the province of psychology. By this people generally understand something modern, scientific, measured and rational. Psychology has for many replaced religious dogma, and it is concerned more with the mind than the soul. But we should be wary of the temptation to write off all talk of angels as projections of our own imagination. In 1996, a priest and a physicist sat down together to discuss the reality of angels.[3] Their conversations, ranged through ideas presented by the Bible, by Dionysius, Aquinas and Hildegard of Bingen, and through modern cosmology, photons, electromagnetic force, contemporary thought and feelings, and the art of all ages. They were searching for objective, not subjective, experiences of angels, and were hoping to formulate a new relationship with angelic intelligences so as to put right some of the social and ecological problems in the world. They asked interesting questions about celestial intelligence and the ever-expanding, ever-evolving universe. They even formulated an agenda for action where most of us are still only feeling our way. But at least two of their underlying premises are unimpeachable: firstly, that any consideration of the angelic world worth undertaking must relate to our ordinary everyday thinking, and secondly, that we should take account of the angelology of the high Middle Ages.

Angelology

For medieval philosophers and theologians many questions that now seem obscurantist were matters of intense rational concern. We already noted that the old chestnut, 'how many angels can dance on the head of a needle', reflects a broader question of whether angels have physical bodies that occupy space. Similarly Aquinas asked whether angels could

see God, how they knew what they knew, whether they had knowledge
of particular things, how they moved, and whether time affects them.
People wanted to know how many angels there are, and exactly when
they were created – or if they are still being created.

Arguments about when they were created go back a long way. Hebrew
commentators discussed the meaning of Genesis 1:26, 'And God said,
Let us make man in our image.' What kind of a plural is intended by
'our' image? Is it simply a 'plural of majesty' or does it include the angels,
already created?[4] In whose image, then, are we made? Rashi interpreted
it as a consultation with the angels, and hence as a sign of divine humility,
assuming that the 'likeness' is to be of the angels, and that angels might
consequently be jealous of man. In *Pirke de Rabbi Eliezer*, which regards
the consultation as being with the Torah, God is said to have led the
angels in their new ministry towards humankind:

> On the day when the first man was created ... the Holy One,
> blessed be He, said to the ministering angels, 'Come, let us
> descend and render loving service to the first man and to his
> help-mate, for the world rests upon the attribute of the service
> of loving-kindness.'
>
> *(Pirke de R. Eliezer*, 13)[5]

The loving-kindness they were to establish, setting an example for
mankind, would mean more than the entire sacrifices and burnt-
offerings of the future. Obadiah Sforno (*c.*1475–1550) advanced the
view that man is to be like the angels in understanding, but unlike them
in possessing free will. Others considered mankind more like God than
like the angels.[6]

It is, in fact, reasonable to suppose that we are created in the image
of God rather than the angels, since the following verse confirms it
(Genesis 1:27). Nevertheless, the involvement of angels at the time
of man's creation was the subject for intense speculation. A Talmudic
midrash says:

> When the Holy One, blessed be He, wished to create man,
> He first created a company of ministering angels and said to
> them: 'Is it your desire that we make a man in our image?' They
> answered, 'Sovereign of the Universe, what will be his deeds?'

'Such and such will be his deeds,' He replied. Thereupon
they exclaimed, 'Sovereign of the Universe, What is man that
thou art mindful of him, and the son of man that thou thinkest
of him? (Psalm 8:5)' Thereupon He stretched out His little
finger among them and consumed them with fire.

The same thing happened with a second company. The third
company said to Him, 'Sovereign of the Universe, what did it
avail the former angels that they spoke to Thee as they did? The
whole world is Thine, and whatsoever that Thou wishest to do
therein, do it.'

(Babylonian Talmud, *Sanhedrin* 38b)

When it came to the great flood, God was asked whether the first angels
hadn't been right all along. His reply is full of compassion for human
failings.

Another midrash describes dissension between God and the angels
over the creation of man:

Rabbi Simon said: When the Holy One, blessed be He, came
to create Adam, the ministering angels formed themselves into
groups and parties, some of them saying, 'Let him be created,'
while others urged, 'Let him not be created.' Thus it is written,
'Love and Truth fought together, Righteousness and Peace
combated each other.' [Psalm 85:11]: Love said, 'Let him be
created, because he will dispense acts of love'; Truth said, 'Let
him not be created, because he is compounded of falsehood';
Righteousness said, 'Let him be created, because he will perform
righteous deeds'; Peace said, 'Let him not be created because he
is full of strife.' ...

While the ministering angels were arguing with each other
and disputing with each other, the Holy One, blessed be He,
created him. God said to them, 'What can you avail? Man has
already been made!'

(*Midrash Rabbah*, 8:5)

The Platonists sometimes asserted that 'God formed angels by Himself,
but souls by means of angels'.[7] Religious authorities made God's
creation of man direct. Nowadays, all such speculations are of course

swept away as we try to accommodate the concept of evolution in our thinking about the creation story.

Angelology, or the study of angels, is said to have reached its high point in the Middle Ages, accompanied in Christendom by a wonderful visual commentary in religious art and architectural decoration. In Judaism and Islam, doctrinal aversion to figurative art kept the speculations mainly to philosophy and poetry, but at certain periods and especially in manuscript illuminations, visual angels are to be found there too. (See Figures 4 and 11.)

In Judaism, Maimonides (1135–1204) marks a high point in the attempt to understand angels, though his views were not universally shared. For him, all angels are conscious beings, constantly active, and all good. They are divided into two classes, permanent and perishable. The former he called Intelligences, in the sense used by Aristotle and Avicenna: that is, the spiritual intelligences that move the spheres and influence the creation from a high level. He disagrees with Aristotle who denied that the heavenly bodies create a music of the spheres, citing Pythagorean and Jewish interpretations of their singing, but allows space for disagreement on such topics, suggesting that 'for speculative matters everyone treats according to the results of his own study, and everyone accepts that which appears to him established by proof'.[8] He also defines what he means by a sphere, and the correct enumeration of the spheres, of which there are nine, seven of them with planets, one for the fixed stars, and one all-encompassing sphere beyond the stars. The tenth intelligence is the Active Intellect.[9]

In the first book of his great compilation, *Mishne Torah* (Code of Law), Maimonides discusses angels' forms:[10]

Everything that God created in His world can be placed in one of three classifications. Firstly, there are those creations, such as the bodies of men and animals, plants and metals, which have matter and form which come into being and then perish. Secondly, there are those creations which have matter and form which does not vary from body to body or in appearance, like those in the first category do, but their form is fixed forever in their matter and can never change. These are the spheres and the stars contained therein. Their matter and form are not like any other matter or form. Thirdly, there are those creations which have a form but no matter at all. These are the angels, which have no bodies, but they are forms that are separate one from another.

This is all very clear and analytical, but needs to be applied to religious tradition:

> What, then, did the Prophets mean when they said that they saw angels of fire with wings? This is in the vision of the prophecy, it is the way of a codeword to indicate that it is not a body and it has no weight. As it is written, 'For the Lord your God is a consuming fire'. But He is not a fire. It is just the way of analogy. As it is said, '… who makes the winds His messengers'.[11]

Returning to scientific logic, he continues,

> How, therefore, are their forms separate if they have no bodies?

He goes on to consider what is meant by difference, and by 'high' and 'low' when all of them owe their existence to God but some additionally owe it to those 'above' them.

> The phrase 'some being below others' does not refer to positions in physical height, but just as one person can be more learned than another and we say that he is 'above' the other, and just as we say that one set of circumstances is 'above' another, so is the meaning of this phrase.
>
> (Maimonides, *Mishne Torah*, I, *Hilchot Yesodei ha Torah*
> (Laws of the Foundations of the Torah) II, 3-6)

Though 'high' and 'low' are not to be taken spatially, Maimonides still ranks the angels. Dionysius had enumerated nine ranks, arranged with Trinitarian symmetry in three hierarchies, and he supplemented four Hebrew names from the Old Testament with five names from St Paul. Maimonides finds ten ranks of angels, for the ten intelligences governing the cosmos, and takes all his names from Hebrew scripture:

> There is a change of names of angels, according to their level. The highest level consists of the *Holy Chayot* then come

the *Ophanim*, the *Erelim*, the *Chashmalim*, the *Seraphim*, the *Malachim*, the *Elohim*, the *Bnei Elohim*, the *Cheruvim* and the *Ishim*. These are the ten names that the angels are called by, according to their ten degrees.

The highest level is that of the *Holy Chayot* and there is none other above it, except that of God. Therefore, in the Prophecies, it is said that they are underneath God's throne. The tenth level consists of the *Ishim*, who are the angels who speak with the Prophets and appear to them in prophetic visions. They are therefore called *Ishim* (men) because their level is close to the level of the consciousness of human beings.

(Hilchot Yesodei ha Torah, II, 7)

The *Chayot*[12] and *Ophanim* are the Living Beings and Wheels of Ezekiel's vision, and *Erelim* are Thrones. *Chashmal* is the mysterious substance in Ezekiel's vision, sometimes translated as amber.[13] *Seraphim* and *Cheruvim* are more familiar (see Chapters 5 and 6), and *Malachim* are the messenger angels we have already met. Perhaps the *Cheruvim* appear so apparently low in the list because of their presence among mankind, as for example on the cover of the Ark of the Covenant.[14] *Elohim* are undefined divine powers, but the use here echoes that in the Qumran texts, meaning just 'angels'. The new category here is the *Bnei Elohim*, their sons. Yet angels are created each for a specific task and do not procreate – unless perhaps these may be the 'sons of God' of Genesis 6:2?[15] The last rank are the *Ishim*, and they derive their name from *Ish*, a man.

All these forms live and know their Creator exceedingly well; each form according to its level and not according to its size. Even those on the topmost level cannot comprehend the reality of [the existence of] God for the reason that their intellect is insufficient for them to do so, but they understand and comprehend better than those on the levels below theirs do. Even those on the tenth level have some understanding of God, but it is beyond the capabilities of Man, who comprises both form and shape, to understand as well as those on the tenth level do. None know God the way He Himself does.

(Hilchot Yesodei ha Torah, II, 8)[16]

In his *Guide to the Perplexed*, II, 6, Maimonides extends the term angel to include a variety of natural forces, including the elements, especially wind and fire. He also includes human agency: 'every one that is intrusted with a certain mission is an angel'. So when the Prophet Daniel says 'My God has sent his angel and has shut the lions' mouths, and they have not hurt me' (Daniel 6:22) we do not have to imagine a winged being standing beside Daniel in the lion's den, but can relate the action to his own powers, implanted in him, of course, by God. The natural forces of the individual, however, including the powers of the soul, are perishable angels, not eternal ones, hence the saying 'Every day God creates a legion of angels; they sing before Him, and disappear' (quoting the third-century commentary on Genesis, *Bereshit Rabbah*, 78). In the same chapter he also calls our imaginative faculty angel, recalling the rabbinic dictum, 'When a man sleeps, his soul speaks to the angel, the angel to the cherub'. The angel here is the imagination, the cherub is the intellect. Likewise, he says, when people refer to the angel of lust tempting someone, they are speaking of his (or her) own lustful disposition.

Maimonides went so far that his near contemporary and fierce critic, Nachmanides (1194–c.1270), accused him of dismissing all angelic happenings as 'events that took place of themselves' and of describing all conversations relating to them as 'in a vision'. In his own stricter reading, allegorical interpretations are shunned: 'Such words contradict Scripture. It is forbidden to listen to them, all the more to believe in them.'[17] Maimonides himself had warned,

> The first Sages commanded us not to discuss these topics with more than one person and that person should be exceedingly wise. When teaching someone these topics, one teaches him first what is contained in the beginning of these chapters in small quantities, and he should be able to deduce further details on his own. These matters are extremely deep in nature, and not everyone can understand them.
>
> (*Mishne Torah*, II, 11-12)

Considering the centrality of angels in scriptural texts, one can have sympathy for Nachmanides's view, which undoubtedly reflected the position of earlier influential thinkers. Among the prayers enshrined in the traditional Jewish rite from very earliest times and recited daily even now are paragraphs about holy beings 'that exalt the Almighty, constantly proclaiming God's glory and holiness'. God is blessed as

> Creator of the ministering angels, all of whom stand in the universe's heights, proclaiming together, in awe, aloud, the words of the living God the eternal King. They are all beloved, all pure, all mighty, and all perform in awe and reverence the will of their Maker. All open their mouths in holiness and purity with song and psalm, and bless, praise, glorify, revere, sanctify and declare the sovereignty of the name … All accept on themselves, one from another, the yoke of the kingdom of heaven, granting permission to one another to sanctify the One who formed them, in serene spirit, pure speech and sacred melody, and all, as one, respond, saying in awe, 'Holy, holy, holy is the Lord of hosts: the whole world is filled with His glory.'
>   Then the Ophanim and the Holy Chayot, with a roar of noise, raise themselves toward the Seraphim and, facing them, give praise, saying: 'Blessed be the Lord's glory from His place.'
>   (*Daily Morning Service* of the United Synagogue)[18]

Nevertheless, Maimonides insists that angels are to be understood as non-corporeal intelligences. He refuses to consider them as independent beings, with continued existence, sometimes assuming human form and becoming visible to human beings. In the *Guide to the Perplexed*, he specifically dismisses the idea of healing by angelic intercession, and also downgrades to the rank of prophet the 'angel' in Exodus 23:20-21 whom Israel is to obey.[19]

Maimonides advances some further unusual arguments. He decides that Jacob's ladder had only four steps (though some say seven), and he cites ancient commentaries for the existence of only four angels upon it, two ascending and two descending – but all standing on the same rung. This leads to a paradox: the ladder must be of enormous width, since each angel is said to be equal to one third of the world. The four angels thus occupy four thirds of the world! With imperturbable logic he reminds us that 'angel' is clearly one third of the world since the creation consists of three parts: (i) pure intelligences, or angels, (ii) the bodies of the spheres, and (iii) matter, which constitutes all the bodies below the spheres that are in constant flux.[20] He invites us, if we understand these dark sayings, or if we desire to understand them, to raise ourselves up to the angels, for we who enquire are awake, and can shake off our forgetfulness. Let others 'swim in the waters of their ignorance'.[21]

He also challenges the idea that angels have no free will. He thinks that they have conscious choice, and freedom of will in the sphere of action entrusted to them. How they go about their allotted task and to whom they impart their gifts are choices within their own control. Maimonides also maintains that everything in the universe comes into being only through the participation of angels. This is not just a reference to those passages where God appears to be speaking to someone, as in 'Let us make man in our image' (Genesis 1:26) or 'Let us go down, and confound their language' at the Tower of Babel (Genesis 11:7) which tradition interprets as God consulting with his heavenly host. Instead, he takes the example of a baby growing in the womb. This is accomplished, he says, in all its precise detail, by an angel. Not in the sense that an angel, which can be as large as one-third the size of the universe, and consists of burning fire, flies into the womb of a woman to form the foetus – though he thinks many religious people might be prepared to believe even that, as a miracle – but he calls the formative power of the seed itself 'angel', because of the miraculous nature of the unseen creative powers held there. He ruefully notes that people find it much harder to believe this kind of miracle than the more spectacular version. Yet such forces reside everywhere, in the individual and in the cosmos, and should be considered as 'angel'. It also follows that one angel does not perform two things; nor are two angels ever sent to perform one thing, because it would be out of keeping with their nature as creative forces.[22]

This highly philosophical or metaphysical way of considering angels is challenging. Not for nothing does Maimonides call his biblical source texts 'dark sayings', and reminds the reader to 'note and consider well all we have said', as well as limiting the teaching of such things.[23]

In Islam, discussion of angels had already reached a peak with the works of Al-Farabi and Avicenna. As described in Chapter 2, the creation of the world flows from a triple contemplation. The highest angels are the cherubim, and the Angels of Magnificence. These are the heavenly intelligences Maimonides spoke of. As we saw, the angel associated with the moon is Gabriel, of great significance in Islam (as Jibra'il). Below the moon, are human souls, illuminated by the angels above, but primarily by the 'tenth angel', the 'active intellect' shared in common by all humankind.

This idea was interpreted by subsequent thinkers, East and West, to suggest that the more one can empty the mind of its natural preoccupation with the sensory world, and still it from its natural perturbations, the more light it will be able to receive and to reflect. We find this not only in the mystics of Judaism, Christianity and Islam but also more widely. For example, in Ficino: when a person's mind is clear, level and at rest, in the very moment of reflecting back the divine ray, the living soul is itself carried upwards to union with the divine:

> If a ray, descending from God Himself to the soul on the
> perpendicular, lights upon a soul [set aslant] at an irregular
> angle, it bounces off it sideways, and naturally does not
> reveal God, but some empty flash in the soul … But if it has
> found a soul that is inwardly level and horizontal, it springs
> back straight to God, and takes the soul with it to the happy
> embrace of its own object and end, where the mind at last
> enjoying God, enjoys itself also, that is, finding itself for itself in
> the Ideal form.
>
> (Ficino, *Commentary on the Epistles of St Paul*, ch. 8)

However for Avicenna it is reunion with the tenth angel that is seen as the final stage of human life. This reunion is considered a natural effect rather than a specially undertaken goal.

Avicenna's tenth angel became the 'agent intellect' of scholastic thinking, a kind of shared collective consciousness – though the extent of collective versus individual consciousness would be hotly disputed among philosophers of the Renaissance.

The two greatest medieval authorities on angels from the Christian point of view are the Dominican monk, Thomas Aquinas (1225–74), later known as 'the Angelic Doctor', and his contemporary Franciscan leader, John of Fidanza, or Bonaventure (1221–74), later known as 'the Seraphic Doctor'.[24] Aquinas embraced Aristotelian science, but also drew substantially on the Church Fathers, Avicenna, Maimonides and other Neoplatonic sources, through Latin translations of the Arabic versions of the Greek originals. Aquinas himself commissioned some of these. Bonaventure's interests were more focused on the way of devotion.

Aquinas approached the topic in his *Summa Theologiae*, dealing systematically with such subjects as the nature of angels, their powers, their number and types, by a series of questions, objections and answers. Questions 50 to 64 of the first part of this massive work are concerned with angels. He then returns to them in questions 106 to 109. The first point to note in his view is that the existence of angels is actually required for the universe to reflect perfection:

> There must be some incorporeal creatures. For what is principally intended by God in creatures is good, and this consists in assimilation to God Himself. And the perfect assimilation of an effect to a cause is accomplished when the effect imitates the cause according to that whereby the cause produces the effect; as heat makes heat. Now, God produces the creature by His intellect and will.[25] Hence the perfection of the universe requires that there should be intellectual creatures. Now intelligence cannot be the action of a body, nor of any corporeal faculty; for every body is limited to 'here' and 'now'. Hence the perfection of the universe requires the existence of an incorporeal creature.
>
> (Thomas Aquinas, *Summa Theologiae*,
> Part I, Question 50, article 1)

He also states that they are here for our sake, to 'give evidence of that intellectual companionship which men expect to have with them in the life to come'.[26] He argues for immense numbers of angels, far beyond all material multitude, but every angel is a single species. They cannot be grouped together and divided by matter, because they have none. Nor, for the same reason, are they corruptible. They can assume bodies, as when they appear and are seen by more than one person. To say that they do not assume bodies would be to make such appearances mere imagination, which he rejects. This is very far from the view of Maimonides.

Though angels assume bodies, they do not have full bodily functions, so that their bodies are somewhat lifeless. They do not eat, even if occasionally they seem to. They appear to speak, but it is a fashioning of sounds in the air rather than proper organs of speech being used; and they do not perceive with the senses, but directly with intellect. Though they appear to move, their movement belongs to the bodies and is therefore only 'accidental'. Real movement for them would be more like the heavenly bodies, but these do not altogether change their places, since they move only partially in relation to one another. Their relationship to space and place is therefore tenuous, and they may be very large or very small according to the body taken. It is, however, finite. An angel cannot be everywhere. Two angels cannot occupy the same place at the same time, not because they would fill it in some bodily sense, but because the application of one angel's power to the place in question sufficiently fills it so that there is no need for a further angel in that place. Angels' movement can be continuous, or non-continuous. If the latter, there is no need for them to pass through the space in between, yet their movements are not instantaneous.

Aquinas then examines questions of intellect: how angels know and what they know. Can they know individual things? Can they see the future? Can they read the secrets of the human heart? Of the future, angels can know causes, but not specific outcomes. Of God,

> Since God's image is impressed on the very nature of the angel in his essence, the angel knows God in as much as he is the image of God. Yet he does not behold God's essence; because no created likeness is sufficient to represent the Divine essence.
> (Aquinas, *Summa Theologiae*, Question 56, article 3)

He calls such knowledge 'specular', meaning that the angel is a mirror image of the divine. He continues through matters of will, love, grace and error. Can an angel sin? (no). Did as many stay loyal as fell? (more stayed loyal), and so on. Demons, unlike angels, are deprived of all knowledge of truth; they are obstinate, unhappy and undergoing punishment.

Such simple summaries of Aquinas's thinking do little justice to the complexities of his carefully weighed and balanced arguments. His method is to gather what others have held on each question, which may yield a wide variety of views in conflict one with another, and after considering all the alternatives, to arrive at a reasoned, closely argued resolution. He raises points that all later discussions will feel obliged to follow, and one can say that almost all European discussion of angels starts from his text. Yet his questions cover far more detail than most people want to know today, especially when he delves into the distinctions between potential and actual, and whether a lower angel can illuminate a higher one.

For Bonaventure, angels had matter, but it was of a spiritual kind. More importantly angels were a constant presence. By their example of combining activity in the world with perfect contemplation of the divine, they set the model for devout human life. Franciscan worship made a special place for contemplation of the angels. For if an angel could engage in work in the world while still contemplating God throughout his activity, humans could at least aspire to serve in worldly work while holding angels in mind. Franciscan angels have less of the cosmic intellect about them than those of Aquinas; they are very much ministering angels and the key texts for Bonaventure are Luke 16:22, where the angels carry the beggar Lazarus to the bosom of Abraham, and Isaiah 6:2-3 where the seraphim spontaneously cry out their praise. Bonaventure's own writings are full of angelic contemplations and the first steps of the soul's journey to God are on the rungs of Jacob's ladder. His angels do have some cosmic functions, but they are linked to their human ministry:

> According to the theologians, the ruling of the universe is
> attributed to the angels, in relation to the work of restoration,
> under the dominion of the most high God. Hence they are
> called 'ministering spirits, sent for the sake of those who inherit
> salvation'.
>
> (Bonaventure, *The Soul's Journey into God*, 2.2)

They may also illumine the minds of all who are engaged in the work of ministering to the poor and needy. Bonaventure called St Francis, the Order's founder, the 'Angel of true peace' and he relates the saint's special fondness for a church where he felt angels dwelt, together with his belief that food begged for in holy poverty was the 'food of angels'.[27]

Both Aquinas and Bonaventure look back to St Augustine, who famously remarked that it is easier to know what angels did than what they were,[28] and to the great codification of angels accomplished by Dionysius.

Angels of the Reformation

Moving now to the long era of church reform, a few examples selected from across the confessional divide will represent a huge field.

George Benigno (1446–1520), a leading spokesman for the Franciscan Order in Renaissance Rome, produced some thoughts on angels in the context of an important debate on prophecy, determinism and free will.[29] Responding to ideas articulated by Ficino, that mankind could receive prophecy from God, through a single ray that passes from God through the angels and into human minds,[30] he stressed the fact that the true prophet received his prophecies directly from God. Angels are only transmitters. This argument had immediate relevance while Savonarola, the controversial Dominican friar, was claiming to be God's prophet for the spiritual regeneration of Florence. Benigno's work on *Angelic Nature*, completed after Savonarola's death, was a substantial volume, running to nine books. It rehearsed much of the standard medieval thinking on angels, but also introduced more recent medical opinion on prophetic ability and possession by demons, as well as considering the whole range of intermediate beings proposed by Ficino's revival of Neoplatonic doctrines on daemons. Although Benigno defended Ficino's work at Rome, he felt constrained to challenge his teachings on daemons, so he emphasized the division between mankind and angels, dismissing all demons as evil spirits, and ranking any miracles they seem to perform as mere *mirabilia*, not *miracula* (admirable but not miracles). Yet he conceded that angelic foreknowledge of events has much to do with the stars, and even astrologers may attain a certain amount of such knowledge through art and experience, and may put it to good use, especially in medicine.

By contrast with this substantial reworking of ideas, a small pamphlet published in Frankfurt in 1553 seemed sufficient to sum up all that needed to be known about angels. Wilhelm Sandfurt, a German Protestant pastor, reduced the topic of angels to 20 questions. Are there angels? What do they signify? What of their name? When were they created? Only on the fifth question does he ask, what are they? And the perennial question, how many are they? Four questions follow on the devil, before he returns to guardian angels and some practical questions: Do they pray for us? Can we invoke them? How should we honour them? Then a rather pointed question: Will the faithful become like them? Do they each have special names? And, perhaps looking over his shoulder, Do they see and know everything? Finally, are there distinct choirs of angels? All these enquiries are answered plainly and simply in a mere 43 octavo pages, but compared with what went before there is nothing new except brevity.[31]

It is not surprising if for others things were less clear-cut. In 1572, the Catholic Hannibal Rosselli of Calabria turned his attention to angels, and, working intensively during the weeks around Christmas, wrote several hundred large folio pages reviewing all the different arguments of the great authorities. The book grew even further in the following months, and formed the second volume of six in a huge commentary on the *Pymander* and *Asclepius* of Hermes Trismegistus, that was in fact more of an encyclopaedia of philosophy. At the time, Rosselli was teaching theology to the Franciscan Observants at Todi. It was only when he was appointed Professor of Theology at the order's house in Krakow, the Bernardine monastery on Castle Hill, that the work was printed. The various volumes appeared from 1584 to 1590, each dedicated to a distinguished patron in Italy or Poland. The angel volume was dedicated to Cardinal Ferdinando de' Medici, in 1585.[32]

There are many surprising aspects to this work: the prominence given to angels, the detailed study of Hermes by a devout friar, his willingness to draw on such a wide variety of pre-Christian and pagan sources, and the agreement of the authorities to publish such a work. Much had changed since Ficino's time, with the Council of Trent (1545–63) drawing stricter boundaries on what might or might not be written and read.

Rosselli quotes the Hermes text one short passage at a time, painstakingly assembling the arguments of ancient and medieval philosophers for and against every point, and resolving disagreements where possible. In other words, he is applying the scholastic method of the past and using the Hermetic texts as an interface between Christian and Platonic thinking. In Hermes, angels are called spirits and daemons; to Rosselli they have the same dignity as Christian angels, 'more noble than other creatures'. Topics of extended debate include the number of angels, what it is that they move and whether they are material or immaterial. Rosselli draws on numerous poets, Latin and Greek, on the Church Fathers, and on Plato, Plotinus, Aristotle, Democritus, Zeno and Averroes among philosophers. He concludes that the spheres are moved by their own intrinsic form, obeying the will of God alone. At most one might call them intelligences. However the angels also move in circuits, embracing the world of sensory existence. Angels can illumine human minds, and they rejoice in the meditation of the human mind, making man a participant in their own ranks.[33]

Where Hermes speaks of the 'seven governors', Rosselli takes these to be the seven planets, which influence the character and fate of individuals and nations. The constellation that forms the head of the Dragon is none other than Lucifer, and the great sin of Lucifer was pride.[34] Mankind, beasts and insensate matter all take their place in descending order beneath the angels, but all are composed of the same elements, falling further from the condition of reason towards that of matter. Most curious of all is the way in which he ends the various sections, not with 'Praise be to God', as one might expect, but 'Praise to the divine Pymander'. One can only imagine that he understood Pymander as 'shepherd of men' and identified him with that other Good Shepherd, Christ.[35]

Such detailed considerations of angels were by no means restricted to the Catholic Church. Within the universities of certain Protestant towns in Germany disputations continued to be held on the subject of angels well into the seventeenth century. At the Lutheran Academy of Giessen, one such disputation was held in 1616, when Boethius Petri Diethmarsus defended 32 propositions before a number of guests with the professor of Metaphysics, Logic and Pedagogy presiding. The professor, Christoph Scheibler, was a leading philosopher and theologian, and wrote a book on angels himself in 1632,[36] but we know nothing of the defender. His arguments are mainly scholastic and concerned with definitions. He equates the 'minds' and 'intelligences' of 'the Ethnics' with fully-fledged Christian messenger-angels.[37] He states first that they are clearly spiritual, not material. But this does not mean they are 'nothing'. He puts them in the category of 'possible' things. Precisely what they are (their 'quiddity') is best approached through what they do. Being immaterial they can appear to men in prison – doors and windows do not shut them in, or out – but so can demons. Their spirit is finite: even though they have no body to limit it; it is of long duration rather than eternal, but requires some special act of God to end it. Their knowledge is limited. As regards the future, they can see what arises from 'necessary causes' – like a mathematician having foreknowledge of an eclipse. But they do not know what is not revealed. They cannot read the innermost secrets of the human mind, unless those are betrayed in signs or visible emotions. He even hints that they can only know one thing at a time. He ascribes a sort of free will to them, but one that is directed towards the good. He is uncertain how they speak, or how they move, but he is sure they do not get from one place to another instantaneously or without passing through what lies in between. They cannot create anything, procreate, or digest food, but they can cause things to happen by moving other beings.

A similar document from Wittenberg examines angels with pedantic thoroughness, again manipulating the thinking of the scholastics. The author, Jacob Musselius, reflects the concerns of his milieu with a section on succubus and incubus, those demons of folklore that seduce men and women in their sleep, together with a list of herbs which might help guard against them.[38] This disputation, of which only two copies survive, was held in the university's faculty of Philosophy, starting at seven o'clock in the morning.

In another debate, held at the academy of Marburg at the 'accustomed time' on the morning of 17 December, 1625 (so these debates were a regular part of university life), Wigandus Mogius raised 39 points about angels. He tried to restrict himself to their functions rather than their nature. This presentation took place in the department of Philosophy, under its Professor of Physics, Johannes Henricus Tonsoris.[39] After a suitable résumé of biblical texts, he notes that angels are part of the creation, they have a fiery nature, which accounts for their readiness and agility in service, and they move so swiftly to accomplish their work that they are said to fly and have wings. He insists that it is an intolerable error to think of them simply as movements in the minds of men, because their accomplishments would be impossible if they had no existence in and of themselves. These accomplishments include many wonderful actions that are outward and exposed to our senses. So he concludes they either assume some bodily shape, or take on real created bodies.[40]

Mogius thinks that angels are numerous, though their number is known only to God, and that hierarchical order exists among them, but only according to the different kinds of task they fulfil, not according to differences in excellence or dignity, 'as if some are worthier than others'. All angels were the same in the beginning. Some fell, but the good ones persisted in their primal integrity and are now so confirmed in it that they cannot fall short of it or fall into sin. The fallen ones are called *Belial*, which means 'without yoke and discipline'[41] and *poneroi*, giving their whole attention to malice. Even these do the will of God, taunting the wicked to turn them in their tracks, or training the righteous to move towards their salvation. But they are obliged to wander the elemental word, with no fixed abode. The remainder of Mogius's points are corollaries, concerned with how these evil angels take on forms and deceive people, from the Witch of Endor to *lamias*, marsh lights, and werewolves (a lamia is a female demon who eats children), and whether alchemy works. So angel studies in this period are tipping over into witchcraft and magic, but they still retain the attention of distinguished scholars.

The same year, 1625, saw the publication in the Netherlands of a compendium of Calvinist theology assembled by the four top professors of theology. One of its 52 sections is a discussion of angels, good and bad, written by a young preacher from Rotterdam, Adrianus Hasius (1601–50), supervised by Antonius Walaeus (1579–1639), a prominent church leader.[42] Hasius takes the view that angels do not have bodies, heavenly, fiery or airy, yet they were created at or near the beginning of time – we should not get too exercised about exactly when – out of nothing, and that they were all created good. They can take on the bodies of others, and they are endowed with intellect, will and wisdom, but still, they cannot know the secrets of the human heart, nor should we appeal to them or grant them adoration. From the gospel (Luke 20:36) he infers that angels cannot die, and cannot be dissolved into constituent parts because they are pure and simple. This applies also to the evil angels but, he reassures us, they are held 'in everlasting chains under darkness unto the judgment of the great day' (Jude 6).

On angel intellect and will, Hasius sweeps away the speculations of the Scholastics, with a flurry of Greek to display his own learning. All his arguments are based on scripture, which causes him to disconnect both angels and demons from the movements of the heavenly orbs: they cannot cause the sun to stand still, alter the course of the moon or stars or perform miracles. The pious should know that no good angels will come to them except by God's decree, nor any evil angels except by God's judgement and permission. So a good Calvinist need not pay angels much heed, but should leave them to their tasks, especially that of standing round God's throne uttering praises. The Dionysian hierarchy has no place in this bold attempt to sweep religion clean from all the accretions of interpretation. In its total reliance on the pure biblical text this chapter is a forerunner of fundamentalism.

On the Catholic side again, another tract issued from the Royal Printing Press of the Kingdom of Naples in 1646. Unlike the short Protestant disputations, it runs to 619 pages, re-investigating all the traditional questions. It was part of a much larger theological project, to revive the teachings of Duns Scotus (1265–1308) in opposition to the doctrines of the Dominicans based on Thomas Aquinas. It was written by Clemente Brancaccio of Carovigno, a Franciscan and raises a few unusual questions: whether angels are able to sin while 'on the way', and whether demons sin, since they have already been relegated to the ranks of harmful beings and no longer have much option in their actions. Lucifer had been among the seraphim. His offence was to have risen above the stars to the divine throne, seeking equality with God. Detailed discussion follows on why he was called 'the prince', what precisely was his rank, and who fell with him.

In his final section, Brancaccio tackles the vexed question of angel numbers, scouring philosophers ancient and modern for guidance. He reports that some say Avicenna thought there were only a few – overlooking the fact that Avicenna was talking about heavenly intelligences rather than angels when he set the number at ten. Brancaccio then claims that Aristotle proposes 47 angels based on the total number of heavenly spheres (*Metaphysics,* XII, 7-8), and that Avicebron and Maimonides follow him. This too is a misreading of the texts, unless it is based on a commentary tradition no longer familiar to us. Aristotle is obscure, mentioning 55 rather than 47 sources of motion; in Maimonides and Avicebron the heavenly spheres certainly transmit motion, but I have not so far come across any reference to Brancasius's 47.[43]

As the seventeenth century advanced and Enlightenment ideas took root, discussion of angels became more important, not less so. Since rational enquiry challenged simple belief, churchmen were increasingly concerned that religion itself might be undermined by the fashionable tendency towards scepticism. They called the doubters of the court and London coffee shops Sadducists and Libertines, and tracts appeared defending all aspects of religious sentiment from their attacks. Along with pamphlets asserting the reality of enchantment and demons came books on the truth of the Christian religion and on angels, good and bad.

In 1702, George Hamond published *A Modest Enquiry into the Opinion concerning a Guardian Angel* in the form of a long letter, answering someone's reasonable doubts. At first he preserves a neutral approach, trying to avoid contention. However he soon adopts a position, arguing for recognition of the angels' role in the administration of the universe, as evidenced by their constant comings and goings. He encompasses both Jacob's ladder and Homer's golden chain of connections, subscribing to a view which he attributes to 'the philosophers':

> [They] make some to be the Presidential Angels of Kingdoms, others of Provinces, others of Cities, others of Particular Families, and Last of all every Man's particular Genius, or Guardian Angel. Nor is it unreasonable to think that there should be some to preside over Brute Animals, and that no one Species or kind, though of the smallest and most contemptible Insect, should be exterminated or lost out of the Creation. As likewise some to take care of the Fruits of the Earth for the use and benefit of Men, which Origen somewhere calls, *aogatas georgas*, Invisible Husbandmen. Some they will have to Cure Diseases, others to counsel and advise, and extricate Men out of ambiguous and perplex Affairs; some afford Men their assistance in the invention of Arts … and others are the invisible and Friendly Companions of them in their travels.[44]

He defends these angels robustly:

> For anyone to think that these were Evil Angels or Devils, with Bats wings and Long-tails, is contrary to that sense that all Men have of the Goodness of God, which would not deliver whole Nations to be governed and instructed by the Devil, unless upon enormous provocations and despightful Rebellions against the Divine Light and Life.[45]

Hamond's authorities are scripture, the ancient philosophers (Pythagoras, Plato, Aristotle, Apuleius and Arrian), the Church Fathers (Origen, Basil, Chrysostom and Jerome), and anecdotal confirmation.

The anecdotal evidence is in my view the least convincing. It consists of three rambling episodes, one taken from the French Catholic Jean Bodin (1530–96), one from the German Protestant, Melanchthon (1497–1560), and the third a melange of dreams, visions and letters, relating to Marcus Aurelius, the second-century Roman emperor, and to a friend of the author.

Guiding spirits are either angels or they are returning souls that once were human themselves. Either way, they protect us, raise our morale, and are with us to the last – though he is not sure if one spirit is with us from birth or whether we can change our protector to a higher one. Though he cannot ultimately prove their existence, he exhorts us all to act as though we knew for certain. Remembering our angel then becomes like that Pythagorean injunction 'Reverence thyself. Do nothing below the honour and dignity of a rational soul', because even when we think ourselves most alone, our angel is standing by and taking note of all we do.[46]

Finally, he urges us to slight no man, however mean, vile and abject he may appear to the World, for he is honoured and assisted with a guardian angel who beholds the Face of God and may vindicate any wrongs against his charge. In Hamond's view, full-scale interventions on a biblical scale are still possible, for if we ignore this principle in our dealings with others, such an angel will 'withstand the Perverseness of thy way as the Angel of old did the Aramitick Sorcerer', namely Balaam (Numbers 22:32).

Hamond was also responsible for the publication of a more comprehensive discussion of angels written by Richard Saunders, who died in 1692. Little is known of Saunders beyond his reputation as a physician and astrologer, and his participation in the running of the church of St Mary's, Kentisbeare, in Devon, either as a minister or a lay preacher. After the Restoration and the 1666 Act of Uniformity, men like Hamond and Saunders could no longer remain as ministers, though Hamond was retained as schoolmaster.[47] When he died, Saunders left his unpublished manuscript on angels to Hamond, and Hamond published it.

Entitled *Angelographia*[48] *sive Pneumata leityrgika, Pneumatologia: A discourse of angels, their nature and office, or ministry*, it was printed in London in 1701. Saunders's work is arranged in 15 chapters, divided into short sections, which Hamond heartily approves. Its aim is to lead people towards an angelic life. Hamond adds in the preface that this tract is of particular use because angels were being so little attended to, having passed out of fashion on account of the Scholastics (i.e. Aquinas and his followers) 'who intruded into things not seen, vainly pufft up by their fleshly minds' and who ended up worshipping angels. Now, the rise of irreligion, scepticism, materialism and 'Sadducees', who 'deny, or pretend to doubt whether there are indeed any Immaterial beings at all' has made a new investigation necessary.

Well versed in Hebrew and Greek, Saunders leads the reader through a detailed analysis of texts and key words. Angels are messengers, sent of God; they are *elohim*, 'all ye gods', which was explained by the apostle to mean 'angels', with *el* denoting their strength or might. In Job 38:7 when 'all the morning stars sang together, and all the sons of God shouted for joy' he takes the second phrase as explaining the first: the sons of God, or angels, are then morning stars, lucid, lightsome and full of knowledge, created right at the beginning of time.[49] He thinks they are called seraphim because, like fire, they are most active and swift; and *cheruvim*, either from *ke-roov*, 'like a youth', for their swiftness and agility, or *ke-rabbim*, 'like a rabbi', for their knowledge. He takes these names as applying to all angels, being unimpressed by Dionysius's division into different ranks. Following Daniel 4:13, he says they are called 'watchers' because they need no sleep and are ready to stir others; and the names of 'principalities and powers' do not indicate rank or degree but only allude to their authority in the world.

He notes that what Aristotle called intelligences, and Plato called demons, the Romans called *genii*, 'because they take care of our birth and are to us as genitors, or fathers'. But any proper names that have been given to angels are 'nothing but idle dreams ... of Cabbalists.' So names like Gabriel and Raphael simply describe what those angels were doing at the time (e.g. in the case of Raphael, healing).[50]

A chapter is devoted to how angels help us at the time of death. He includes numerous anecdotes here about the death of martyrs, several of whom, it seems, were known to him: a Mr Hawks, burned at the stake, James Bainham, a Mr Holland. When we die, the angels receive our soul and carry it to heaven, we know not how, where more angels will joyfully welcome it. But first they have to get it past the territory of the devil, prince of the air, so they apparently travel in convoy.[51] He specifies how to honour angels and what to do if you think you have seen an angel – though it is far more likely to be a spirit of delusion. We may treat angels with love and reverence but not worship, nor should we obey if they tell us to do anything against scriptural law.[52] Among their many virtues we may aspire to imitate, patience and integrity stand out, together with an enviable 'unweariedness'!

Another defence against the 'Sadducees and Free thinkers' appeared in 1714 as a threepenny tract entitled *The Seraphick World*.[53] It bears no author's name, but affirms the existence of angels against those who 'resolv'd these glorious Beings into meer Qualities and Dispositions of the mind', so that when a prophet was bidden by an angel, they say he was just 'inwardly persuaded'. Graphic descriptions of angel encampments around Elisha and Elijah are brought as evidence, but so too is the fact that angels 'attend here in Places of Publick Worship'. This is then used to inveigh against immodesty of dress and disrespectful conduct in church (such as failing to pay attention, or whispering). 'Is this a fit Behaviour,' he asks, 'in the Presence of Angels?'

Despite dismissing the idea that an angel is an inner prompting, he attributes our unexpected good impulses to the secret influence of invisible spirits.[54] Invisibility should be no obstacle to belief, since we do not see God either. But what did the ancients see that made them so sure about angels?

> a magnificent, stately Appearance of bright Curling clouds,
> with perfect Walls of transparent Light, rang'd and opening one
> behind another and forming so many Courts like a kind of First,
> Second and Third Holy, and at the End of all (as on a throne)
> the refulgent emanations of the Divinity.[55]

With astonishing circularity of argument he then claims that from visual descriptions of the heavenly hosts we can draw conclusions about the presence of their General, 'though it is impossible to see Him with mortal Eye'.[56] Finally, he reminds his readers of their duty to assist the angels by supporting the church schools newly built for the education of the poor.

This was one of the more outspoken, less reasoned tracts. More typical is that of the Puritan divine Isaac Ambrose (1604–64), *Ministration of, and Communion with Angels*, which was republished many times in the seventeenth century and revived by John Wesley in the eighteenth. Much material is familiar, but Ambrose emphasizes the fact that our angels are appointed to us in the womb and we have duties towards them arising from their ministrations to us.[57]

Nineteenth-century Angels

My own favourite among the Church of England treatises is the delightfully written *Service of Angels* by Henry Latham (1821–1902).[58] On a perfect spring day in April, 1885 in Siena, he encountered a lizard. Much taken with its beauty and that of his surroundings, Latham entered into a meditation on whether it matters if there is beauty and no one sees it. This led to a contemplation of joy, greatly enhanced when he met some children. He concludes that goodness and happiness, besides blessing their possessors, exhale a moral beauty. We cannot add to God's joy, but if there are angels watching the doings of men, any human act of kindness could add to their joy, and is therefore well worth undertaking.

Latham declares that he can offer no proof, and will solve no mysteries. 'I only hope to be of a little practical use', in particular, against despair. He is writing not for the convinced, who had John Keble's triumphant hymns to guide them, but for those in doubt or uncertainty.

On guardian angels, he notes that there is room for differences of belief. It is likely that no one particular angel can appropriately care for a particular human being, from beginning to end, but since God does not relinquish care of us, Latham settles rather for a collective guardianship. He warns against blaming one's own misdeeds on one's guardian angel, or attributing the success of a rival to a more efficient one. He also warns against offering petitions to a guardian angel, lest it become a sort of household god because God seems too distant. No one, he says, is too low or vile to offer prayers or praise to God. With regard to children, and Christ's words, 'Take heed that ye despise not one of these little ones; for I say unto you, That in heaven their angels do always behold the face of my Father which is in heaven' (Matthew 18:10), Latham wonders whether 'their angels' might imply the angels into which those who die as children pass – the pure, original 'type' of the child, 'that which it was created to be', and what God sees whenever he looks. This view of childhood had important educational implications, which Latham did not hesitate to apply.[59]

The happiest of men, he says, do not need angels as intermediaries. They are serene in knowledge that the infinite God cares about every detail. But what can we know of ubiquity or eternity? or even of living in an everlasting present? We cannot imagine the divine scale, attending to everything all at once, existing without a beginning. Perhaps angels have been imagined for the purpose of sharing in the glories of the divine world, as company, rather than as supernatural agents, just as the Greeks imagined dryads, naiads, sylphs and nymphs, to enjoy the hidden beauties of lonely Thessaly. He draws a distinction between the messenger angels of the Pentateuch, and the witness angels of Daniel, Enoch, Tobit and other later works. The former are messengers with a definite commission. They come, they perform it, there is no sorrow over human lapses and no joy in human repentance. They simply appear, as if people are familiar with them, and perhaps they are manifestations of the Lord himself. He is aware of new findings on Babylonian aspects of angel lore, as well as rabbinic, and readily praises the work of other scholars.[60]

Latham grants angels no independence of will, and even sees their perfection as angels as somehow bound up with our willingness to let them play their part. We may also join in their work. He wonders whether our interest in angels is a question of awakening to some recollection, or intimation of what awaits our own souls. Our ideas about the resurrection are too earthbound, but that is nothing to be ashamed of: it is the natural result of our human condition, and besides,

> We are not intended to lap ourselves in delicious reveries about the future, but to bestir ourselves in doing all the good we can while we are here. In a life of ecstatic contemplation more than half our faculties would waste from disuse and we should fail to learn the lessons for which our earthly existence is the special school.[61]

He invents a fable of a caterpillar who dreams about being a butterfly in the future. While absorbed in watching a butterfly sip nectar from a flower, it is eaten by a thrush. This leads to another meditation: what is dead does not know God – but what does not know God is also dead. Latham, the educational reformer, seeks every opportunity to encourage people to 'do angels' work', because he is convinced that in doing so they will find delight. Chasing happiness for itself yields little fruit, but we may find great happiness on the way. In this, our own self can be the main obstruction, along with the youthful desire to possess. Angels have no 'self', therefore no obstacles to delighting in the good of others. The elderly often become spectators in life and may more easily live by reflected happiness, seeing good with the inward eye as the outer eye begins to fail. Yet even a child has what he calls 'here am I' moments.

In his experience, 'boys of a certain age have an imaginary existence running by the side of their actual one, which gets confused it with now and then'. This is like a kind of stage performance concurrent with ordinary life. For adults, however, the confusion is harder to untangle: 'social, professional and what-not are so mixed up, and have been acting upon one another in complex ways so long …' that it is hard to separate the man from his parts. We get 'stiffened' in these roles, making them our own, and we want to die if we fail in the thing we are reputed good at. But angels are after the real self.[62]

On the eternity of angels he observes that it is easier to imagine an infinite host of finite beings than a single infinite being, cognisant of all doings in all worlds.[63] Becoming aware of angels watching us can give us a palpable sense of time and eternity: 'We feel less ephemeral when we have made friends with an Angel who saw the pterodactyl's first attempt at flying, or who, possibly, put the notion into his head.'[64] He notices, too, that our own idea of heaven is what shapes our character. If we regard it as a haven of rest, work will be a molestation. If we expect a paradise of delights, we will strain the imagination trying to enjoy it in advance. But if we regard it as a continuance of the exercise of our mental and moral faculties, we will preserve our own energies and foster those of others. This is what Tennyson calls 'the glory of going on, and still to be'.[65] It is mischievous, Latham says, to regard future bliss as a reward when what is being offered is the heritage of life:

One who looks to helping Angels in their work should make this world a school for lovingness. Let him begin by loving 'what he has seen' – every living thing that comes in his way – and he will go on to love the Angels too; for they also love God's creatures, and treasure up the good and happiness that is brought to light. Thus he may be brought, by easy steps, through Christ to love God, and, loving God, to come to know Him, which our Lord tells us is eternal Life.[66]

Any disenchantment people have with the idea of immortality is the result of what kind of immortality seems to be on offer:

> It is the frivolity of our lives that renders it hard to believe in immortality. If a man feels that his life is spent in expedients for killing time, he finds it hard to suppose that he is to go on for ever trying to kill eternity.[67]

The good that we do, and the evil, do not pass out of existence as though they had never been. They are a 'field of operation for the angels'. Finally, while we cannot understand angels fully, we can be messengers ourselves, whispering guiding or illuminating thoughts to others. These need not be religious thoughts, for the whispers may come in the form of science. This, he says, will help us keep our energies alive to the end.[68]

By the time Latham's book was in print, angels seemed to have found a new equilibrium at least in English life. In 1898, John Burnham compiled for popular use a service of narrative and hymns called *Whispering Angels*.[69] Mary Watts trained the villagers of Compton to help her decorate a cemetery chapel with mysterious angel figures and faces (1898–1904),[70] and Edward Burne-Jones's magnificent angel stained-glass windows were radiating light in a series of churches across the country (see Figure 5).[71] This was no mere medieval revivalism.

Demons

> As night enters and spreads her wings over the world, numerous dazzling, demonic guardians stand poised to emerge and rule the world … As soon as morning arrives and brightens, they all vanish and rule no longer, every single one entering his place, returning to his site.
>
> (*Zohar*, 1:203b)[72]

We have already seen how spirits fill the space between heaven and earth. Good daemons and bad daemons share the same origin, differing only in how they use their powers. In the early years of Christianity, good daemons disappear from view and evil 'daemons' become 'demons', that is, spirits wanting only to pervert and corrupt. It was widely accepted that the heavens were full of angels and the air around the earth was full of demons, a source of danger, capable of tempting a person away from higher aspirations, even if worse harm could be avoided. Gnostic texts are full of evil spirits as well as good angels. Even in Judaism, there were demons.

One Muslim philosopher, Nāṣir-I Khusraw (1036–94) believed that demons were human souls who could not quite break free of the world when their bodies died, because of the intensity of their physical desires. So they enter hideous bodies, and traverse the world, luring people to destruction, or prompting them to commit evil. To Khusraw, such satanic spirits are far more problematic than the *jinn* or *parīyān*, as he called them. (*Jinn* is an Arabic word meaning 'hidden'; *parīyān*, the plural of *parī*, is its Persian equivalent.) The *parīyān* are regarded as lower than the angels, but in Khusraw's view are still potential angels. Created with natural beauty, they may become fully-fledged angels by practising obedience. However, if they practise disobedience they become devils, as indeed does mankind.[73]

Khusraw realized that he was somewhat out of step with 'the philosophers' on this, but there is a practical point to his system: each person has within himself two devils that deceive him, two *satans* who tempt him; these are the concupiscent soul and the irascible soul; but each person also has a rational soul, which is a potential angel, a *parī*. So if a man allows his rational soul to prevail over the tempters, he can become an angel. To confirm this, Khusraw reports at length the conversation of the 'chosen Messenger' who appears in the Qur'an, in the narrative of Adam. The Messenger, an archetypal messenger-angel, also had two satans within him, even though he was an angel. But God gave him victory over them, and made them surrender. Iblis, on the other hand, had been an angel but became a devil through failure to obey.[74] Human beings, in this view, are potential angels and potential devils, and the world is replete with actual angels and actual devils.

Khusraw may have been inspired by a similar conception of the satans and how they might be overcome in Avicenna's recitation, the parable of Ḥayy ibn Yaqẓān (Living Son of the Awake). Ḥayy's two companions may be readily interpreted as the concupiscent and irascible souls, who are to be overcome by the patient application of restraint and wisdom.[75]

For Maimonides, who was also familiar with Arabic literature, bad angels, like their good counterparts, were to be understood allegorically. Such a view has antecedents at least as far back as the early centuries CE. For example, Hermes lists tormenting spirits as being within:

> TAT: Do I have tormentors within me, father?
> HERMES: More than a few, my son. In fact there are many and they are fearsome.
> TAT: I am not aware of them, father.
> HERMES: This ignorance, my son, is the first of these tormentors. The second is sorrow; the third is intemperance; the fourth lust; the fifth injustice; the sixth greed, the seventh deceit; the eighth envy; the ninth treachery; the tenth anger; the eleventh recklessness; the twelfth malice. These are twelve in number, but besides these there are many others, my son. They compel the inner man who dwells in the prison of his body to suffer through his senses. These tormentors depart one by one from the man who receives God's mercy. This constitutes the manner and teaching of rebirth.
>
> (*Corpus Hermeticum*, XIII, 7)[76]

The writings of Hermes had also carried a special warning of what may happen if we lose our reverence for the divine and fall wholly into a materialist way of life:

> How grievous will be the withdrawal of gods from men! Only the evil angels will remain. Mingling with humanity they will force those wretches into all the evils of violence: wars, robbery, fraud and all those things which are contrary to the nature of souls.
>
> In those days the earth will not be stable, nor will the sea be navigable. Heaven will not be crossed by the stars, for the course of the stars will cease in the sky. Every divine voice will … be stopped. The fruits of the earth will wither, and the land will no longer be fertile. The very air will hang heavy in lifeless torpor.
>
> (Hermes, *Asclepius*, 25)[77]

According to Hermes, demons take possession of us from the very moment we come into being and receive a soul. Each demon is attached to a star, and their influences may therefore be studied through astrology. They can cause public disorder and revolution, but they also work within the individual:

> They reshape our souls to their own ends, and they rouse them, lying in ambush in our muscle and marrow, in veins and arteries, in the brain itself, reaching to the very guts. ... From moment to moment they change places, not staying in position but moving about.
>
> (*Corpus Hermeticum*, 16:14-15)[78]

Luckily for humankind, their activities can be resisted: for 'the rational part of the soul stands free of the tyranny of these powers and remains fit to receive God'.[79] Furthermore, angels, such as those who fill the eighth realm of heaven with silent singing, may exercise a countering force.[80]

Porphyry confirms that the evil demons engage in sorcery, wonder-working, enchantment and deceit. They are able to draw people to themselves through foolish desires for riches, power and pleasure. Demons, for him, operate through revelations in dreams or false prophecy. They further compound their mischief by contriving to make the blame for it fall on the gods:

> One of the very great injuries inflicted by the daemons who do evil is that, although they themselves are the authors of the tragic sufferings which befall earthly creatures, sufferings such as plague, famine, earthquake, drought, and similar disasters, they persuade us that the gods are responsible for these things, whereas the gods are the authors of the exact opposite ... They [the daemons] evade blame themselves: their primary concern is to do wrong without being detected. Then they prompt us to supplications and sacrifices, as if the gods were angry with us.[81]
>
> (Porphyry, *On Abstinence*, II, 40)

They then help themselves to the meat and drink of the sacrifices.[82] But he distinguishes between these evil demons and the good ones. The good ones partake in divine power and never abandon their duties. They do their best to indicate the dangers threatened by the evil demons, through dreams, inspiration or other means, but not everybody recognizes the significance of their signs.

The frequent appearance of the devil and demons in Christian texts is well known, and examples could be quoted in abundance from every century. The Jewish demons are less familiar. They make their first appearance in scripture in Leviticus 17:7, with the call to cease sacrificing to *se'irim*, a kind of devil or goat-demon. Throughout the ancient Near East it was believed that uninhabited lands were home to all manner of noxious creatures – not just the natural fauna of the desert, such as snakes, serpents and scorpions, but many demonic beasts whose hunger was for souls as well as bodies.[83]

The *se'irim* are mentioned again in II Chronicles 11:15 where Jeroboam appoints priests for their worship, and in Isaiah 13:21: at the destruction of Babylon, 'their houses shall be full of ferrets; and ostriches shall dwell there, and demons shall dance there'.[84] Again in Isaiah 34:14, the goat-demon will cry to his fellow, and the night monster (the mythical demon Lilith) will find a place of rest.[85] In Psalm 91:6, a psalm already noted for its angels, a demonic presence lurks in the form of *ketev*, often translated as 'destruction', especially that of oppressive heat, but *ketev* also refers to a malign Babylonian deity, Ketev Meriri.

In I Samuel 16:14, an 'evil spirit' (*ruach ra'ah*) descends upon Saul. Taken by some as a disorder of his own mind, to others it is something more tangible, lurking in the shadows. In I Kings 22:20-23, a 'lying spirit' (*ruach sheker*) in the court of heaven volunteers to carry the message that will draw Ahab to his destruction. Spirits of the dead or ghosts (*mazzikim*) make their first appearance in the Mishnah, reflecting rabbinic debates of the first and second centuries CE. Created at dusk on the sixth day, they have a twilight existence.[86] In the Talmud and midrashic commentaries (i.e. those using legend and allegory), much is made of angels and demons. It is even claimed that Moses composed Psalm 91, with all its angels and demons as protection when he ascended Mount Sinai.

Another name for demons in rabbinic literature is *shedim*, derived from *shadad* (to devastate or ruin).[87] According to Nachmanides, who records many mystical traditions, these creatures, are not made up of four elements like everything else in creation (following the ancient tradition of earth, water, fire and air) but only of two, fire and air.

Consequently their bodies have a delicacy and lightness that enables them to fly through fire and air, and they cannot be perceived by our five senses. Angels are also made of only two elements, fire and ice (water), and the *shedim* are like the ministering angels in three other respects: they have wings, they fly and they know the future. Angels know the future because they 'hear from behind the curtain of heaven' what is to be, but for the demons it seems to be more a matter of eavesdropping while they fly about, or drinking in the powerful forces held in the atmosphere. Furthermore their knowledge is limited only to the immediate future, and therefore enchanters who consult them are getting little useful information.

They are also like humans in three respects: they eat and drink, procreate, and die. They die when the two elements of which they are composed separate. Their eating and drinking is to replenish their moisture, and consists of water vapour and 'the odours of fire'. He gives no detail of their procreation. In general, he believes the demons have no strength or power, and we do not need to fear them. But, unlike Maimonides, he does not doubt their existence.[88]

In the Talmud their existence is taken for granted: 'They are more numerous than we are, and they surround us like the ridge around a field.' Demons are responsible for the clothes of scholars wearing out – through rubbing up against them! A remedy is suggested for this, involving the sprinkling of ashes. Another recipe, involving the roasted and ground placenta from a pure bred black cat, will enable one to see the demons – but speaking of what is seen may bring harmful consequences.[89]

Persistent fear of demons reflects in rabbinic literature. Rabbi Jose ben Halafta (second century CE) relates:

> I was once travelling on the road, and I entered into one of the ruins of Jerusalem in order to pray. Elijah of blessed memory appeared and waited for me at the door till I finished my prayer. After I finished my prayer, he said to me, 'Peace be with you, my master!' and I replied, 'Peace be with you, my master and teacher!' ... I learned from him three things: One must not go into a ruin; one may say the prayer on the road; and if one does say his prayer on the road, he recites an abbreviated prayer.
>
> (Babylonian Talmud, *Berachot* 3a)

The spirit of Elijah, a benign presence, waited for him at the door, not inside. From this tale the rabbis adduce three reasons for not entering ruins: 'because of suspicion, because of falling debris, and because of demons'. Suspicion would include superstition and unlawful congress, with either spirits or human beings. Falling debris is indeed a risk. More surprising is the assumption of a real presence of demonic beings capable of causing harm. A thousand years later Joseph Caro indicates that the strictures had lost none of their force.[90]

In this context, we should now acquaint ourselves with Azazel, a demonic character who slips in and out of view in biblical commentaries. The key text is the chapter describing the annual rituals of atonement to be followed by the high priest on behalf of the people (Leviticus 16:7-8). Besides offerings of bullocks and incense, Aaron is to select two goats, and set them before the door of the tent of meeting. 'And Aaron shall cast lots upon the two goats: one lot for the Lord and the other lot for Azazel.' The one for the Lord is prepared for sacrifice, the other, the 'scapegoat', is sent out into the desert alive,[91] to the dwelling place of Azazel. The medieval commentator Rashi explains here that he was to place the two goats one on each side of him, and then put both his hands into a lottery urn and draw out two lots, placing one on each goat. One lot was inscribed for the Lord and the other for Azazel. The derivation of Azazel's name is clear enough: *azaz* means 'strong' and *el* is 'God' or 'mighty'.[92] Yet the identity of Azazel is a mystery. Is he an aspect of God, or a demon? Rashi also gives an alternative derivation of his name as 'severe' or 'austere' for *az* and 'strong or harsh' for *el*.[93] Does Azazel represent impurity, set up as an opposite power to the good, in some form of Manichean dualism?

Various attempts were made to explain this difficult passage. According to the Talmud, the name Azazel denotes not a person or power but a steep cliff some ten miles east of Jerusalem to which the goat was led and over which it was hurled (Mishnah *Yoma* 6:4-8). According to others, including Chief Rabbi, Dr J. H. Hertz (1872–1946), *azazel* simply means 'dismissal'. In the Septuagint, it is translated as 'the one to be sent away'. But a strong tradition developed that saw Azazel as a spirit in the desert, perhaps even one of the primeval hairy goat-demons, or *se'irim*, who dwelt in the wilderness. These creatures are mentioned again one chapter later, when all the proper sacrifices have been described and improper ones are being prohibited: 'And they shall no more sacrifice their sacrifices unto the *se'irim*, after whom they go astray. This shall be a statute for ever unto them, throughout their generations' (Leviticus 17:7). *Se'irim* are often translated as 'satyrs'. They have been called 'demons of a hairy appearance' (Abraham ibn Ezra),[94] or 'deluded persons in the form of goats' (Nachmanides). The goat in ancient Greece, Rome and Egypt was regarded as a nature spirit, and associated with dark arts and the devil. Not surprisingly, therefore, Azazel came to be regarded as a devil or fallen angel. Some even identified Azazel as one of those angels who were attracted to the daughters of men and were lured into sexual relations and hence into rebellion, as recounted in Genesis 6:2. In the Ethiopian *Book of Enoch*, Azazel is mentioned by name: the Archangel Raphael is instructed to bind him hand and foot and place him under rocks in a chasm in the desert at Dudael, for a perpetual punishment (1 Enoch 10:4-6). Though he was not one of the leaders in going astray after women, Azazel's sins are listed there as having taught mankind the use of swords and shields, the mining of metals and manufacture of jewellery and cosmetics – all of which led to unbridled desire and bloodshed (1 Enoch 6–8).

A tale is told in a late rabbinic source that once, on the Day of Atonement, Azazel accused Israel before God, saying, 'Why do you show them mercy when they have provoked you? You should destroy them instead.' God's reply was that if he were a human, he would sin too. Azazel, outraged by this, asked to be put to the test. He descended to earth. When he became involved with a beautiful woman this was deemed to be a sin, and so, unable now to return to heaven, he was condemned to remain in the desert until the end of time.[95] This is advanced as a reason for the ancient Atonement Day ritual, but it also sounds a warning to those who accuse others of sin and would condemn without mercy.

In the second and third centuries CE, Apuleius, Plotinus and Iamblichus all wrote on daemons, covering both the good and the bad kind.[96] Plotinus says that we are each guided by a spirit from one plane higher than our normal level of existence, and that we somehow choose it, according to our nature. It is even perhaps an expression of our own soul. It is partly indwelling, and partly external. His biographer Porphyry relates that Plotinus's own spirit guide was summoned up for him, one day, in visible form:

An Egyptian priest who came to Rome and made his
acquaintance through a friend wanted to give a display of his
occult wisdom and asked Plotinus to come and see a visible
manifestation of his own companion spirit evoked. Plotinus
readily consented and the evocation took place in the temple of
Isis: the Egyptian said it was the only pure spot he could find
in Rome. When the spirit was summoned to appear a god came
and not a being of the spirit order.

(Porphyry, *Life of Plotinus*, 10, tr. A. H. Armstrong)

No more could be learned about the god, however, because the assistant
took fright and accidentally strangled the birds he was holding as part
of the ritual.

Iamblichus confirms that the soul chooses its daemon, but thinks it
does so before taking on an embodiment, which the daemon will help to
shape and form. He also advocates theurgic rites, to obtain for ourselves
a better daemon, perhaps like Plotinus even a god, to help in our human
task of reuniting with the divine world of intelligence from which the
pure soul originally came.[97]

According to a Hermetic fragment, it was an angel Amnael who
revealed the mysteries of alchemy to mankind.[98] In *Asclepius*, Trismegistus
tells his pupil how their ancestors discovered the art of animating statues
by enticing gods and demons into them:

Since they could not make souls they summoned the souls of
demons or angels and implanted them into sacred images ...
in holy rituals. By virtue of these they were able to create idols
having both good and evil powers.

(Hermes, *Asclepius*, 37)

Being composed of a mixture of divine and earthly elements, such gods
are easily provoked to anger. The earthly part derives from herbs, stones
and spices which have in them a natural power of divinity. The celestial
part needs frequent sacrifices, hymns, praises and sweet sounds in tune
with the celestial harmony, in order to be able to endure long periods of
contact with humanity (*Asclepius*, 38).

The early Christians of Upper Egypt looked askance on all such
ideas and practices. Constantly inveighing against Egyptian sorcery,

they took delight in exposing its weak points. In the fourth century, Bishop Macedonius once boasted about a visit to the temple at Philae while the priest was away and only his sons in charge. Pretending that he wanted to make a sacrifice, he set the sons to prepare the fire. While they were busy, he chopped off the head of the mechanical bird whose moving beak was manipulated to give oracular pronouncements and he threw it into the flames.[99] Yet the same desert fathers constantly tell of how they themselves were saved by angels, or received communion from angels.

The Romans called the tutelary spirit a *genius*. Allotted to every person at birth, the *genius* was capable of influencing a person's character and the fortunes he or she would meet. The *genius* was considered an individual instance of a universal divine nature, with its own quality that could be imparted to the person under its care. (The modern meaning of 'genius' as a person of exceptional ability makes hidden reference to this innate divine power.) A family could have a *genius* protecting all its members, and so could a particular place. In the classical revival of the eighteenth century, the *genius loci* was celebrated in poetry by Alexander Pope and consulted, at least conceptually by the great landscape gardeners, alongside questions of soil, air, light, water and plant selection, in order to design gardens that would nurture the human spirit. Depictions of the *genius loci* or of personal and family *genii* on ancient altars, vases or shrine paintings depict the *genius* as a male figure with wings, although in one fresco at Pompeii, the *genius* appears as a snake. It was sometimes supposed that a person was governed by two opposing spirits, a good *genius* and an evil *genius*.

This *genius* has sometimes been connected with the idea of a 'genie', such as the one summoned by Aladdin's lamp, to do his bidding. However these powerful spirits are more properly thought of under their Arabic name *jinn* (جن) coming from the root *j-n-n* meaning to hide or be hidden.[100] The singular of jinn is jinnī. The jinn were from the beginning a separate class of beings, distinct from angels. They are mentioned in the Qur'an as being created out of fire, alongside man who was created out of clay (suras 55:14-15 and 15:26-27). They share with human beings the capacity for exercising free will to the extent that they may accept or reject guidance and they may serve God or serve themselves. By contrast, angels are created out of light, and can only serve God. Whether Iblis (the devil) is a jinn or was originally an angel who then fell from grace is a question still debated (sura 18:50 but see also 38:71-89 which implies his angelhood).[101] Some people consider the jinn as simply hidden qualities present in human beings, others regard them as unseen spirits operating alongside human beings, with power to intervene forcibly in human affairs. The special power of an evil jinnī is to cast evil suggestions into the hearts of human beings. Other jinn may be good or neutral. In the sura entitled *The Jinn* (sura 72), some are in obedience to God and seek rectitude, some have 'deviated' and become 'firewood for Gehenna'. The principal message of the sura is that prayer should be addressed to God alone: no other power comes near him; his messengers carry out his will, with watchers appointed to ensure that everything is accomplished.

Attendant upon the jinn are a whole class of demonic servants called *ifrit*, *afrit*, or *efreet*. In sura 27, a throne is transported from the Queen of Sheba to King Solomon: 'An efreet of the jinn said "I will bring it to you before you rise from your place. And verily, I am indeed strong, and trustworthy for such work"' (27:39-40). These beings are portrayed with great strength and power, but they are essentially mischievous or evil, and often rather like monsters, dwelling in a dimly lit, marginal world or underworld.

It is quite likely that the jinn had their origin in a pre-Islamic mythology of wild creatures of the forests, deserts or jungles, and owe their fantastic forms and wonderful deeds to these older legends. They feature prominently in the tales which have come down to us as the *Arabian Nights*, a blend of ancient myth and legend, reflecting a range of cultures from Arabia, Persia, India and Egypt. Some are from the tenth century, but some are much older, showing ancient Mesopotamian and Greek influences.

Some interesting quirks in the history of demons are found in early scientific works. Through the study of optics, and especially 'catoptrics', which is the study of reflections and mirrors, it was possible to produce images of demons in the air with which to frighten one's enemies. The principles for doing this, using cylindrical convex mirrors (which produce an image that appears outside the mirror), are described in several works. One is the *Perspectiva* of Friar Witelo, written in the 1270s, drawing on the scientific works of Aristotle and the great Arab authority on optics, Ibn al-Haytham (965–1040), known to the West as Alhacen or Alhazen.[102] In *The Secret of the Philosophers*, a widely-read handbook compiled in England between 1300 and 1350, instructions are also given for creating images in the air, by converting a convex mirror into a concave mirror. The Venetian physician and engineer, Giovanni Fontana (*c*.1395–*c*.1455), explained the theory of such reflections in his book *On Perspective*. In another work, *Instruments of Warfare*, Fontana shows practical applications, ending with a small demon etched onto a magic lantern being projected forwards as an image magnified a hundredfold, capable of striking alarm into the unwary beholder (see Figure 6).[103] This sort of device fascinated another wonder-worker, the Englishman John Dee (1527–1609), who describes a 'marveilous Glasse' owned by his friend S. W. Pickering, which could allow one man to seem to be a whole army, and can make a person start at his own shadow. If you stand near this glass and make as if to lunge at it with a sword or dagger, a similarly armed image will appear in the air between you and the glass, lunging right back at you.[104] Dee counts such works as 'Thaumaturgie', that is, the raising of spirits. He revelled in such magic or trickery, although he was under no illusions about it. In fact, he publicly urged Pickering to make his glass available to the public 'that longeth ardently for the wisedome of Causes Naturall'.

Demons were certainly feared. Old liturgies contain prayers for protection and in the *Discoverie of Witchcraft* by Reginald Scot (1538–99) we find a round-up of such evil spirits:

> In our childhood our mothers maids have so terrified us with an ugly devil having horns on his head, fire in his mouth, and a tail in his breech, eyes like a basin, fangs like a dog, claws like a beare … and a voice roaring like a lion, whereby we start and are afraid when we hear someone cry 'Boo!' and they have so fraied us with bull beggars, spirits, witches, urchins, elves, hags, fairies, satyrs, pans, faunes, sylvans, kit-with-the-candlesticke, tritons, centaurs, dwarfs, giants, imps, calcars, conjurors, nymphs, changelings, incubus, Robin Good-fellow, the spoorn, the mare, the man in the oak, the hell-wain, the firedrake, the puckle, Tom Thumb, hobgoblin, Tom Tumbler, boneless, and such other bugs, that we are afraid of our own shadows.[105]

Angels at the Edge

Besides the demons there are a few other lowly angels that deserve a brief mention (apart from the fallen angels who will have a chapter of their own). First there are some modern angels who seem to straddle the border between angel and demon. Among these I would single out Paul Klee's strange and disturbing *Angelus Novus*, painted in 1920, to which the essayist Walter Benjamin was deeply attached, and the terrifying angels of Rainer Maria Rilke's *Duino Elegies*, begun in 1912, which may have helped to inspire Klee (see Figure 7).[106]

Interpreting this picture Benjamin calls it the Angel of History. Writing in 1940, under Nazi persecution, Benjamin expresses a melancholy view of history as a progressive trampling of human ideals:

> [It] shows an angel looking as though he is about to move
> away from something he is fixedly contemplating. His eyes are
> staring, his mouth is open, his wings are spread. This is how
> one pictures the angel of history. His face is turned toward the
> past. Where we perceive a chain of events, he sees one single
> catastrophe which keeps piling wreckage upon wreckage and
> hurls it in front of his feet. The angel would like to stay, awaken
> the dead, and make whole what has been smashed. But a storm
> is blowing from Paradise; it has got caught in his wings with
> such violence that the angel can no longer close them. The
> storm irresistibly propels him into the future to which his back
> is turned, while the pile of debris before him grows skyward.
> This storm is what we call progress.[107]

Benjamin prefaces his interpretation with lines from his close friend, the pioneer of Kabbalah studies, Gershom Scholem, entitled *Angelic Greetings*:

> My wing is ready to fly
> I would rather turn back
> For had I stayed mortal time
> I would have had little luck.[108]

From the safety of the post-war era, the British artist Cecil Collins (1908–89) portrays angels from mystical dream visions, calling them 'the spiritual intelligence that connects all worlds'. Their role is to unify the worlds, by transforming our awareness. In an early painting, *The Fall of Lucifer* (1933), he shows a red figure plunging from the sky, and winged angels intervening on a human battlefield. However, his later angels are creatures from whom light and love radiate, and through whom mankind, often shown archetypally as a Fool, might be able to find his way back to a lost paradise.[109] Despite a long history of presumed masculinity among angels, for him the angel represents the feminine. Angelic intelligences awaken the creative imagination, and help humanity shake off negative energies. Collins expresses concern that our present civilization is the only one in history not to be based upon a metaphysical reality. Our friendship with nature and our relationship with the divine world are broken and need to be recovered.[110]

Seven Angels, a new opera by Luke Bedford, with a libretto by Glyn Maxwell, also occupies a mid-zone between the demonic and the divine. Set in an apocalyptic time, it presents a sequel to Milton's epic, starting with the fall of seven angels from heaven. They fall for so long that they forget why they have fallen. To help them remember they devise a story, a play within the play, which is an allegory of greed and neglect, set to suitably dramatic music. This opera in turn spawned a five-minute demonic fantasia, *An Extra Angel in the Foyer*, which had its first performance in July, 2011. Neither met great critical acclaim, but they do at least show that angels of various kinds are still inspiring new work in the arts, even if they have lost their foothold in philosophy.[111]

Chapter 4

WINGS OR NO WINGS?
ANGELS AS MESSENGERS

Angels and messengers
Sanctify and bless
The King of kings.
They prepare and make ready
Their wings, a shelter;
Each day they enthrone
The King of kings.

>   (Amittai ben Shefatya of Oria, Italy, ninth century)[1]

As messengers, angels fly back and forth, but in this ninth century hymn their wings also provide a shelter and a throne for the Most High.[2] How important are wings in our conception of angels? People who report seeing angels often speak of winged figures, but is this based on expectation determined by medieval poetry and art? Are wings essential, or just a metaphor for swift movement? What do we really know of how angels should look?

To answer such questions, let us recall some of the evidence considered in Chapter 1. Three angels came to Abraham's tent as three men (Genesis 18:2); the angel who appeared to the wife of Manoah was described as a 'man of God', only being recognized as an angel when he ascended in the smoke of the sacrifice (Judges 13:20-22); when the Archangel Gabriel appears to Daniel, he has 'the appearance of a man' (Daniel 8:15 and 10:18), and the Archangel Michael is 'one of the first princes' (Daniel 10:13). Jacob saw angels going up and down the ladder, but did they have wings? If so, why did they need a ladder? And when Jacob struggled with the angel, he is first described as a 'man', and later it is said he had 'striven with God and with men' and prevailed: no wings are mentioned. These examples cast doubt on the idea that wings are a necessary characteristic of angels.

Certainly cherubim and seraphim have wings. We are told so in the biblical texts, though we may puzzle over why some angels have two wings, some four and some six. More puzzling still is the verse in the Qur'an,

> All praise is due to Allah, the Originator of the heavens and the earth, the Maker of the angels, messengers flying on wings, two, and three, and four;
>
> (Qur'an 35:1)

It is hard to envisage a three-winged angel, unless perhaps it means three pairs – but if so, we meet here for the first time eight-winged angels. The next sentence reassures us that 'Allah increases in creation what He pleases; surely Allah has power over all things.' Besides, according to Jewish legend Satan has 12 wings (*Pirke de Rabbi Eliezer* 12). But in general, should winged angels be considered a special class, and others envisaged without wings? Artists generally thought otherwise: even the three wingless angels of Abraham, are usually depicted with wings, as in the famous icon of Andrei Rublev, *The Hospitality of Abraham* (1425–7) in Figure 8.

His elegant angels have definite golden wings, and by choosing symbolic colours for their robes he allows identification on two levels: not only are they three angels enjoying Abraham's hospitality, but they also represent the Trinity. The Angel of God, on the left, in shimmering tones, is the first person of the Trinity; the central angel wears the customary colours of Christ, a dark red robe with a gold border band and a blue cloak; the third angel, with blue robe, gold wings and a cloak of green, which signifies soul, vitality and youth, represents the Holy Spirit.[3] Earlier icons on this theme had included the figures of Abraham and Sarah between the angels. By excluding them, Rublev could represent the Trinity through the three angels, avoiding theological prohibitions on depicting God. Since the original story provides grounds for taking one angel to be

God, this new shift is no surprise, and the panel was soon known as *The Trinity*. Indeed, it was commissioned for the Monastery of the Trinity founded by St Sergius of Radonezh (1322–92), who laid emphasis on contemplation of the Trinity, and on creating a harmonious fellowship of love. Angels are certainly natural candidates for a fellowship of love.

The Holy Spirit is also usually depicted as possessed of wings. Sometimes these are the wings of a dove, on the body of a dove, but there is also a branch of early Christian discourse that sees the Holy Spirit in angelic form. For some considerable time there was fluidity between the doctrines of the Holy Spirit, of Christ and of the angels.[4] The four symbols of the Evangelists also have wings: the angel (or winged man), winged ox, winged lion and eagle are the four creatures mentioned round God's throne in Revelation 4:7, identified with Matthew, Mark, Luke and John respectively.[5] In Ezekiel's vision, all four faces are on each of the four heavenly creatures, human, lion, ox, and eagle (Ezekiel 1:1-14). The book of Daniel recalls visionary beasts, of which the lion and the leopard are both winged (Daniel 7:1-8). St Augustine says of John that he 'soars like an eagle above the clouds of human infirmity, and gazes upon the light of the unchangeable truth with those keenest and steadiest eyes of the heart'.[6] The eagle is also a symbol of Christ's resurrection and an analogy for Christ who gazes at God the Father and raises men up to contemplate divine brilliance. According to the Roman naturalist, Pliny the Elder (23–79 CE), the eagle was the only creature that could gaze upon the sun with unflinching eyes, and it trained its young to do likewise, bearing them up on its wings, and turning them to face the sun.[7]

It was believed that the eagle's youth was constantly renewed, as in Psalm 103:5. Some writers accounted for this by habits of moulting, apparent fasting, or shedding its old, overgrown beak. However in a popular account written around 1210, the renewal is linked with heat, light and purity:

> The eagle is the king of birds. When it is old it becomes young
> again in a very strange manner. When its eyes are darkened
> and its wings are heavy with age, it seeks out a fountain clear
> and pure, where the water bubbles up and shines in the clear

sunlight. Above this fountain it rises high up into the air, and fixes its eyes upon the light of the sun and gazes upon it until the heat thereof sets on fire its eyes and wings. Then it descends down into the fountain where the water is clearest and brightest, and plunges and bathes three times, until it is fresh and renewed and healed of its old age.

(Guillaume Le Clerc, Bestiary)[8]

Dionysius relates the eagle to royalty, might, speed, agility, cunning and contemplation, as well as unswerving observation of the divine sun.[9] To Isidore of Seville (560–636), an eagle's head and wings on a lion's body formed a creature of immense strength and power which dwelt in the far-northern Hyperborean mountains. Eagles' wings are symbolic of strength and undoubtedly formed the model for many artists' wings for angels.

But not all angel wings are eagle wings. In some of the paintings of Sandro Botticelli (1445–1510), rings of angels dancing through sky have only the most modest of wings. Their movement is expressed by their billowing robes and outstretched arms. However, the majority of angels in Christian art are clearly shown with a strong pair of wings, often of myriad hue, and certainly impressive. From the rooftop angels of medieval churches to Renaissance candelabra and the angels in the spandrels of St Paul's Cathedral, we can find strong muscular angels with healthy wings. Exactly how a powerful wing can join on to a human body is an anatomical problem. Some painters avoid the problem, others have resolved it. Sculptors in particular have had to rise to the challenge.

Some Islamic angels are said to have wings of emerald. Fra Angelico's famous Angel Gabriel in the upper corridor of the monastery of San Marco in Florence has wings that sparkle with mineral deposits embedded in the fresco, giving extra life and vibrancy. Sadly, the sparkle never shows in reproductions, but the line, form and colour gradations can still be appreciated (see Figure 9).

Like Rublev's, this painting is iconic, in the sense of being one of the best known images of religious art, and in the original sense, too, of an image designed for religious contemplation. Here the Angel Gabriel bows to the Virgin Mary. Both figures are imbued with modesty and grace, but while Mary personifies stillness and humility, the angel's power of movement is emphasized by the folds in his robe, and his compact but impressive wings. Some have considered angels like this to have a feminine appearance, or to be without gender, but Gabriel is generally considered to be male.

Islamic depictions of the Archangel Israfil blowing the trumpet for the Day of Judgement usually boast a splendid pair of wings. Other Islamic angels are equally resplendent. Similarly, the heavenly beings of the Dunhuang frescoes on the Silk Road between India and China are shown flying, though without feathered wings. These wonderfully fluid beings probably had their origins in the Hindu apsarasas, celestial musicians and dancers who are generally portrayed without wings, though they have their home in the clouds. At Dunhuang, in the Mogao caves, they are mostly shown with long trailing scarves fanned out in the air, suggesting the power of flight without actual wings. Over 6,000 of these angel figures adorn the cave complex, mostly in ceiling designs or borders at the tops of walls, in frescoes spanning several centuries. In India the apsarasas were noted for their sensuality, but at Dunhuang, Confucian and Buddhist influence makes them more modest merging with the Chinese *Feitian,* a 'fragrant goddess with sweet voice'. In Japanese mythology, from at least the eighth century there are similar flying maidens who transform to and from birds, and come to earth shedding their feathered mantles.[10]

If angels sometimes have wings and sometimes do not, what about other parts of their anatomy? For instance, can angels bend their knee? As so often, it depends on which biblical source is uppermost in the mind. For those who base their angel views on the visions of Ezekiel, the leg is definitely 'straight', and possibly single, while the foot is 'round', like a calf's hoof (Ezekiel 1:7). For those who principally recall the seraphim, hands are of human type (Isaiah 6:6) and possibly feet as well. If angels are elemental – as in the winds and the storm cloud – hands and feet are harder to imagine. Abraham's angels are human in form, and so too is the angelic scribe Metatron who before his translation to heaven was the human being Enoch (though admittedly his form may have changed: see below) and his partner Sandalphon.[11] Given the obvious variations in the physical appearance of the various classes of angel, we should perhaps at this point review our definition of what an angel is.

It seems fair to say that an angel is a spiritual being. Although they were created (whether before the first day, or on the second, third or the fifth day, according to different accounts) they do not reproduce, and do not die.[12] Their natural home appears to be not so much on earth as in heaven, though human beings may rely upon them for protection here on earth. We may not be too clear about what is meant by 'heaven', but at the very least it can be considered as a realm where existence does not rely on the possession of a physical body. Thus it may be 'angelic mind', that great universal realm conceived by the followers of Plato, home of ideas of which the things on earth are but the shadow. The reality of those ideas is such that if every horse were to disappear off the face of the earth, the ideal form of horse would still exist in this realm. Or it may be the realm in which person-shaped angels come and go, on the wing, at the bidding of the divine; at one moment they are gathered round the throne, engaged in songs of constant praise, at another they may be sent on errands, one task at a time, according to their level and instruction.

While we think of angels in the second way, wings are clearly part of the picture. They provide the means for an angel to appear suddenly just where and when it is needed and to fly between the invisible and the visible realms, heaven and earth. Yet what of those accounts where angels are indistinguishable from human beings? Abraham's messengers, Jacob's angel, Manoah's 'man of God', and even Raphael in the Book of Tobit: these are all messengers with something specific to convey that emanates clearly from the divine world, yet is brought by visitors in human form. Can such messengers equally be human beings? In the cases mentioned, we are told specifically, at some point in the story, of their angelic status. Frequently their names are kept concealed, and mostly they do not eat or drink, though these characteristics are not essential: Gabriel and Raphael declare their names, and Abraham's angels eat what he sets before them. But what about more human angels? The term 'angel' has passed into common use, to describe a fellow human-being who has assisted us in some particular way, but who certainly has no wings. Perhaps we need to consider angelhood as more of a spectrum, reaching from those mythical or mystical entities at one end, including the winged figures of the seraphim and cherubim, to purely human carriers of angelic virtues at the other end, for whom wings are not a necessary part of angelic status.

There is also an interesting historical perspective. In the earliest centuries of Christian art, wings were not attached to every angel. A panel survives from the third century in the Catacomb of Priscilla in Rome that shows the Angel of the Annunciation (Luke 1:28-38) as a man, without wings. There was also a strong tradition against taking biblical descriptions of wings literally. John Chrysostom (*c.*347–407), a Father of the Church, says, 'When you see the seraphim flying around that exalted throne, their sight walled around by the projection of their wings, hiding their feet, backs and faces ... do not think wings and feet, and that they are winged. For these are invisible powers.'[13] The wings are simply a means of expressing exalted, ethereal qualities as well as lightness and speed. Likewise, Gabriel's wings are not part of his power, but remind us that he 'descends from realms on high, and returns to his abode whence he was sent'.[14] Even Dionysius insists that wings are allegorical, just as later the whole idea of angels was allegorical for Maimonides.

The adoption of wings by artists as a universal symbol for angels was nevertheless a natural development. Yet it seems to have been influenced not so much by the stately winged guardian figures of Near Eastern courts, as by the numerous representations of winged messenger figures in Graeco-Roman culture. The messenger god Mercury, giver of eloquence and intellect, is borne swiftly hither and yon by his winged sandals, and sometimes a winged hat. The goddess of victory, Nike, or her Roman counterpart Victoria, is a female figure with outstretched wings and flowing robes. She is associated with Athena, goddess of wisdom, and like angels, she often carries a lyre. When the whole of Olympus was under attack by the storm giant, it was Nike who encouraged Zeus not to give up the fight and she became his chariot-driver. Nike presided over contests and games. Her images are found on vases and oil flasks, coins and medallions, and numerous statues in the Greek colonies of Italy. They were certainly a common sight in the early Christian centuries. One particularly fine pair of earrings in the British Museum, surviving from the third or fourth century BCE, shows Nike in full flight. The wearer would surely be invoking her protection much as one might invoke a guardian angel.[15] (See Figure 10.)

Other winged figures which may have influenced the form angels took in art are found on Greek and Roman sarcophagi, especially of the second century, depicting the departed human soul. Known as *spiritelli*, they are of particular relevance to the changes that took place in the representation of the cherubim (see Chapter 5).

The angels who predominate in the earliest centuries of Christian art are stocky figures, with or without wings. The angelic powers shown in mosaics in Byzantium, or under Byzantine influence in Italy, such as the ceiling of the Baptistery in Florence (from 1225) are powerful muscular figures in jewelled robes with big wings. Images of the Archangel Michael in this period show a short, stout warrior figure, as for example atop the basilica of his name in Lucca (thirteenth to fourteenth century). A favourite story in the Eastern Church celebrates his miracle at Chonae, where he single-handedly carved a chasm in the rocks to carry away flood waters. Yet at some point angels became more willowy figures. Henry Mayr-Harting, Regius Professor of Ecclesiastical History at Oxford, pinpoints the change to the end of the eleventh century, following Anselm, Archbishop of Canterbury's argument that the devil had no rightful dominion over man and his significance in church doctrine should be reduced. Mayr-Harting describes the effect of this change graphically: 'As the devil was pushed, not out of existence of course, but more down into hell, by a kind of pulley effect the angels were pulled up into heaven.'[16] In effect, angels ceased to walk the earth and were confined to heaven. 'From the twelfth century onward, angels would look more heavenly and their messages would sound more heavenly.' They change in appearance from the swarthy figures of the tenth and eleventh centuries to the amiable hermaphrodites of the thirteenth or even, as one monk reported, comely maidens.[17] By the time of Aquinas, angels do not 'have' bodies as we have bodies, but assume them according to need, by condensing air, which then assumes both shape and colour, as clouds do.[18]

As for flight, Gregory the Great brings interesting logic to bear on this. For while angels depart from the divine presence in order to be with us, they only do so externally. Internally they retain the power of contemplation, continuing always to look on the face of the Father.[19] So even their wings are only conveying part of the angel's presence into our realm.

Useful glimpses of the appearance ascribed to angels of the highest rank can be gathered from the story of Enoch related in the various books that bear his name. Building on the brief mention in Genesis that Enoch, son of Jared, 'walked with God and he was not, for God took him' (Genesis 5:24), these books describe his journeys in the heavens and his transformation from a human being into an angel. In 3 Enoch, which belongs to the *hekhalot* literature of the fourth or fifth century CE,[20] we are told that his body was changed from flesh into fire, that he was given wings, numerous eyes, and a change of stature to cosmic proportions, and that he was clothed with garments of glory, replete with every kind of light and splendour (3 Enoch 9:2-5; 12:1-2; 48:6-7).

The Bible itself gives some guidance on angels' apparel: Daniel's angel is 'clothed in linen' with a girdle of fine gold (Daniel 10:5). St John the Divine saw one with a gold crown and many with sickles (Revelation 14:14). In Revelation 4:4, 24 elders sit around the divine throne clothed in white raiment with gold crowns on their heads. In Revelation 1:20 angels can be stars, held in the hand of an angel clothed in a long robe bound with a golden girdle. At the transfiguration, Christ's glistening white raiment is a sign that he has been speaking with angels (Luke 9:29-31).[21]

Angels can appear in other guises as well as shimmering white robes. Theologically it has been said that they are clothed in garments of light. But this light can also take on various hues. Thus angels have been portrayed in many colours. Among my favourites are the vivid angels portrayed in manuscripts of *The Marvels of Nature*, by Zakaria al-Qazwīnī (Baghdad, 1203–83). These vary from one angel to another and one manuscript to another. One wears colourful blue and red robes over pleated yellow pyjamas, on his head a turban, and his wings are edged with feathers of red flame.[22] Another manuscript shows an angelic trumpeter, the Archangel Israfil, with vibrant blue-striped wings, a red and green gown and yellow boots, with a sash that takes on a life of its own in movement. A further example is shown in Figure 11. Angels' vestments clearly assume form and colouring according to the cultural conditioning of the beholder. Another traditional interpretation of angels' clothing is simply that they are clothed with a body, to become manifest to human beings. Any garments added to that body would then be purely incidental, dependent upon the role for which the angel has been sent.

So, whether angels are created beings, able to assume semi-corporeal form, or whether they are simply attributes, and their manifest forms mere figments of the beholder's imagination, it remains true that they appear in many different kinds of garb. To say how an angel looks is thus a very personal matter and we cannot say how angels are 'supposed' to look. The metaphysical poet John Donne brings us back to the essentially mysterious nature of angels when he speaks of a 'shapeless flame' and says, 'Some lovely glorious nothing I did see …'[23]

Chapter 5

THE GREAT PROTECTORS

Come and see. As the sun sets the cherubim standing in this
place, dwelling miraculously, beat their wings above and spread
them out, and the melody of their wings is heard above.

(*Zohar*, I, 231b)[1]

It is now time to turn to that class of beings called cherubim. In the
medieval *Zohar* (Book of Splendour), the cherubim initiate the constant
daily cycle of praise, joined by angels and man. It says they were created
on the second day of creation, ready to welcome the arrival of human
beings. Together with the *ophanim* (wheels) and the *chayyot* (living
beings) they emanate directly from the divine presence, which is called
'fire consuming fire'.[2] In the Bible, cherubim are set to guard the Garden
of Eden, golden cherubim are made for the Ark of the Covenant and
huge cherubim decorate King Solomon's temple. While all angels may
have protective roles, cherubim in particular are the great protectors. Yet
these great beings reappear in Renaissance art as chubby winged infants,
who in turn help shape Victorian ideas of childhood and immortality.
This seems to be a major change of role, even if the name stays the same.
This chapter will therefore be devoted to an exploration of their history
and significance.

Origins of the Cherubim

Unlike some of the messenger angels, the cherub is always a winged
figure, usually with two wings, but sometimes four. Some say that the

cherub owes its promotion to the rank of angel only to the Christian mystics, and especially Dionysius in the sixth century, but descriptions of cherubim when they first appear already suggest recognizably angelic qualities. That is to say, their protective powers and semi-divine status would lead to their inclusion in any reasonable definition of angels.

Dionysius clarifies their special attributes of knowledge and contemplation. These are not obvious from the cherubim in Genesis or Exodus, but come mainly from Ezekiel and later writings. He says that their name means 'fullness of knowledge' or 'outpouring of wisdom'. They have

> the power to know and to see God, to receive the greatest gifts of his light, to contemplate the divine splendour in primordial power, to be filled with the gifts that bring wisdom and to share these generously with subordinates as a part of the beneficent outpouring of wisdom.
>
> (Dionysius, *Celestial Hierarchy*, 205c)

They are pure, not in the sense of being innocent of earthly imaginings, but because they transcend all weakness, and are firmly established within their own order, which is close to God and in constant motion round Him. The motion is powered by their love for God, and that love is undiminished by a constant generous flow to lower beings. Being filled with light they are also filled with 'a transcendent and triply luminous contemplation of the one who is the cause and source of all beauty' (208c). Following this description, medieval paintings often depict cherubim and the seraphim as winged heads, without any other body parts, but ranged around the source of light or some holy scene. The seraphim are coloured red, to denote their association with fire, while the cherubim can be recognized by the colour blue, which would thus appear to be the colour of knowledge.

Going back, however, to their earliest traceable predecessors in Mesopotamian art, we find something very different: mysterious animal bodies with huge wings, representing formidable powers of protection. Standing at the entrance to sacred spaces or palaces, these figures sometimes have the body of a lion, the wings of an eagle and a human head. Or the body may be that of a bull, and the head human or eagle. They have a superhuman aspect, designed to terrify intruders (see Figure 13).[3]

The name cherub, and its plural cherubim (rendered awkwardly as 'cherubims' in the King James Version) are taken directly from biblical Hebrew, though the pronunciation there is *keruv* and *keruvim*. But where did it come from before that? The Hebrew origin of the name is steeped in mystery. Cruden's *Concordance* (1737, but continuously in print ever since) offers no real explanation of the name. Robert Young's *Analytical Concordance* (1879), gives the meaning of cherub as 'one grasped or held fast'. An etymology is offered from the Greek *cheroubim*, but this is perhaps conjectural, or mistakenly identified with an assumed form *cheiroubim* from *cheiros*, a hand. Cherubim do have hands beneath their wings (Ezekiel 1:8; 10:7 and 10:21) but no biblical passage describes them as 'held fast'. Advances in scholarship soon after Young's work allowed new connections to be explored. One of these was to link the Hebrew *keruv* or *kerub* and the Assyrian *karâbu*, 'to be gracious to, to bless'. A similarity was also noticed with *karûbu*, meaning 'great' or 'mighty'. Nineteenth-century anthropologists saw the Assyrian winged bull, called *shedu* or *kirubu*, and the Persian gryphon, or griffin, as ancestors of the biblical cherubim. The gryphon had the head and wings of an eagle with the body and hindquarters of a lion; it was believed to inhabit the furthest reaches of Scythia and to guard the gold that is there. But lexicographers, perhaps by nature more cautious in their scholarship, rejected some of the wilder speculations. The standard *Lexicon of the Old Testament*[4] casts doubt on any connection with the Assyrian winged bull, even though connection through the name *kirubu*, lingers on in the literature. The *Lexicon* also doubts linkage with the Persian gryphon, whose name, transmitted through Greek as *Gryps*, had been considered by some to be sufficiently similar to *k'rub*, for the sound of the Greek '*y*' is very close to a Semitic '*u*'. Some had even proposed that the gryphon was related to the bird of Vedic mythology, mighty eagle-chariot of the god Vishnu, whose Sanskrit name is *Garuda*,[5] but all this is a step too far for the dictionary. More surprisingly, it suggests that the seraphim of Isaiah and the creatures before the throne in Revelation 4:6-8 may be another form of cherubim – but the seraphim will have a chapter of their own.

Other linguistic explanations of the name have been put forward. One is that it changed by an inversion of letters (a linguistic phenomenon known as *metathesis*) from *rekhuv*, 'chariot' to *kheruv*. This might explain why God 'rode upon a cherub and did fly' (Psalm 18:10; II Samuel

22:11). It might also link the cherubim with the *ophanim* or wheels described in Ezekiel 1:15, where they are counted (together with the seraphim) as 'those that sleep not, and guard the throne of His glory'. Another linguistic approach traces derivation from the Aramaic word *karov*, 'to plough'. This might account for the face of an ox suddenly appearing in one of the descriptions of a cherub (Ezekiel 1:10). A third sees the Akkadian *karibu*, 'to bless', as an inversion of the Hebrew *baruch*. A fourth suggestion, that has been around since the third century, sees the word *keruv* as being derived from the particle *ke*, meaning 'like' and *ruv*, or the related *ravya*, Babylonian Aramaic for 'a child or youth'. This would explain why a cherub (*keruv*) may be considered to have the face or form of a youth.[6] The biblical scholar S. M. Paul considers the most plausible derivation to be from Akkadian *karibu* or *kuribu* (both formed from *karabu*; 'to pray or bless') but interprets this to suggest an intercessor who brings the prayers of humans to the gods (or, in a biblical context, to God). However modern scholarly consensus follows the more cautious suggestions of Samuel Driver, focusing on the twin aspects of graciousness and great might.[7]

This would still link our cherubim to the winged creatures placed at the entrance of Babylonian and Assyrian palaces and temples. In Akkadia, such creatures (*karibu*) mediated between man and god, bringing prayers before the deity as well as guarding holy places. Two winged sphinxes flank the throne of Hiram, king of Byblos, the Phoenician king to whom Solomon turned for expert assistance in the building of the Temple.[8] Winged protectors appear on incense altars from Taanach and Megiddo, and in the art of Carchemish, Calah and Nimrud, in ivory plaques from Samaria, and on other items excavated at Aleppo, and Tell Halaf. One Hittite gryphon with the wings of an eagle and the body of a lion, is a serene seated figure, imperturbable guardian of holy things. A few show a winged human: one bone handle from Hazor, dated to the eighth or ninth century BCE, depicts a youth with four large wings, holding on to the fronds of a small tree on either side of him.[9] Perhaps we can find in him a hint of the ancient cherub, but even in the first century CE Josephus observed that no one knew or could even guess what the cherubim really looked like.[10]

Cherubim in the Bible

In the Bible, the first cherubim we meet are at the entrance to the Garden of Eden, to prevent Adam and Eve from trying to re-enter it after they have been expelled:

> He drove the man out, and stationed east of the garden of Eden the cherubim and the fiery ever-turning sword, to guard the way to the tree of life.
>
> (Genesis 3:24)[11]

The flaming sword is not necessarily being brandished in the hand of the cherubim. On the contrary, the cherubim are plural and there appears to be but one sword, leading some to identify it with bolts of lightning. The cherubim are described only in terms of their function. Nevertheless images of cherubim were chosen for the covering of the Ark of the Covenant in the Tabernacle, and later for the decoration of the Temple. Those that were to be placed on the cover of the Ark of the Covenant were to be fashioned from beaten gold (hammered work), and placed one at each end facing each other, but with their eyes cast down. Their wings were to be spread out, shielding the cover, which was also known as the mercy seat. God's presence would rest between the two cherubim. Sometimes the ark cover is described as God's footstool, meaning the footstool of his throne (Exodus 25:18-22).

How to make the ark is precisely delineated, and the posture of the figures fashioned by Bezalel is described in Exodus 37:7-9. But at neither point are we really told what they look like. This suggests that everyone already knew, and implies that our Mesopotamian conjecture is correct, since figures regarded as too familiar to warrant description are likely to be those of the lands from which the Hebrew people had come. Abraham was born among the Chaldaeans, near the mouth of the Euphrates, at Ur in Sumeria. Yet the cherubim of the ark were not to be the threshold. Their place was within the very innermost part of the sanctuary itself. The unseen God was to speak as if from his throne, seated upon the cherubim.[12]

Those who wish to find a practical function for the cherubim take their lead from interpretations of the Ark of the Covenant as a kind of 'thunder-box', as in the film *Raiders of the Lost Ark*, or a giant capacitor. The cherubim, according to this view, being made of pure gold, would have been conductors of the electromagnetic force in which God's presence was thought to reside. Thus the ark becomes a potent source of energy, dangerous to anyone who is not appropriately prepared to come near it. The sons of Aaron who approached the Holy of Holies with 'strange fire' were struck dead on the instant (Leviticus 10:1-3);[13] likewise in King David's time, when the ark was set upon a cart to be carried to his encampment against the Philistines, one of the drivers, Uzza, put out his hand to steady it when the oxen stumbled and he, too, was instantly struck down (II Samuel 6:6-7 and I Chronicles 13:7-11).

A symbolic function was proposed by Philo of Alexandria, for whom the two cherubim of the mercy seat are the same as the two cherubim who guard Paradise. They are an allegory for the universe, where the ever-changing motion of the planetary spheres confronts the unvarying sameness of the realm of fixed stars. Alternatively, they represent the two hemispheres of heaven, one 'above' the earth and one 'below', whose continuous rotation gives us day and night, with earth between them, and the flaming sword as the sun. Or, he suggests, on a deeper level, they indicate God's two chief powers: sovereignty and goodness. If we can appreciate these two powers, through the flaming sword of reason, we in turn can be filled with cheerful courage and reverent awe. The cherubim are therefore vehicles of recognition and knowledge. Appreciating the twin aspects of sovereignty and goodness allows us to steer a measured course in life and to know that divine judgement is tempered with mercy. It should also remind us when things go well not to claim 'high thoughts' for ourselves, detracting from divine majesty; and when things go badly, not to despair.[14]

This interpretation gave rise to a curious later development in which the cherubim were imagined as embracing one another. The original description states that the cherubim will have their wings outspread screening the ark cover, and their faces 'one to another, toward the ark-cover'. God would then speak to the people from between the two cherubim (Exodus 25). It would not be surprising if at such time the cherubim's faces would be averted from the brilliance of the divine presence. But Talmudic commentaries speak of how the cherubim turn their faces lovingly towards one another and embrace. The curtain behind which they were concealed might then be raised to show this to worshippers as a symbol of how much God loved them (Babylonian Talmud, *Yoma* 54a). Kabbalists elaborated this further, and said the cherubim represent the mysterious union of heaven and earth. The embrace became a sexual embrace, expressive of the intensity of God's love.

Such commentaries fail to take account of the fact that while the temple still stood, the cherubim of the ark cover were out of sight of everyone except the high priest. However, their image was repeated in embroidery on the curtain which separated the Holy of Holies from the larger inner sanctum (i.e. the 'holy place' as opposed to the 'most holy place'). This would have been seen by a few more, though still only by the priestly class, since the rest of the people gathered only in the courtyard outside the holy enclosure. The curtain is described as a veil 'made of blue, purple and crimson (or scarlet) yarns, and fine twined linen with a design of cherubim worked into it' (Exodus 26:31 and 36:8): blue to represent the sky, crimson/scarlet perhaps as the redness of earth, and purple to denote the place where the two realms meet, where human and divine encounter one another. Outside the temple, visible to all, stood a large water pool on a base decorated with lions, oxen and cherubim, all wrought in brass (I Kings 7:23-37).

The cherubim on the ark were actually quite small: the cover on which they were to stand was two and a half cubits long and a cubit and a half wide (approximately 125 cm x 75 cm).[15] Those on the temple walls were much larger. Twin cherubim ten cubits high (i.e. over 5 m high) were made for the inner sanctum, and more were carved on the outer walls, on the outer doors, and on the olive-wood doors leading to the inner sanctum, together with palm trees and flowers, all overlaid with gold (I Kings 6:23-35). The ten cubits of those on the inner sanctum were measured wing-tip to wing-tip. This is nearer to the scale of the colossal Assyrian guardians, or human-headed lions and winged bulls at Nineveh, or Khorsabad.

Bible commentators have asked how images of this kind could have had a place in a cult where images were in all other cases strictly forbidden. Flowers and leaves were acceptable, but not living beings. The memory of it in later ages lent weight to the arguments of those who wished to allow images in churches, against those who wished to remove them, as for example during the Iconoclast controversy of the eighth-century Church. It may therefore ultimately be to the Hebrew cherubim that we owe many centuries of figurative Christian art. There are even occasional historic periods when figurative art was allowed in Judaism and Islam, especially in manuscript illumination. But no entirely satisfactory explanation has ever been put forward for allowing such figures in the Holy of Holies. It is hardly reasonable to argue, as some have, that the cherubim belonged to an older mythological tradition that could not be entirely dislodged, so it was limited and contained within the inmost sanctum. Some would say that explanations are not needed since holy writ is beyond human powers of understanding. Others may conclude that escaping the strictures of the second commandment proves that the cherubim had no real existence on earth or in heaven, or at least that there was no risk of worshipping them, any more than the palm frond, pomegranate, almond or flower also prescribed as decorative elements – or than the brass oxen and lions.[16] Certainly there are no recorded incidents of idolatrous worship of cherubim, unlike the golden calf (Exodus 32) or the brazen serpent (II Kings 18:14).[17] Nevertheless, after the destruction of King Solomon's temple, nothing more is heard of such decorations. Indeed, it is thought that the Ark of the Covenant, with or without its golden cherubim, had no place in the second temple, and its whereabouts became the subject for numerous legends. According to the Book of Revelation, it is in heaven with God (Revelation 11:19). The Ethiopian Church of Axum and the Lemba people of Zimbabwe both claim to have possession of it. Other claims have been made for Languedoc in France, Warwickshire in England (both through the intervention of Knights Templar) and the Hill of Tara in Ireland. There is also confusion between a simple wooden Ark of War and the golden creation of Bezalel which may never have left Jerusalem. However, we are unlikely to see the ark or its cherubim again, since according to the second book of Maccabees, which predates all these other sources, it was taken by the Prophet Jeremiah to a cave on Mount Nebo and buried there (2 Maccabees 2:4-10).[18]

Another way in which cherubim occur in the Bible is as a divine steed or mount. When his wars with the Philistines were finally over, King David uttered a song of thanksgiving to the Lord, who 'rode upon a cherub, and did fly: yea, he did fly upon the wings of the wind' (II Samuel 22:11, repeated in Psalm 18:10). From this verse, taking the two halves of it as a composite, comes the tradition of identifying cherubim as personifications of the wind. Support for such a notion has been found in Babylonian art. In one relief, a winged figure, who looks like an angel, is shown hand-pollinating date palms, a task which in nature is carried out by the wind.[19]

If cherubim can be divine steeds, how do they relate to chariots? The cherubim of the water pool outside King Solomon's temple stood upon brass wheels like chariot wheels (I Kings 7:27-37). In Ezekiel's vision the cherubim are in some kind of complex relationship with the wheels (*ophanim*) and the living beings (*chayyot*), moving all together in conjunction.

Ezekiel's cherubim have four faces and four wings, with the likeness of a man's hands under their wings; he now says these are the same as the 'living beings' he saw at the water's edge (Ezekiel 1), but now he knows them to be cherubim (Ezekiel 10:20). However some details have changed. Earlier, their four faces were of a man, a lion, an ox, and an eagle, (Ezekiel 1:10). Now they are those of a cherub, a man, a lion and an eagle.[20] Why the change? Is it to indicate the inconstancy of dream images? But if so, why is he so especially concerned to repeat the name of the location, a name that has no known occurrence outside the book of Ezekiel?[21] Ezekiel's message will be further discussed in Chapter 7, but it is worth noting here that the complexities of description in the two parts of this first vision (Ezekiel 1 and 10) gradually develop into a composite, whose confused forms blend into a general impression of a chariot: we see a 'sapphire throne' mounted above the heads of the cherubim, between whom are emerald wheels and burning coals. When the prophetic message that needs to be heard has been spoken, the holy presence departs:

> Then did the cherubim lift up their wings, and the wheels were beside them, and the glory of the God of Israel was over them above. And the glory of the Lord went up from the midst of the city ...
>
> (Ezekiel 11:22-23)

All this is a dream vision, however, and we cannot expect exact detail. Even our happy associations with the brilliant translucent sparkle of a fine blue sapphire may be wide of the mark: modern scholarship suggests that sapphire as we know it was scarcely to be found in ancient times, and the stone intended by the name סַפִּיר (*sapphir*) is probably lapis lazuli, a dark, opaque blue-green stone with flecks of gold.[22]

Ezekiel had a second vision involving cherubim and the temple. Transported in this vision to a high mountain in Jerusalem, Ezekiel sees the ruined temple being restored, and an angel acts as his guide and interpreter (Ezekiel 40:1–44:4). The new temple is of exquisite beauty, echoing the original temple of Solomon, and its stone walls are ornamented with panelling decorated with an alternating design of cherubim and palm trees. Likewise the temple doors (Ezekiel 41:25). These cherubim each have two faces, one of a man, and one of a young lion (Ezekiel 41:18-20).

Yet another cherub image occurs in Ezekiel 28. Here the prophet is inveighing against Tyre which has fallen due to the pride of its ruler, formerly known for his beauty, wisdom and wealth, Ezekiel berates the prince, saying,

> Thou wast the far-covering cherub;[23] and I set thee so that thou
> wast upon the holy mountain of God; thou hast walked up and
> down in the midst of stones of fire.
>
> (Ezekiel 28:14)

Summing up the appearances of cherubim in the Bible, we have noted an assumption at the outset that everyone knew what a cherub looked like, but which was then challenged by the divergence of the actual descriptions. They may be large or small; they may have two wings each or four; and one face, two faces or four. When they have four wings, the upper two may be spread out above them, one cherub just touching another. They may be used as a chariot or stand tall and free. One particular cherub is vast, and walks in fire.

Alice Wood's study of cherubim, brings together biblical texts, linguistic evidence and archaeological parallels.[24] Her conclusions suggest that the earliest cherubim had animal bodies, but not the later ones. She finds little evidence for cherub thrones in surrounding nations, therefore she interprets biblical descriptions of God 'seated upon the cherubim' symbolically. She also finds indications of an awareness among craftsmen and writers that divine beings cannot be constrained by any fixed corporeal reality. Her etymological evidence, though far from certain, suggests that the primary function of pre-biblical cherubim was guarding sacred space, without any intercessory role. But by the time of the Babylonian exile (which corresponds to the writing of Ezekiel and Chronicles), cherubim have become more like seraphim. On the whole Dr Wood is unconvinced of likenesses between ancient Near Eastern art of other nations and the cherubim of the Bible. However, in another recent study, analysis of a cylinder text called *Gudea's Dream* allowed Rabbi Yuval Keren to identify important similarities between the composite winged creatures of Sumerian tradition and Ezekiel's chariot.[25] There is still room for discovery.

Cherubim after the Bible

In post-biblical literature the emphasis shifts to the function of praise. In the *Book of Enoch* we hear of 'cherubim of fire in a stormy sky', presided over by Gabriel, singing praises. They never sleep but constantly watch the throne of God's glory. In the Qumran *Songs of the Sabbath Sacrifice*, cherubim are described as those who 'know', and who declare the splendour of God's kingdom according to the knowledge they have been given:

> Separating light from deep darkness
> by the knowledge of His mind He established the dawn.
> When all his angels had witnessed it they sang aloud,
> for He showed them what they had not known.
>
> (Scroll fragment Qumran, Cave 11)[26]

Through their total absorption in knowledge of God and praise, and because of their closeness to God, the cherubim became an object of focused contemplation. While Moses de Leon was just beginning to teach the *Zohar* in Spain, Bonaventure (1221–74) in Paris was already meditating upon the cherubim of the Ark of the Covenant. Seeking to see what each cherub saw in turn, he, like Philo, found a natural pairing of essences. The cherubim, for him, represent unity and diversity: absolute lack of division on the one side, and the substance, power and operation of the Trinity on the other. By contemplating these mysteries the soul could ascend towards union with the divine, contemplating God through the light of the mind, with the cherubim representing two modes of contemplation of what is invisible and eternal.[27] Bonaventure's practices found many followers. He himself drew upon an earlier tradition, which goes back to the *Celestial Hierarchy* of Dionysius, and had found expression in Paris at the Abbey of St Victor.[28] Richard of St Victor (d. 1173) in particular created a tradition of meditating upon the various angels as symbols for elevating the mind and soul towards God. For him the cherubim are a vehicle for exploring matters that transcend human reason. Because the cherubim of the ark were made of beaten gold, he felt that human beings too must undergo the repeated 'hammering' of sighs and lamentations to reach higher knowledge. In *The Mystical Ark*, his aim is to surpass the normal limitations on knowledge and moral purity, through engagement with the cherubim, in an 'angelization' of the human soul.

Moving from monastic contemplation of the twelfth and thirteenth centuries to Renaissance art, we find cherubs in another totally different form, one perhaps more familiar to us today. Here are the chubby, winged infants, whose origin is far different from the protective figures of Babylonia. They derive from the *spiritelli*, or 'sprites', who graced Greek and Roman tombs. These figures originally indicated the non-physical aspects of a person: his *genius* or spirit, separable from the body at death and therefore shown as having wings. This form is forever young – generally a small boy (*putto*). Such youthful figures began to be copied in sculpture and then in painting. Agostino di Duccio (1418–81) has *spiritelli* playing harp and organ, dressed like young angels in robes and wings. But generally they are naked in form, like their classical forebears. From tombs and fountains they spread to paintings, manuscript illuminations and even altars (see Figure 14).[29] Often they are mischievous or playful. Andrea del Verrocchio's *putto* with a dolphin manages to combine playfulness and purity in a fountain sculpture. Sometimes these *putti* were considered to be *erotes*, or little 'loves', like Cupid, who is also a small winged boy. Sometimes they were clearly intended to be angels, and the category of cherubim seemed most appropriate for such little figures, for cherubim had often been portrayed in medieval art as just heads with little wings. From the fifteenth century these cherubs begin to appear everywhere, often carrying garlands, wreaths or musical instruments, supporting medallions or creating a humorous subplot, as in Botticelli's *Mars and Venus* in the National Gallery, London. It is also no accident that the character of Cherubino in Beaumarchais's play, *Marriage of Figaro* (1784), and Mozart's opera (1786), was given such a name.

The childish figures of these cherubs in turn shaped ideas of childhood and immortality, which can be traced not just through funerary art but also through poetry and literature of the seventeenth, eighteenth and nineteenth centuries.[30] When Thomas Traherne (1637–74) speaks of the angelic experience of childhood, it is this kind of cherub that comes to mind:

> How like an angel came I down!
>   How bright are all things here!
> When first among his works I did appear,
>   Oh, how their Glory me did crown!
> The world resembled his Eternity.
>   In which my soul did walk;
> And every thing that I did see
>   Did with me talk.
>
> (Traherne, *Wonder*, verse 1)

Echoed just over a century later in the words of William Wordsworth (1770–1850), the cherubic image once again seems best to fit the description of the soul of the child, descended from its heavenly source:

> There was a time when meadow, grove, and stream,
>   The earth, and every common sight,
>   To me did seem
> Apparell'd in celestial light,
> …   …   …
> But trailing clouds of glory do we come
>   From God, who is our home:
> Heaven lies about us in our infancy!
>
> (Wordsworth, *Intimations of Immortality from Recollections of Early Childhood*, verses 1 and 5)

Such views reinforce the sense that childhood is a time of innocence and purity. Any more wayward behaviour has its origin in some accretion of earthly matter. Hence the great stress laid on cleanliness and purity in the Platonic fable (and sharp satire), *The Water Babies* by Charles Kingsley (1863). When Tom the chimney sweep falls in the stream and drowns he sheds the shell of his body and becomes a water baby, with a 'pretty little lace collar of gills about his neck'. In illustrations to the various editions, these gills often appear as little cherubic wings, an analogy that artist and author no doubt intended.

While Kingsley's high Victorian tale has largely fallen out of favour, the cherubs certainly have not. Raphael's two cherubs from the bottom border of the Sistine *Madonna* must be among the most popular of reproduced Renaissance images. Their combination of innocence, slight boredom and potential mischief strikes an especially endearing tone. But such cherubs, as emblems of childlike purity, are a far cry from the powerful protectors and knowers who are their earlier namesakes.

CONSTANT PRAISE

… to recount Almighty works
What words or tongue of Seraph can suffice?
(John Milton, *Paradise Lost*, VII, 112-13)

Unlike the cherubim, seraphim make few appearances in the Bible, occurring only in Isaiah's vision and the reflection of that vision in Revelation 4. Yet they were accorded high rank and a special place in hymns, literature and art.

An early relief from Tell Halaf in northern Syria, from the tenth century BCE shows a divine being with six wings. In medieval paintings and manuscript illuminations seraphim are sometimes depicted as noble figures of human form with wings, but more often just as heads with wings of fire. Sometimes the word 'seraphic' is used in ordinary speech to denote ecstatic bliss or an otherworldly sense of beauty. The heroine of Disraeli's novel, *Sibyl*, is 'that seraphic being, whose lustre even now haunts my vision',[1] while Milton's seraphs, such as Abdiel, are majestic celestial beings of great wisdom and power (*Paradise Lost*, V–VI). But we should more properly reserve the term for those beings in Isaiah's vision, singled out among the 'train that filled the temple'. They stand over the throne of God, in attendance upon Him. They have three pairs of wings, feet and hands. No other detail of their anatomy is given, though we can perhaps infer human shape as one of the seraphim carries to Isaiah a glowing coal in his hand, touches the prophet's lips and speaks to him.

Before exploring how the seraph interacts with the prophet, however, let us look at the derivation of the name seraph, because it has given rise to two quite different strands of interpretation. The name denotes fire, being formed from the Hebrew root *s-r-f* which means to burn. One line of interpretation links this with *saraf*, a serpent, others link it with the fire itself.

Taking the serpent first, the name *saraf* is especially applied to the flying serpents of Isaiah 14:29 and 30:6 (*saraf me'ofef*), said to be the deadliest, on account of their burning venom. Serpents such as these are like dragons, winged, scaled, and breathing fire; or like the monstrous python (*draco*) slain by Apollo at Delphi. According to this reading, seraphim were originally some kind of winged-serpent protector, differing from the cherubim in form rather than function

Winged serpents appear as guardians of sacred places in the ancient Near East. Herodotus, in the fifth century BCE, also speaks of hordes of small flying serpents among the spice groves of Arabia: they had to be smoked out with storax before the people could gather the frankincense.[2] He saw for himself their skeletons when he travelled to the border of Arabia and Egypt, where they were said to be devoured by flocks of Egyptian ibises whenever they tried to leave Arabia and enter Egypt. Herodotus was intrigued by the skeletons, but did not see any live creatures. He called them *ophies amphipterotoi*, or 'serpents with two pairs of wings' – one pair less than Isaiah's seraphim. Aelian, writing in the second century CE, tells us such creatures fly by night and emit urine that causes a festering wound on anyone on whom it drops.[3] *Ophis* or *ophies* (plural) was the Greek word used for serpents in the Gospels, Epistles and Revelation as well as translating the flying fiery serpents of Isaiah 14:29. Later writers have been as intrigued as Herodotus, but by the winged serpents of biblical account, and have attempted to identify them. Proposals have ranged from alleged living relics of prehistoric pterosaurus, of which modern sightings are claimed in the remote islands of Papua New Guinea,[4] to the horned viper (*aspis* or *cerastes*) or the saw-scale viper (*echis*) of the Arava desert, the one with a fiery venom, the other with a propensity to leap at its prey.[5]

Serpents without wings have a mixed reputation: the serpent in the Garden of Eden (which is *nahash*, rather than *saraf*) was the deceiver (Genesis 3:1), though the Gnostics saw it in a more positive light: *On the Origin of the World* presents the serpent as a hero sent by Wisdom to guide mankind towards enlightenment. Fiery serpents (who are both *nahash*, and *saraf*) beset the Israelites as they wandered through the wilderness and many died from their bites (Numbers 21:6). Yet the serpent (*sarpa*) is a protector in Hindu myth, and Naga snakes decorate and protect temples from India to Bali and Angkor. The Sanskrit name for a snake, *sarpa*, is cognate with our own 'serpent', and by the assimilation of *p* and *f* may also be cognate with *saraf*. Even in the wilderness story, a cure for the serpents is provided in the form of the magical copper (or bronze) serpent made by Moses (the *naḥash neḥoshet*, Numbers 21:9), which was thought to possess healing powers.[6] This serpent is later destroyed by Hezekiah, King of Judah, on the grounds that the people had begun to make sacrifice to it (II Kings 18:4). This implies that it was being worshipped as a god, or at least as a representation of God (as was sometimes the case with bulls at this time in the sister Kingdom of Israel). It also reminds us that some have questioned whether angels themselves may represent gods demoted in status during a transition in early times from polytheism to monotheism.

In Canaan and Babylon we know there were serpent cults. In Egypt serpents loomed large among the many hazards of the *Am Duat* (equivalent to our idea of an underworld), but could also have more positive functions. For example, the protector goddess Wadjet, sometimes represented as a serpent with wings, protected Lower Egypt and provides the famous symbol of sovereignty, the *uraeus*, a stylized, upright cobra – capable of spitting fire. It may be no coincidence that the centre of Wadjet's cult was at Buto, where Herodotus first found his fiery serpents.

Another mythical creature of Ancient Egypt is known as *serref* (with obvious linguistic echoes of *seraf*). These were guardian griffins, with head and wings of an eagle and the body of a lion, or sometimes a lion's head, or that of a vulture. They carried dead kings to heaven, and were transmitters of prayer. The Greeks believed that they were the same as the Scythian gryphon that kept watch over the gold. Throughout their legendary history, which continued into medieval Europe, they have been ascribed a grim, unloving, watchful aspect. Despite a superficial similarity of name, scholars have been inclined to liken the *serref* to the cherubim rather than the seraphim.

Following these lines of interpretation and etymology one might think that a seraph is just a kind of serpent. Yet in my view all these explanations are less than wholly convincing, and we should now follow that other aspect of the word *saraf* in its sense of burning. The Hebrew lexicon, while not denying possible mythical origins as serpentine deities, interprets seraphim rather as personifications of lightning, in particular as the lightning's strike.[7] A parallel is advanced with the Babylonian solar deity Nergal, one of whose epithets is *Sharrabu*, and who is associated especially with the destructive heat of midsummer that parches and burns.[8]

The word *saraf*, 'to burn', refers mainly to a particular kind of burning, meaning 'consumed utterly by fire' – the kind of burning from which no residue remains. Seraphic fire would thus burn away all impurities. It might even consume the sense of a separate individual existence. This appears to be Isaiah's experience when the seraph brings him a burning coal. So the seraph in his vision of the royal throne is not a winged serpent but a fiery agent of purification.

The setting for Isaiah's vision is the Temple in Jerusalem, and the year 739 BCE.[9] Although the vision does not appear at the beginning of his book, it does record the beginning of his ministry:

> In the year that King Uzziah died I saw the Lord sitting upon a throne high and lifted up, and his train filled the temple. Above him stood the seraphim; each one had six wings: with twain he covered his face, and with twain he covered his feet, and with twain he did fly.
>
> (Isaiah 6:1-2)

These majestic beings in attendance upon God on his throne seem to be of human form, but with six wings. Only two of these wings are for flying. The other two pairs are traditionally connected with reverence and modesty. Even as ministering angels, the seraphim do not venture to gaze upon the divine presence but cover their faces with wings. Nor do they expose their bodies. Some commentators suggest that the covering of the feet is a euphemism for covering their private parts. But much debate ensued as to whether angels in fact have organs of generation. If they do not, why would they need to cover that part of their anatomy? Questions were also raised about whether such beings wear white robes, as specified for the 'elders' in Revelation, or whether they were 'clothed' simply in a visible form, perhaps even a naked one. Midrashic commentators suggest that covering the feet is related to the fact that their feet were as Ezekiel had described them, 'like the sole of a calf's foot' (Ezekiel 1:7), an embarrassing reminder of the sin of the golden calf (Exodus 32).

The position of the seraphim, standing above the throne denotes being in attendance, but they are clearly free to move about, and indeed one flies to Isaiah, to administer to him the burning coal. Static or in motion, they are engaged in constant refrain, expressing praise and adoration: 'Holy, holy, holy, is the Lord of hosts; the whole earth is full of His glory' (Isaiah 6:3).[10] As the seraphim sing, the door posts, or the foundations of the house, are moved and the Temple is filled with smoke. It is never quite clear how many seraphim there are. Some have said only two; Milton calls them 'numberless';[11] there were clearly enough of them at least to create an impressive effect.

Their refrain is part of the *Kedusha* (Sanctification) in Hebrew, and is called *Trisagion* (Thrice Holy) in Greek. It became central to divine service in both Judaism and Christianity. It is the *Sanctus* of the Catholic mass and some Protestant communion services. It is understood as the moment at which human voices join with the angel voices that are always singing, could we but hear them. In fact, when the *Sanctus* is sung in some medieval churches and chapels we do hear them, for the architecture enhances the voices of the choir, creating overtones and resonances that blur the boundary between human and divine in a truly ethereal experience. In Jewish ritual, it is traditional for worshippers to close their eyes, turn their inner eye towards heaven, and rise on tiptoe at each of the three soundings of the word *kadosh* (holy), a little higher each time, as if to reach up to join the angels who, faces covered with wings, are hovering round the throne of glory.[12] In churches too, the presence of the angels is understood to be tangibly experienced through the recitation of the equivalent prayer.

Isaiah, caught up in an ethereal moment, is naturally concerned at what he, a mere mortal, is doing in this company, and feels that he is doomed, for not only is his own age corrupt, but 'man shall not see God and live' (Exodus 33:20). Then the seraph flies to him 'with a glowing stone (*ritzpah*) in his hand, which he had taken with tongs from the altar'. With this, the prophet's impurities are burned away, and he is free to undertake his mission. Thus the seraphim are instrumental in preparing him to undertake the role of prophet. Once his lips have been cleansed with the burning coal, Isaiah is able to speak when the voice of God calls:

'Whom shall I send,
And who will go for us?'
Then I said: 'Here am I; send me.'

(Isaiah 6:8)

By accepting the mission, Isaiah becomes himself a messenger from God. Prophets and angels begin to look extremely alike! When God proposes a message of desolation and destruction, Isaiah speaks up on behalf of the people, 'Lord, how long?' Not only is he being sent with a message for humans from the divine, but he speaks back to God on behalf of the people too. Again we face the question: can human beings serve as angels? And not just in the dim and distant past of King Uzziah's reign, but also here and now? If so, does it require a grandiose vision with lights and smoke, shaking of foundations and purification with burning coals? Or might it rather be in a still small voice such as the Prophet Elijah heard – after the storm, after the fire, after the whirlwind – the voice that speaks from within?

Meanwhile, the seraphim, closest of all angels to the divine throne, are on fire with love of God. Through this burning love they express the reverence and praise for which they are invoked daily in the Christian *Sanctus* and the Jewish *Kedusha* prayer. The importance of reverence and praise are underlined in many sources, from the Psalms to the philosophers. Plato argued eloquently for the powers of human reason, but never elevated it above reverence for the gods. One modern philosopher describes reverence as 'the well-developed capacity to have feelings of awe, respect, and shame when they are the right feelings to have'.[13] Lack of it was described in the writings ascribed to Hermes Trismegistus:

Irreverence is mankind's greatest wrong against the gods ...
Whatever else humans dare to do – out of error or daring or
compulsion or ignorance – all these the gods hold guiltless.
Irreverence alone is subject to judgment.

(*Corpus Hermeticum*, XVI, 11)

The companion of reverence is not fear, as Plato's Euthyphro discovers, but love. Perhaps that is why the seraphim have always been held in such deep affection by theologians, contemplatives and mystics. For their perpetual song of praise is an expression of love.

An entire tradition of mysticism was built on Isaiah's vision together with Ezekiel's dream and some later accounts.[14] But for now we shall pass straight on to the first appearance of seraphim in Christian literature, in the Book of Revelation. Here the dream imagery is more complex. Round the throne are 24 elders, clothed in white raiment, wearing crowns of gold and seated. But 'in the midst of the throne, and round about the throne' were four 'beasts'. Each beast has six wings and many eyes, in fact, they are 'full of eyes within'. They have animal form, of a lion, a calf, and an eagle, though one has the face of a man. They sound more like the composite Babylonian and Egyptian figures that we compared to the biblical cherubim, and they bear a close parallel to the four-winged creatures of Ezekiel's dream. Yet by their six wings and their song of praise, echoing Isaiah's seraphim, they are surely intended as seraphim too, for 'they rest not day and night, saying, Holy, holy, holy, Lord God Almighty, which was and is, and is to come' (Revelation 4:4-8).

It has been argued by some Jewish theologians that cherubim and seraphim should be considered as a separate class of beings, and not as angels, since they seem to play no role as messenger or intermediary in the world of mankind. However, Dionysius clearly included them, and so too does the much earlier 1 Enoch. When Enoch's spirit was translated into the heavens, he saw 'holy sons of God', in white garments, their faces shining like snow as they were stepping on flames of fire. The Archangel Michael leads him up to see all the secrets of the heavens, including a structure of crystals interspersed with tongues of living fire and surrounded by streams of fire:

And round about were Seraphin, Cherubin, and Ophannin:
And these are they who sleep not
And guard the throne of His glory.
And I saw angels who could not be counted,
A thousand thousands, and ten thousand times ten thousand,
Encircling that house,
And Michael and Raphael and Gabriel and Phanuel,
And the holy angels who are above the heavens,
Go in and out of that house.

(1 Enoch 71:7-8)[15]

The fire and light associated with the seraphim have sometimes been described as so bright that it entirely hides them from our view. How many the seraphim are is still unclear, but we are left with the impression that of all angels they are not the most numerous.

Dionysius focused attention on the purifying role of the seraphim, achieved through lightning flash and flame, but he insists, too, on their role as 'carriers of warmth' (*Celestial Hierarchy,* 205c). He describes their 'perennial circling around the divine' in a movement that never falters or fails, and he refers to a penetrating warmth, an overflowing heat. The seraphim have the capacity to arouse in others the flame that burns in themselves. Their very presence removes every obscuring shadow. They receive the divine light and can hold it unveiled and undiminished. In Dionysius's view, they have been initiated into an understanding of divine works, and enjoy a perfection and splendour above all other angels. In our own age one can but wonder how Dionysius was able to achieve such certainty of knowledge about the divine realms! His own explanation is the most plausible, for although he asserts that the angels are intermediate intelligences carrying out the will of the Most High, he also reminds us that the goal of a hierarchy is to enable beings to be as like as possible to God and to be at one with him (165a). All the images he describes are of 'beings so simple that we can neither know nor contemplate them' (137c) but they are 'for the purpose of lifting ourselves up' (137a-c), to the ray that never abandons its own nature (121b). His *Celestial Hierarchy* is not so much a geography of the heavenly realms as a contemplative exercise to train the human mind in the apprehension of divinity.

Nevertheless, the images, all of which had scriptural authority, gained in power through succeeding centuries. After Dionysius, seraphim held an unassailable ascendancy in Christian angelic thought. In addition, they became associated with the movement of the first of the celestial spheres, the crystalline heaven or *primum mobile.* They also continued to hold sway in the Jewish mystical tradition, but not as principal characters in the literature of spiritual ascent. Other angels and archangels play that part. Apart from Isaiah's special moment, seraphim have no mediating role to play among human beings.

In some traditions Lucifer, the morning star who fell from grace, was originally chief of the seraphim and head of the order of virtues. Gregory the Great is among those who regard him so, though attributing to him twelve wings instead of the usual seraphic six. But many, from the Greek Church Fathers to Aquinas and Milton, do not agree with this.[16]

Among poets, seraphim exemplify all that is brightest and best, most faithful and true. When Solomon Ibn Gabirol (1021–55) speaks of 'lively, light-refracting angels, rainbow-girt in lustrous rays' among them are the seraphim, magnifying God's glory.[17] Dante, in the realm of Venus, is encouraged to join their song:

> What stays thy voice, whose song charms Heav'n, and rings
> Tuned to those burning quires perpetually
> Who worship, hooded in their six-fold wings?
>   (Dante, *Divine Comedy*, *Paradiso*, IX, 76-78)

Even in popular song, the name of Jerusalem still scorches the lips like a seraph's kiss.[18]

The seraphim, whose home is in highest heavens, are not confined there totally beyond our reach, nor are they just the stuff of visions or dreams. They may be present among us, at least in a religious, liturgical context, at the sounding of the *Kedusha* or *Sanctus* and through song and psalm. They are certainly connected most fully with the function of praise as, for example, in Figure 15.

Chapter 7

THE CHARIOT AND THE THRONE

Visions of the divine chariot and the heavenly throne are central to Kabbalistic speculation and mystical endeavour. This chapter will take a closer look at the vision of Ezekiel, and how its image of the chariot, together with ideas about the throne of glory, influenced certain kinds of mystical tradition.

With all its fire, light, noise and commotion, the book of Ezekiel is a key text for connecting angelic visions with human aspirations. Unusually for an ancient prophecy, we have a precise date: the fifth day of the month of Tammuz in the fifth year of the captivity which followed the fall of Jerusalem in 597 BCE.[1] The location is the 'river Chebar' or Kevar, a waterway flowing down from Babylon to rejoin the Euphrates at Nippur, a place of forced resettlement in what Ezekiel calls the land of the Chaldaeans.

Ezekiel was the son of a priest and trained as a priest before the destruction of the Temple. The vision marks the start of his ministry as a prophet, warning the people of destruction through their iniquities but promising the eventual downfall of their oppressors, and their own redemption. His vision begins with the approach of a terrible storm-cloud and enveloping fire, at the heart of which was 'the colour of electrum' (Ezekiel 1:4). The Hebrew says 'as the eye of *chashmal*'. 'Eye' is appearance, and hence colour. *Chashmal* appears in no other context, so its meaning cannot be adduced from elsewhere, but it may be electrum, a brilliant natural alloy of gold. Modern Hebrew has adopted *chashmal* as the word for electricity. In the King James Version it is translated as amber, which has a golden glow and some electrical properties. Both electrum and amber were called

Figure 2. Winged figure of *Ma'at*, Egyptian Spirit of Truth, ink on paper, Naomi Spiers.

Figure 3. Zoroastrian winged *Fravashi*, ink on paper, Naomi Spiers.

Figure 4.   Islamic angel, after illustrations in illuminated manuscripts of
Al-Qazwīnī (Persian physician and astronomer, 1203–83). Ink
on paper, Naomi Spiers.

Figure 5.   Stained glass window by Edward Burne-Jones, made in
the William Morris studio, 1878, for St Martin's Church,
Brampton, Cumbria.

Figure 6. Demon created by magic lantern. Giovanni Fontana, *Bellicorum instrumentorum liber*, c.1420.

Figure 7.   Paul Klee, *Angelus Novus*, 1920. Indian ink, coloured chalk and
brown wash on paper, 318 x 242 mm.

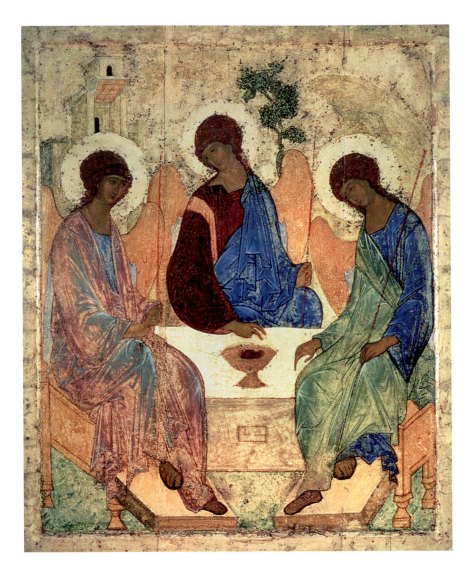

Figure 8. *Hospitality of Abraham* by Andrei Rublev, sometimes known as *The Holy Trinity*, 1425–27, tempera on wood.

Figure 9. Fra Angelico, *Annunciation* (*c.*1445), fresco. Museo di San
Marco, Florence.

Figure 10. *Nike.* Gold earrings made either in Bolsena or Taranto,
fourth–third century BCE. British Museum.

Figure 11. *Archangel Israfil 'Lord of the Horn'*, detached manuscript folio
from *Aja'ib al-Makhluqat* (Wonders of Creation) by Al-Qazwīnī;
early fifteenth century, opaque watercolour, ink and gold on
paper (32.7 x 22.4 cm).

Figure 12. *Annunciation*, from Christ Church, Oxford, MS 101, *The Wolsey Epistle Lectionary*, folio 13 verso.

Figure 13. Colossal statue of a winged lion from the North-West
Palace of Ashurnasirpal II, Neo-Assyrian, Nimrud (Iraq),
ninth century BCE.

Figure 14. *Relief from an Altar*, by Benedetto da Rovezzano (1474–1554).
Florence, marble, 1507–12.

Figure 15. *Levites at the Temple*, accompanied in prayer by seraphic beings, papercut by Naomi Spiers.

Figure 16. Scorpion men encountered by Gilgamesh, guarding the Mountains of Meshu. From an Assyrian engraving, drawn by M. Faucher-Gudin, in G. Maspéro, *History of Egypt, Chaldea, Syria, Babylonia, and Assyria*, ed. Sayce, tr. (London: 1895) vol. 3.

Figure 17. *Annunciation*, detail from Figure 12 above, MS 101, *The Wolsey Epistle Lectionary*, folio 13 verso.

Figure 18. *Yahoel leads Abraham to heaven*, from *The Apocalypse of Abraham* in the Sylvester Codex, first half of fourteenth century, fol. 351.

Figure 19. *Schutzengel* (Guardian Angel), Fridolin Leiber (1853–1912).

Figure 20. *Death as a winged youth*, *c.*325–300 BCE, from the Temple of Artemis, Ephesus, now in the British Museum.

Figure 21. Detail of the *Nativity with the infant St John*, Piero di Cosimo, *c.*1500.

elektron in Greek, therefore both versions are valid. Talmudic sages drew attention to the strange nature of this substance, out of which everything else seems to appear. But they pursued a different puzzle. Noting that *chashmal* appears to have a four-letter root, *ch-sh-m-l*, which is contrary to the laws of grammar (roots should be formed of two letters or three), they broke it down into two constituents, *chash* and *mal*, both abbreviations, rendering one of two meanings 'living creatures talking fire', or 'silent, speaking' a combination of opposites.[2]

Arising from this substance are the four living creatures that flash like lightning: they are human in form but with four faces, four wings and those curious straight feet of burnished brass. One pair of wings is stretched up, joining them one to another, while the other pair covers their bodies. They move forwards and back, without turning (Ezekiel 1:5-12). These are no ordinary angels. Their four faces, of man, ox, lion and eagle, which would later provide the symbols for the four Evangelists, perhaps reflect Babylonian influence. Their wings, however, remind us of the cherubim of the Temple in Jerusalem where Ezekiel had been a priest, and at the reprise of the vision in Ezekiel 10 these creatures are in fact called cherubim. Their appearance was like burning coals, and they move like flashes of lightning (1:13). But their main function is connected with locomotion: 'And they went every one straight forward; whither the spirit was to go, they went; they turned not when they went' (1:12). Any idea of a primitive rustic vision must recede before this description of flashing lights and frenzied motion which is more akin to some neon chariot devised in Las Vegas. Or perhaps he is thinking of the intensity and linear motion of a meteor, which can cross the sky in a straight line while burning with preternatural brightness? The aim is certainly to describe the chariot upon which the divine presence is about to depart from the people, though its wheels defy any attempts at mechanical understanding:

> Now as I beheld the living creatures, behold one wheel at the
> bottom hard by the living creatures, at the four faces thereof.
> The appearance of the wheels and their work was like the
> colour of an emerald;[3] and they four had one likeness; and
> their appearance and their work was as it were a wheel within a
> wheel.

When they went, they went toward their four sides; they
turned not when they went. As for their rings, they were high
and they were dreadful; and they four had their rings full of eyes
round about.

And when the living creatures went, the wheels went
hard by them; and when the living creatures were lifted up
from the bottom, the wheels were lifted up. Whithersoever
the spirit was to go, as the spirit was to go thither, so they
went; and the wheels were lifted up beside them; for the spirit
of the living creature was in the wheels. When those went,
these went, and when those stood, these stood; and when
those were lifted up from the earth, the wheels were lifted up
beside them; for the spirit of the living creature was in the
wheels.

(Ezekiel 1:15-21)

It is hard to visualize each component, let alone the relationship between
the four 'living creatures' and the wheels. The 'emerald' (or beryl, or
topaz) is named in the text simply as 'eye of Tarshish', a variegated
transparent or semi-transparent stone. It could equally be yellow jasper.
That the wheels had eyes gave them an intelligence. The 'rings' or rims,
and the 'height' seem to be connected with the power to lift themselves
up. The arrangement of wheels within wheels has been interpreted in
different ways, but it seems that the purpose was to allow motion in any
direction, and that each creature had one wheel. Later these wheels were
accorded the status of a special rank of angel with the name of *ophanim*
אוֹפַנִּים (wheels) and they are classed with the seraphim and cherubim,
attending upon God (1 Enoch 61:10 and 71:7). The name for the 'living
creatures' is *chayyot* חַיּוֹת, related to *chai* חַי, 'alive'.

After the chariot, Ezekiel describes the indescribable:

And over the heads of the living creatures there was the likeness
of a firmament, like the colour of the terrible ice, stretched forth
over their heads above …

And above the firmament that was over their heads was the
likeness of a throne, as the appearance of a sapphire stone; and
upon the likeness of the throne was a likeness as the appearance
of a man upon it above …

> As the appearance of the bow that is in the cloud in the day
> of rain, so was the appearance of the brightness round about …
> (Ezekiel 1:22, 26, 28)[4]

The cherubim are circling the chariot-throne, with one pair of wings stretched out, while the second pair covered their bodies. The reverberation of their outstretched wings produces a thunderous tumult; there is light and fire and more electrum; but at the sound of a voice, the cherubim let down their wings, and Ezekiel can see the central part of the vision, the divine presence seated on the throne. This is so far beyond the power of words to express that it is described at three removes, as the 'appearance of the likeness of the glory of the Lord' (1:29).

Further strange episodes follow, for example, when a scroll is unrolled before the prophet and he is ordered to eat it (3:1-3). Ezekiel's text contains many puzzling features which present endless difficulties of interpretation.[5] Nevertheless it exerted a powerful appeal to mystics through the ages, and especially to those engaged in the esoteric disciplines of Kabbalah. It was in the hopes of a glimpse of the glory Ezekiel described that mystics directed their contemplation towards 'the work of the chariot' (*ma'aseh merkavah*). They spoke of 'descending' to the chariot, rather than ascending, but only because one had to reach the heights of heaven above it first. A vast body of literature and practices grew up around the *merkavah* and the *heikhalot*, the 'palaces' or heavenly realms of which Isaiah's vision had given a foretaste.[6]

In the *merkavah* and *heikhalot* literature angels multiply, acquire names and specific natures, act as intercessors, and are the holders of knowledge that they may or may not bestow upon the aspirant according to how he approaches them. Such knowledge is generally about divine law, rather than any specific information or assistance. Since a feature of mystical practice was the idea of working towards a transformation of one's being we find various approaches to purification, through devotion and the singing of hymns as well as other disciplines. The aim was to participate at least as a witness in the celebration of divine glory. One example of what the adept might see is given in *Heikhalot Rabbati*, 189:

Each and every day when the afternoon prayer approaches,
The adorned king sits and extols the Holy Creatures (*chayyot*).
Even before the speech from his mouth is completed,

> The Holy Creatures come forth from beneath the throne of glory,
> from their mouths the fullness of rejoicing,
> with their wings the fullness of exaltation;
> Their hands playing instruments
> And their feet dancing.
> They go around and surround their king,
> One from his right and another one from his left,
> One from in front of him and another one from behind him.
> They embrace and kiss him
> and they uncover their countenance.

In response, the king of glory covers his own countenance, while the topmost heaven bursts open 'like a sieve' because of the strength of the angels' radiance, beauty, form, desire, compassion and longing, while they sing the *Kedusha*.[7]

Warnings duly accompanied the study of these texts. Only men were allowed to engage, and to be accepted by a teacher they had to be of mature age and good character. Even then, the teachings were to be passed on only to one person at a time, and in a whisper. The need for a spiritual guide was taken seriously, partly for practical reasons but also because an adept might expect to encounter all sorts of angelic beings, not all of them helpful. Visions could be dangerous, with fire streaking down from heaven to consume the unwary, or dancing angels leading him astray. Physical dangers included, for example, the control of breath by prolonged cycles of recitation combined with postural techniques designed to inculcate visions and trance, as taught by Abraham Abulafia (1240–c.1291).

One such warning is contained in the story of the *Four Sages who entered the Orchard*, set in the first century CE. The orchard (*pardes*) is paradise. Of the four great scholars who make the ascent, one goes mad, one dies, one becomes an apostate. This is Elisha ben Abuyah who mistook Metatron for a second god and all his merits were destroyed on the instant. To this day, he is spoken of as *Acher* ('the other'), as a sign that even his name was obliterated. Only Rabbi Akiva emerges from the visionary experience unscathed (though arguably the one who dies is also rewarded, with a peaceful death of the best possible kind).[8]

It was the sight of the angel Metatron seated in the heavenly court that led Elisha ben Abuyah into error, since no heavenly creature might be seated in the presence of God. Indeed some say that angels cannot be seated, as their legs do not bend – though plenty of kneeling angels in art indicate the opposite, and Milton's 'Sons of Light' all take their seats around the throne (*Paradise Lost*, XI, 82). Elisha's mistake was also understandable, since Metatron is sometimes called 'the lesser God' (from God's statement in Exodus 23:21, that 'my name is in him'). The name of Metatron, too, is still not spoken by many people, because of such dangerous associations.

While the followers of the chariot and the throne certainly hoped to ascend, did they also hope to become angels? Enoch and Elijah had become angels, but Isaiah and Ezekiel did not. In the mystical tradition, Enoch's transformation was not so smooth and gentle as the biblical words suggest ('And Enoch walked with God; and he was not, for God took him', Genesis 5:24). In order to become Metatron, angelic scribe and chief angel, enthroned beside the seat of glory, his flesh was turned to flame, his veins to fire, his eye-lashes to flashes of lightning, and his eyes to flaming torches (3 Enoch 48:6).

Elijah's case is rather different. He became aware that it was time for him to die while he was journeying with his disciple Elisha along the river Jordan. Turning to Elisha he said,

'Ask what I shall do for thee, before I am taken from thee.' And Elisha said: 'I pray thee, let a double portion of thy spirit be upon me.'

And he said: 'Thou hast asked a hard thing; nevertheless, if thou see me when I am taken from thee, it shall be so unto thee; but if not, it shall not be so.'

And it came to pass, as they still went on, and talked, that, behold, there appeared a chariot of fire, and horses of fire, which parted them both asunder; and Elijah went up by a whirlwind into heaven.

(II Kings 2:9-12)

Elisha did see it, and began his ministry. Elijah, taken up into heaven, became the angel Sandalphon. Yet tradition maintains that Elijah still comes and goes. He is accessible at the close of the Sabbath, he visits homes on the night of Passover, and he performs other miracles. He will 'turn the heart of the fathers to the children and the heart of the children to their fathers' (Malachi 4:6). In the Christian tradition, he appeared with Moses at Christ's transfiguration, and will appear again before the Last Judgement; in the Qur'an he is a great and righteous prophet, and in the folklore of the Balkans he is responsible for thunder and lightning. Since he was taken up into heaven, yet comes and goes about the earth, he surely has taken on angelic form, even though he is always still called 'prophet'.

Enoch has a place in the heavenly court as chief angel; Elijah is a perpetual intermediary between earth and heaven. Both confirm that humans may become angels. However, they are exceptional, therefore the confirmation is limited. So when mysticism holds out the hope of rising to the angelic ranks, perhaps it is just to move among them for a while, to gain knowledge, rather than to change form. Contemplative effort and purification are still required, but just for the chance of seeing angels, not to become one. There remain vital differences between angels and humans. This is not a question of wings, gender, or knee joints, but of free will. For if only man has free will, then potentially mankind is already above the angels. We are able to choose a good path and commit to it personally, whereas angels have no choice but to obey and carry out the task for which they are sent.

This is implied in the ending of Milton's *Paradise Lost*. Rich as its narration was in angelic forms and supernal struggle, at its end the human protagonists, our ancestors Adam and Eve, have no longer any need of Eden or of angels. They look back, and shed some natural tears for all that they have known in Paradise, but as they leave, the world is all before them, and Providence their only guide.

It also helps to explain another development that interpreted the living creatures of Ezekiel's vision as an allegory for the human condition. Relying on the phrase 'the living creatures run to and fro' (Ezekiel 1:14) the Baal Shem Tov (1698–1760) taught that ascent and descent are inevitable for man. The concentrated state of being totally absorbed in devotion to the divine cannot be maintained all the time.[9] Life, even for the most pious, must consist in periodic alternation between absorption in and distance from the divine. His grandson, Rabbi Moshe Hayyim Ephraim of Sudikov (1748–1800), spells out why:

When a man engages in worship he cannot help having a
picture of God in his mind. But whatever he depicts is totally

inadequate since God is beyond all comprehension. Man must therefore run to and fro in his mind; running to affirm God's existence and then immediately recoiling from the mental picture he is bound to have ... There is an ebb and flow in the mystical life.[10]

Similarly a sense of being very small and shut in (*katnut*) alternates with 'greatness of soul' (*gadlut*).

This thinking was not limited to the Hasidic revival of eighteenth-century Eastern Europe. Moses Cordovero (1522–70) writing 250 years earlier in Safed had already pointed out this almost inescapable 'running to and fro' that occurs in the mind during prayer. He, too, had likened this back and forth motion to the constant forward and reverse of the *chayyot*. Rather than man becoming an angel, angels (or at least the *chayyot* of Ezekiel's vision) have become a part of man.

Ideas of ascent still find their followers among esoteric circles today. There is also much material on ascent in Islamic and Christian mystical sources, some of which has its roots in Ezekiel's vision, some not. Dante's descent to the inferno, and his climb back up through purgatory and heaven draws on many sources. Another popular Christian work reverts to Jacob's ladder. St John Climacus, a monk of Sinai in the sixth century, wrote his *Ladder of Paradise*, giving 30 steps to religious perfection. Illustrated copies show human souls climbing up the ladder with help from angels in the sky, while devils and demons do all they can to pull them off the rungs. Each rung represents a stage of prayer and preparation, and rungs are steeper at the top of the ladder than at the bottom. In one illustration, the robes of the men start to billow out like angels' wings as they reach the top.[11] Perhaps inspired by this ladder, Count Maldolus had his vision of white-robed monks ascending and descending that prompted the foundation of the Camaldolese order. In drawing up its rules St Romuald made contemplation of the ladder central to its spiritual exercises.[12]

In Jacob's dream the ladder was for angels; here humans climb. At all events, the ladder represents the point at which heaven and earth may join or interpenetrate.

Chapter 8

ANGELS AND ARCHANGELS

Angels and archangels
May have gathered there,
Cherubim and seraphim
Thronged the air.
(Christina Georgina Rossetti, *In the Bleak Midwinter*)[1]

Christina Rossetti pictures crowds of angels in attendance upon the scene of Christ's nativity, a moment of tender intensity between mother and child. We have seen how cherubim and seraphim are distinguished from other angelic beings. Now it is time to consider archangels, and those known merely as 'angels'.

By ordinary angels we mean those angels in closest contact with mankind. These are the personal guardians, personal messengers and angels presiding over particular places. This class would include the angel of healing who troubled the waters at Bethesda. John the Evangelist tells how sick people gather at the pool, and whoever comes into the water first when it is 'troubled' by the angel will be healed of his malady (John 5:14). Thornton Wilder (1897–1975) wrote a one-act play exploring this angel's interaction with humans. In his version, a physician who suffers from deep inner anguish and remorse comes periodically to the pool, hoping to be first and to be healed. At the moment that he is ready to step into the water, his way is blocked by the angel:

ANGEL: Draw back, physician, this moment is not for you.
PHYSICIAN: Angelic visitor, I pray thee, listen to my prayer.
ANGEL: Healing is not for you.

PHYSICIAN: Surely, surely, the angels are wise. Surely, O Prince, you are not deceived by my apparent wholeness. Your eyes can see the nets in which my wings are caught; the sin into which all my endeavors sink half-performed cannot be concealed from you.
(Thornton Wilder, *The Angel That Troubled the Waters*)[2]

The angel does know, but will not yield. The physician has spoken of his own 'wings', as if to indicate the angelic potential of the human soul. Wilder's interpretation is instructive:

ANGEL: Without your wound where would your power be? It is your very remorse that makes your low voice tremble into the hearts of men. The very angels themselves cannot persuade the wretched and blundering children on earth as can one human being broken on the wheels of living. In Love's service only the wounded soldiers can serve. Draw back.
(*Ibid.*)

Someone else enters the water and is healed, but as he is about to leave, he turns to the physician and says:

Come with me first, an hour only, to my home. My son is lost in dark thoughts. I – I do not understand him, and only you have ever lifted his mood. Only an hour ... my daughter, since her child has died, sits in the shadow. She will not listen to us.
(*Ibid.*)[3]

Angels have something to teach. They are not simply to be invoked so that we may accomplish our own will. Even among practitioners of angel healing, the majority would agree that the individual needs to attune him or herself to universal forces, rather than summoning an angel to do one's own bidding. Archangels are also sometimes invoked by angel healers, though more traditionally they are considered as conveyers of greater messages or as guardians of whole nations. Michael was said to be the angelic guard of Israel, and was later claimed as guardian of the new Israel, Puritan England. When we use the term 'archangel' its Greek prefix 'arch' conveys the sense of 'first': first in rank, in authority or even in terms of antiquity. Yet in the Dionysian scale they come very near to last, with the ordinary angels. So it is helpful to consider the two groups 'angel' and 'archangel' together, to set the context in which any distinction between them may be valid.

The archangels have been counted either as four or as seven in number: traditions vary. The four are Michael, Gabriel, Raphael and a fourth named either as Phanuel or Uriel. Their names have clear meanings in Hebrew: 'Who is like God?' (Michael), 'Greatness of God' (Gabriel), 'God heals' (Raphael), 'Face of God' (Phanuel) and 'Light of God' (Uriel). In Islam, the first three have Arabic names with cognate meanings: Mikha'il, Jibra'il, Israfil (corresponding to Raphael) but the fourth is considered to be Azra'il, the angel of death. They were all sent out to gather dust from the four corners of the earth from which Adam might be formed, but only Azra'il succeeded – hence our mortal nature.

Four Hebrew archangels feature in a night-time prayer of great antiquity, while a fifth entity, the divine presence, completes the protection:

> In the name of the Lord the God of Israel:
> Michael is on my right, Gabriel is on my left,
> Uriel is in front of me, Raphael is behind me
> and God's divine presence is over my head.
>   (From the evening recitation of the *Shema*, Ashkenazi rite)

In a similar Christian bedtime prayer the angels are unnamed, partly replaced by the four Evangelists:

> Matthew, Mark, Luke and John, Bless the bed that I lie on.
> There are four corners to my bed, Four angels round my head,
> One to watch, and one to pray, And two to bear my soul away.
>   (Traditional, with many variants)

The divine presence (*shekhinah*) mentioned in the Jewish version, is not an angel but is often described as having wings.[4] The angels named may also be regarded as aspects of God – aspects about which we can speak, whereas attempts to speak of God directly can only fail. (Hence the tradition among many religions of four levels of discourse: literal, moral, allegorical and mystical.) At other times, however, archangels seem to be individual beings, with functions of their own to perform.

The Bible tells us little about archangels. We know that one will sound the last trump (1 Thessalonians 4:16) and Michael is named as one in Jude 1:9. The Book of Tobit tells us about Raphael (see below). He is not actually named an archangel, but is clearly an 'angel of the presence': 'I am Raphael, one of the seven holy angels, which present the prayers of the saints, and which go in and out before the glory of the Holy One' (Tobit 12:15). Similarly, in St Luke's gospel, Gabriel introduces himself as an angel that stands in the presence of God (Luke 1:19).

In Revelation 8:2 we meet 'the seven angels who stand before God'. But are these seven archangels? Whether an 'angel of the presence' is equivalent to an archangel is a difficult question. We know from the visions of Ezekiel and Isaiah that other classes of angel were in the immediate presence of the divine throne, including cherubim, seraphim and *ophanim* (wheels). Some ancient sources draw a distinction between 'angels of the presence' and 'angels of sanctification', and distinguish both from all the other angels that come and go, in charge of winds, fire, rain, storm, seasons and the like. An 'angel of the presence' is mentioned in Isaiah 63:9, as being sent in compassion to save the people. He becomes known in Christian tradition as the Messianic Angel, with attributes related to Christ. Also in this group are Metatron and Sandalphon, Raphael and Gabriel. In rabbinic tradition there were 70 tutelary (guardian) angels in 'the presence', though according to the *Zohar* they were later expelled. In Christian tradition, Satan, too, belonged to this band before he fell. According to the *Book of Jubilees*, an 'angel of the presence' recounts the history of the creation to Moses, having witnessed it from the very beginning since he was created on the first day.[5] Among the 'angels of sanctification' are at least two of the archangels, Michael and Phanuel. Angels of the presence enjoy prime place above those of sanctification and above all the lesser ranking angels. Yet as time went by, the distinction between 'presence' and 'sanctification' seems to have diminished, leaving the archangels united in one group as distinct from other angelic beings with other functions. All of the archangels are considered to lead great troops of lesser angels, if indeed any angelic being can be regarded as 'lesser'. According to 3 Enoch, each archangel leads 496,000 myriads of ministering angels, and a single myriad consists of 10,000. Their role as celestial warriors is quaintly celebrated in a genre of paintings that appeared in the last two decades of the seventeenth century in the Andean region of Peru showing a guardian archangel with wings, dressed as a Spanish noblemen armed with a musket (*arcángel arcabucero*).[6]

In 1 Enoch 40, Michael is accompanied as an archangel by Gabriel, Raphael, and Phanuel. In an earlier, older, list of seven (1 Enoch 20), Raguel, Saraqael and Remiel make up the number (but Uriel replaces Phanuel).[7] Plenty of later lists exist, with Michael, Gabriel and Raphael common to nearly all, while the names of the other four vary. For example, Dionysius has Uriel, Chamuel, Jophiel and Zadkiel. Gregory the Great names Uriel, Simiel, Orifiel and Zachariel. An interesting variant from Judah Ben-Barzillai, early in the twelfth century, lists 12 archangels, connected with the signs of the zodiac. But the number seven also embodies astronomical connections, since seven was the number of the planets known to the ancient world – and was a holy number in itself.

Apart from Michael, Gabriel and Raphael, not one of the huge number of angel names recorded in later literature has biblical authority. In the third century CE, the great scholar Resh Lakish noted that names of the archangels were brought back from Babylon.[8] In fact, the very idea of archangels may have come from Babylon, from the seven planetary gods worshipped there, or perhaps even from Zoroastrian lore, which also found followers in Babylon. The six Amesha Spentas, counted with Ahura Mazda, make seven 'Beneficent Immortals'. They are the first emanations from the supreme deity, and it is with and through them that the creation is accomplished. Their names mean good purpose, truth (or righteousness), desirable dominion, holy devotion, wholeness (or health) and immortality.[9] The period of exile, which lasted for much of the sixth century BCE, provided ample opportunity for contact with indigenous Babylonian ideas and adopted Zoroastrian ones from Persia.

The seven Babylonian planetary gods were the main focus of a classic study by Rev. G. H. Dix. He charts their adaptation and transformation into the archangels that we know. Ezekiel's second vision marks an important stage in this process. In Ezekiel 9, six 'men' come from 'the way of the upper gate which led towards the north', and a seventh man is in the midst of them. These figures are armed with weapons of slaughter and are come to wreak divine vengeance. They have come from the 'north', which for Babylonians was the home of the gods. The seventh figure, 'in their midst', is 'clothed in linen with a writer's inkhorn by his side'. His task is to mark the righteous, while the other six will slay those who are unmarked. These 'men' are clearly divine messengers, and Dix argues that they derive from the seven Babylonian gods, now deprived of their godly status, and reduced to agents of the one God.

The man with the inkhorn derives from Nabu, god of the planet Mercury, 'preserver of wisdom, writer of the fates of men upon the starry heavens'. Nabu was a messenger god, and his symbol was the writer's stylus. He becomes Ezekiel's seventh man, chief among them, with the 'inkhorn', and having knowledge of the secrets of every heart.[10]

For the author of 2 Enoch, Nabu's role is given to the Archangel Uriel.[11] The former Babylonian gods have acquired an authentic Hebrew narrative, but their transformation is not complete until the seven are reduced to four. Dix, regarding archangels and 'angels of the presence' as the same, identifies the principal angel of the presence as Phanuel (face of God), also called the Angel of Peace, since the blessing of peace is generally associated with God's countenance (Numbers 6:26). Phanuel was later merged or confused with Uriel, who had hitherto been the principal archangel, long before Michael was accorded that role.

In reducing the seven archangels to four, Dix thinks that Ezekiel's four *chayyot* were the model, together with four constellations, Leo, Taurus, Aquila and Scorpio. They certainly seem to correspond to the four heads, lion, bull, eagle and man, if one takes into account the presence in Babylonian mythology of scorpion-men, fearsome winged creatures that open and close the gates of the sun (see Figure 16).

Dix also notes a separating out into individual archangels of the four attributes of the 'Messianic Angel' of Isaiah 9:6 named as 'Wonderful Counsellor', 'Mighty God', 'Everlasting Father' and 'Prince of Peace', and he cites sufficient likenesses to link these with Michael, Gabriel, Raphael and Phanuel respectively.

But it seems that there may be more than Dix noted. In antiquity, the eagle was associated with Scorpio. We would therefore have no need to invoke scorpion-men, but can take Scorpio as the eagle. This enables us to remove Aquila (eagle) from the list of four constellations and to replace it with Aquarius, who more plausibly represents the man. Our four constellations are now the four 'fixed' signs of the zodiac (Aquarius, Scorpio, Leo, Taurus), giving a four-square figure in the skies. Not only is this reminiscent of that biblical phrase 'the four corners of the earth', but four also has rich symbolic associations connected with life on earth: for example, the four ages of man, the seasons, the elements (fire, water, air and earth). Four was considered an expression of stability. This was doubly so for the four fixed signs, as opposed to the four cardinal signs (Aries, Cancer, Libra, Capricorn) or the four mutable signs (Gemini, Virgo, Sagittarius, Pisces). The constellations, as Dix noted, had the great advantage that they had never been worshipped in Babylon, unlike the planets, so they were free of the taint of being 'foreign gods'. But now we can see they were also more closely related to earth, bringing the archangels nearer than the wandering planetary deities.

It seems that Resh Lakish was right to underline the foreignness of the names of the angels, yet perhaps we are missing the point if we try to pin down too closely what each archangel is called, or even how many of them there may be. They are more like a kaleidoscope rather than a fixed band. The same would apply, all the more, to the ordinary angels. John Dee had a list of several hundred angels he regularly called upon. Gustav Davidson's *Dictionary of Angels* contains many more names.[12] Some of these come from the Enochian writings and some from Gnostic texts of the second and third centuries CE, but many can be traced no further back than an anonymous fourteenth-century Kabbalistic work, *Atzilut* (divine world).

The archangels' names all end in '*el*', which refers to God or power. It is therefore not unreasonable to interpret them as aspects of God's own power. Their presence would then be a token of God's presence, and their separate existence illusory. Yet the archangels have also taken on individual characteristics in each of the religious traditions, so we may now follow their main exploits.

Michael

Michael is generally considered to be the leader of the archangels, having replaced Uriel in this role. In Islam, Mikha'il is an angel of mercy, responsible for rewarding the righteous. He also has charge over thunder and rain, and hence plants. He is named in the Qur'an in a context of mobilizing against enemies, and is identified as one of the three angels who visited Abraham. In Christian tradition, he is both saint and angel,[13] but in either capacity he is renowned as a warrior. In Greek, he is called *taxiarchos*, which corresponds roughly to 'brigadier'. His great victory over the dragon and his angels is described in Revelation 12:7-8. To Milton it is single combat:

> Together both with next to Almightie Arme,
> Uplifted imminent one stroke they aim'd
> That might determine, and not need repeate,
> As not of power, at once; nor odds appeerd
> In might or swift prevention; but the sword
> Of MICHAEL from the Armorie of God
> Was giv'n him temperd so, that neither keen
> Nor solid might resist that edge: it met
> The sword of SATAN with steep force to smite
> Descending, and in half cut sheere, nor staid,
> But with swift wheele reverse, deep entring shar'd
> All his right side; then SATAN first knew pain,
> And writh'd him to and fro convolv'd; so sore
> The griding sword with discontinuous wound
> Pass'd through him.
>
> (*Paradise Lost*, VI, 316-30)

The depiction of Michael slaying a dragon on the obverse of a gold 'noble' coin led to the coin becoming known as an 'angel'. It was used as currency from 1465 to 1642, and for longer as a medal.[14] Until 1712, a gold or silver angel medallion was given to every person coming to be cured of the 'king's evil' (scrofula). Since 1985, angels have been minted again on the Isle of Man, to sell as bullion. They carry an image of Michael, dressed in a loincloth, and slaying a dragon with his spear. An unintended consequence is that notices of 'angels for sale' now appear in certain trade journals!

Michael's feast day, Michaelmas (29 September), was one of the four traditional quarter days for payments of rent, and it used to mark the start of the university year. His role as leader is recognized in the frequent naming of churches for 'St Michael and All Angels'.

He appears in the Bible at first without name. One such appearance is in the book of Joshua:

And it came to pass, when Joshua was by Jericho, that he lifted
up his eyes and looked, and, behold, there stood a man over
against him with his sword drawn in his hand: and Joshua
went unto him, and said unto him, 'Art thou for us, or for our
adversaries?'

And he said, 'Nay; but as captain of the host of the Lord
am I now come.' And Joshua fell on his face to the earth, and
bowed down, and said unto him, 'What saith my lord unto his
servant?'

And the captain of the Lord's host said unto Joshua, 'Put off
thy shoe from off thy foot; for the place whereon thou standest is
holy.' And Joshua did so.

(Joshua 5:13-15)[15]

Although no name is given, medieval commentators were in no doubt
that this was Michael. It was also thought that Michael visits Abraham
and Sarah, wrestles with Jacob and guides Moses and the children of
Israel through the wilderness.[16] It is not until the book of Daniel that
the Bible names him (though several humans named Michael figure in
earlier books). After a period of mourning Daniel has a vision in which
he is assured that the angel Michael, 'one of the chief angels' will
protect Israel and will prevail against the angel of the Persians (Daniel
10:13 and 21). He will stand up for the children of Israel in greater
troubles than have ever yet been known (Daniel 12:1). In the epistle of
Jude, Michael contends with Samael (the devil) at the death of Moses.
According to a tradition recorded in *Midrash Devarim Rabbah* 11:6,
Samael lay in wait to take the life of Moses, while Michael grieved
at the coming death, and tried to prevent it. In the end the soul was
taken by God, directly to heaven – traditionally, by means of a kiss –
while his body was buried in an unknown place (Deuteronomy 34:6).
Michael's parting comment to the devil, 'The Lord rebuke thee', is
taken as a sign of his restraint and humility.

According to another *midrash*, when Samael fell from heaven, he
seized Michael by the wings and tried to bring him down with him.
Michael was injured but escaped.[17] Nor did the injury impair his powers.
Many sources link Michael with effective interventions, from Abraham's
escape from Nimrod's furnace to the near sacrifice of Isaac, rescuing
Lot, wrestling with Jacob, Daniel's fiery furnace and the tribulations

in the book of Esther.[18] So important were his protective powers that prayers were addressed directly to him. The Jerusalem Talmud saw fit to warn, 'When a man is in need he must pray directly to God, and neither to Michael nor to Gabriel' (*Berachot* 9:13a).

One of the most important legends associated with the Christian cult of the Archangel Michael is based on an episode that took place at Chonae in Phrygia. A group of followers of the pagan gods decided to attack the Christian sanctuary by diverting the river Lycus in order to flood and destroy it. Either by lightning or with a spear, Michael carved a chasm in the rocks to avert this flood. Besides saving the sanctuary, the archangel's intervention gave the waters medicinal powers and it became a great centre of healing. He also raised a healing spring at nearby Colossae, in the first century CE.[19] Thereafter he was known as a healer as well as a defender, and many Orthodox churches were dedicated to him. Amongst these was the Chudov Monastery in Moscow's Kremlin, no longer standing, but its Italianate Archangel cathedral (rebuilt in 1505–08) remains.[20]

In the West, another healing episode led to the founding of Castel Sant'Angelo in Rome, when the Archangel Michael brought deliverance from plague. He became a patron saint of the Holy Roman Empire, of various orders of chivalry and of many important churches. Mont St Michel in Brittany, and St Michael's Mount in Cornwall, both claim his special protection for fishermen.

Some theologians identify Michael with one of the cherubim set to guard the Garden of Eden (though Michael generally holds his sword, whereas the sword there is self-turning). He is also considered by some to have proclaimed the Ten Commandments on Mount Sinai, to have been Balaam's angel (Numbers 22:22) and to have put Sennacherib to flight (II Kings 19:35). A role specific to him in the Catholic tradition is that of angel of death, bringing the chance of redemption to each soul, and carrying the souls of the deceased to heaven. In this he is often in conflict with the devil, as in Jude's epistle. He is also associated with justice, especially for the dead, being represented in statuary with a balance as well as his drawn sword and sometimes a slain dragon at his feet. Among Jehovah's Witnesses and Seventh-day Adventists, he is regarded as the pre-incarnate form of Christ.

With all these roles, his precise position in the nine ranks of angels came under dispute. Some of the Church Fathers wished to place him among the seraphim, as the greatest of all angels, while others were content to leave him with the other archangels in the Dionysian hierarchy.

Gabriel

To Christians the angel, or archangel, Gabriel is best known for the annunciation of the birth of Christ to Mary, but he has a long history before that, beginning with his appearance to Abraham, with Michael, as one of the three visitors. Gabriel often takes the form of a man when he appears. He appears as a man to Daniel, to explain his visions (Daniel 8:16 and 9:21), but he is sent to the priest Zacharias serving at the altar as an angel (Luke 1:19): 'I am Gabriel, that stand in the presence of God; and am sent to speak unto thee, and to shew thee these glad tidings.' Zacharias is struck dumb by the experience.

In Luke 1:26 Gabriel is sent to Nazareth in Galilee to deliver the famous words 'Hail, thou that art highly favoured, the Lord is with thee: blessed art thou among women', and in most depictions of this scene he is portrayed as a fully-winged angel. The conversation that follows in verses 28-38 is more two-sided than many angelic encounters: Mary responds to the angel's news with the equally famous words, 'Behold the handmaid of the Lord; be it unto me according to thy word', followed by the *Magnificat* (1:46-55), as shown in Figure 17.

According to tradition, Gabriel stands at the left hand of God and is the angel of revelation, as well as a prince of fire. Several of the interventions that are ascribed to Michael are ascribed by some to Gabriel, such as wrestling with Jacob. The medieval work *Sitrei Torah* (Torah Secrets), by Abraham Abulafia, tells us that Gabriel is robed in red, to denote his connection with judgement, but Daniel sees him dressed in white linen, as a priest. Gabriel also serves as an angel of death, especially for kings. He figures in Milton's *Paradise Lost* as another chief guardian of heaven (besides Michael), wise and measured in his response. In 1 Enoch he is the instigator of war amongst the giants, and in Christian tradition has the task of blowing the trumpet to signal the end of time. But mostly his voice is one of prayer, intercession and supplication on behalf of those who dwell on earth.

In Islam, he is both an archangel furnished with wings and the holy spirit in a created form. It was Jibra'il who delivered the Qur'an to Muhammad the Prophet, in a cave near Mecca, and who returns to earth on the anniversary of that occasion each year during Ramadan on the 'Night of Destiny'.[21] In the Qur'an, too, he makes the annunciation to Mary (19:17). He may come in the form of a man, but according to a *hadith*, if he comes in his own form he has 600 emerald wings and each wing can cover the whole horizon.[22] He is Muhammad's guide through heaven.

Raphael

Raphael's primary function is to bring healing. His name is Hebrew (God heals), yet his origin may be Chaldaean. In the Book of Tobit he accompanies Tobias (whose name, *Toviyah*, means 'God is good') on a journey. This book was immensely popular in the Middle Ages, providing themes for the activities of confraternities, as well as the decoration of hospital buildings. From the early Renaissance to the Enlightenment, the city of Florence had a confraternity called the 'Boys of the Archangel Raphael', which engaged noble youths in religious dramas, pageants and music.[23] The eclipse of the Book of Tobit in more modern times may be due to its relegation to the Apocrypha by Protestant churches. Though never part of the Hebrew Bible canon, it is found in the Septuagint and amongst the discoveries at Qumran.

Tobit, a righteous but unfortunate refugee in Nineveh (in modern Iraq), living in a time of persecution, is accidentally blinded. Sorrows seem to heap upon him, though his faith never wavers. He has an equally unfortunate niece who has lost seven bridegrooms on the eve of marriage, through the work of an evil spirit. Tobit, in great poverty and ready to die, decides to send his son Tobias to Rages (in Iran), where a kinsman Gabael has some money that is owing to him. Tobias is to seek a man to accompany him on the long journey, a hired hand, who is in fact the angel Raphael. They set off towards the river Tigris, where a fish attacks them, and Raphael instructs Tobias to take out and keep the heart, liver and gall of the fish. Travelling on to Ecbatana, where the niece lives, they use the heart and liver to drive out the devil that has beset her. The gall of the fish will provide healing for Tobit's eyes on their eventual return. Meanwhile, they retrieve the money from Gabael in Rages, but their return is delayed, and Tobias's mother, fears that they have perished. The tale is replete with moments of faith, trust, devotion, generosity and sheer goodness which drive away the doubts, fears and compromising actions that would have been all too understandable in the circumstances. Finally, when the father goes to thank Raphael and pay him his wages, Raphael reveals himself and his reasons for coming, pointing out that although he had been with them many days 'I did neither eat nor drink, but ye did see a vision' (Tobit 13:19).

The Tobias story is retold to most touching effect in Salley Vickers's novel, *Miss Garnet's Angel,* in a narration that runs parallel to the adventures of her heroine in modern Venice, in a plot revolving around the Church of the Archangel Raphael near the Giudecca.[24]

Raphael is the principal angel of healing, 'set over all the diseases and wounds of the children of men' (1 Enoch 40), but he is also a guide in the underworld (1 Enoch 22), and is sometimes called the angel of the sun, perhaps in parallel with the Greek god of healing, Apollo (though the title 'regent of the sun' also belongs to Uriel). He seems to bring with him love, joy and light. These aspects of his nature are celebrated by Milton, where his long conversations with Adam convey knowledge, wisdom and encouragement. They even end with a surprising glimpse into a question that has puzzled many: do angels engage in sex? Blushing, Raphael says,

> Let it suffice thee that thou know'st
> Us happie, and without Love no happiness.
> Whatever pure thou in the body enjoy'st
> (And pure thou wert created) we enjoy
> In eminence, and obstacle find none
> …   …   …
> Easier then Air with Air, if Spirits embrace,
> Total they mix, Union of Pure with Pure
> Desiring; nor restrain'd conveyance need,
> As Flesh to mix with Flesh, or Soul with Soul.
>
> (*Paradise Lost*, VIII, 620-29)

Their union is total, an intermingling of breath and being – but no more is divulged, as the conversation is cut short by the setting sun.

Raphael's counterpart in Islam is Israfil (see Figure 11), the archangel who awaits the announcement of the end of days when he will sound the last trump:

> And the trumpet shall be blown, so all those that are in the heavens and all those that are in the earth shall swoon, except Allah; then it shall be blown again, then they shall stand up awaiting.
>
> (Qur'an 39:68)

Beautiful, and possessed of four wings, Israfil is said to be so tall as to reach from earth to the pillars of the divine throne. According to Edgar Allan Poe, his voice is the sweetest of all God's creatures, and his heart strings are a lute.[25]

> None sing so wildly well
> As the angel Israfel
> And the giddy stars (so legends tell),
> Cease their hymns, attend the spell
> Of his voice, all mute.
>
> (Poe, *Israfel* (1831), lines 3-7)

His compassion is said to be infinite: he looks into hell three times a day and three times a night, and his tears would flood the earth if Allah did not stop their flow. Occasionally Israfil has been identified with Sarafiel rather than Raphael, because of the root *s-r-f* in his name which indicates burning, or with Uriel. However, through his healing power and musical voice, it is better to consider him the parallel of Raphael.

The Fourth Archangel

The fourth archangel of Islamic tradition is the angel of death, Azra'il. It is said that he accomplishes the separation of body and soul by holding an apple from the tree of life to the nose of the dying person. This puts a fascinating twist on the biblical tale of Eve's temptation, source of the Christian doctrine of original sin. Was the attraction of the apple beyond a mortal's power to resist? Were Adam and Eve originally immortals? Azra'il is tasked with 'forever writing in a large book, and forever erasing what he writes', inscribing people's names at birth, and erasing them at death, in a Book of Life.

In the Judaeo-Christian tradition the fourth archangel seems, by contrast, to be a defender of humankind before the Almighty, during life. Named as Phanuel, 'face of God', he fends off the demonic accusers of mankind from bringing their suit before the holy court, and he is invoked against evil spirits. Named as Uriel, 'light or fire of God' he has special watch over repentance and salvation, and care of souls at times of terror. It is Uriel who reveals to Enoch the science of the heavenly luminaries and the mysteries of the calendar. Uriel has power over night and day, causing the sun, moon and stars to revolve in their circular chariots and give light to men (1 Enoch 82:7).

According to the Transcendental philosopher, Ralph Waldo Emerson (1803–82), Uriel was one of the angels who fell from grace when his sharp mind led him to question the physical and metaphysical laws of nature. Finding everything round, without a single straight line, he questioned the wisdom of the divine plan, and 'all slid to confusion':

> As Uriel spoke with piercing eye,
> A shudder ran around the sky
> ...   .
> A sad self-knowledge withering fell
> On the beauty of Uriel;
> In heaven once eminent, the god
> Withdrew that hour into his cloud.
>
> (Emerson, *Uriel*, lines 25-26 and 35-38)

In *Paradise Lost*, he is based in 'the sun's bright circle' and renowned for his wide field of vision and keen sight. When Satan wants to initiate his train of mischief, he seeks out Uriel, claiming that he has come alone, 'from the Quires of Cherubim', to admire God's latest handiwork:

> '*Uriel*! For thou of those seven Spirits that stand
> In sight of God's high throne, gloriously bright,
> The first art wont his great authentic will
> Interpreter through highest Heaven to bring,
> Where all his Sons thy Embassie attend ...

   ... ...
Brightest Seraph, tell
In which of all these shining Orbes hath man
His fixed seat, or fixed seat hath none?
                           (*Paradise Lost*, III, 654-58 and 667-69)

Despite his 'sharp sight', Uriel is taken in by Satan's flattery, and directs him towards Adam and Eve. Then Satan's mien changes, and Uriel, realizing the disaster he has unleashed, goes to consult with Gabriel, the 'wingèd warrior', guardian at the Eastern gate of Paradise:

   Thither came Uriel, gliding through the even
   On a sun-beam, swift as a shooting star
   In autumn thwarts the night ...
                           (*Paradise Lost*, IV, 555-57)

Admitting his mistake, he asks for Gabriel's help, and Gabriel, without rebuking him, agrees. The drama unfolds. For Milton archangels are Angels of the Presence – the seven 'who stand before God' (Revelation 8:2). They were created on the first day, witnessing the very beginning of creation:

   I saw when at his Word the formless Mass,
   This world's material mould, came to a heap:
   Confusion heard his voice, and wild uproar
   Stood rul'd, stood vast infinitude confin'd;
   Till at his second bidding Darkness fled,
   Light shon, and order from disorder sprung.
                           (*Paradise Lost*, III, 708-13)

Though entirely fictional, these poetic accounts have helped to shape our perceptions of the angelic world. Milton is not so much read now as in former times, but his influence persists through other writers and through hymns that are sung, which often do more for our religious sensibilities than whole volumes of theology.

But perhaps the final word on angels and archangels should be from 1 Enoch, which claims a precision for which we would search in vain in the canonical books of the Bible:

And after that I saw thousands of thousands and ten thousand times ten thousands, I saw a multitude beyond number and reckoning, who stood before the Lord of Spirits. And on the four sides of the Lord of Spirits I saw four presences, different from those that sleep not, and I learnt their names: for the angel who went with me made known to me their names and showed me all the hidden things.

And I heard the voices of those four presences as they uttered praises before the Lord of glory. The first voice blesses the Lord of Spirits for ever and ever. And the second voice I heard blessing the Elect One and the elect ones who hang upon the Lord of Spirits. And the third voice I heard pray and intercede for those who dwell on the earth and supplicate in the name of the Lord of Spirits. And I heard the fourth voice fending off the Satans and forbidding them to come before the Lord of Spirits to accuse them who dwell on the earth.

After that I asked the angel of peace who went with me, who showed me everything that is hidden: 'Who are these four presences which I have seen and whose words I have heard and written down?'

And he said to me: 'The first is Michael, the merciful and long-suffering; and the second who is set over all the diseases and all the wounds of the children of men, is Raphael; and the third, who is set over all the powers, is Gabriel; and the fourth, who is set over the repentance unto hope of those who inherit eternal life, is named Phanuel.'

          (1 Enoch 40:1-9, tr. R. H. Charles)

Chapter 9

ANGEL GUIDES IN
THE WORLD TO COME

Fascination with the idea of a world to come pervades the literature of many ages. Even a sceptic can draw psychological insight from the imagery of the afterlife taken allegorically. Much was made of other-world journeys by the great ethnologists of the late nineteenth century: Edward Burnett Tylor and Sir James Frazer sought explanations through anthropology and psychology, Emile Durkheim saw them as codifications of social relationships. Ioan Couliano, writing in 1991, links such journeys with ecstasy and techniques of healing. His mentor and compatriot Mircea Eliade, himself a great interpreter of religious experience, described such journeys as attempts 'to obtain contact with the parallel universe of the spirits and to win their support in dealing with the affairs of a group or of an individual'.[1]

A rich body of literature dating from 300 BCE to 200 CE contains accounts of journeys through the heavenly realms, often set within a context of apocalyptic visions and prophecies. These include the books of Enoch we have already met, in which angels often serve as guides. The word 'apocalypse' simply means an uncovering or revelation. It is used in particular for revelations of divine purpose, and these works often celebrate the ultimate triumph of good over evil in order to encourage people to have faith through times of suffering. Apocalyptic views were already present in parts of Isaiah, in Ezekiel and the book of Daniel. But the richest period of apocalyptic writing falls between the end of the canonical Hebrew scriptures and the completion of the Gospels.

The most famous Christian apocalypse is the revelation of the future granted to St John on the Aegean island of Patmos. Known as the Book

of Revelation, it forms the final section of the New Testament. In the
Byzantine rite it is closely linked to the Easter story, being read at the
conclusion of the all-night vigil on 'Bright Saturday', celebrated as the
Saturday following Christ's resurrection.

Characteristic of all these apocalyptic books is the bringing together
of forces of good and evil in confrontation, often in weird depictions
and symbolic dream sequences. Many were written at times of intense
public grief, offering consolation based on the view that an omnipotent
God will vindicate the righteous, if not in this world then in the next.
They are generally narrated in the first person, but feature dialogue
with an angel or angels through which the layers of heaven are revealed,
with visions of a heavenly temple, of justice, and of mysteries. Not
surprisingly such books give rise to much controversy in interpretation,
yet they have caught the imagination of successive generations, perhaps
because their images carry a primordial or archetypal power. For
example, Revelation, with its dragons, beasts, horsemen and seals,
the Lamb, Satan, the Whore of Babylon, piles mystery on mystery,
but speaks of the battle of good and evil that takes place around and
within humanity. As seen by St John, this continual, bloody battle will
ultimately culminate in a healing of all ills, a new heaven and a new
earth. Within that overall tale, however, our interest lies with the role
of the angels.

At the start, we are told that the revelation given to John comes
from God but is 'sent and signified' by his angel (Revelation 1:1). John
was 'in the Spirit' when he heard 'a great voice as of a trumpet' (1:10).
He turned and saw seven golden candlesticks and in their midst 'one
like unto the Son of man', holding seven stars. The stars are angels,
each having the care of one of seven churches, that is, the seven most
important early Christian communities, all located in what is now
Turkey. But it is the 'Son of man' who invites our attention, described
in words reminiscent of Daniel's vision (Daniel 10:5-6):

> dressed in a robe reaching down to his feet and with a
> golden sash around his chest. His head and hair were white
> like wool, as white as snow, and his eyes were like blazing
> fire. His feet were like bronze glowing in a furnace, and his
> voice was like the sound of rushing waters. In his right hand
> he held seven stars, and out of his mouth came a sharp

double-edged sword. His face was like the sun shining in all
its brilliance.

(Revelation 1:13-16)[2]

His appearance is that of an angel, but when he speaks, it is Christ.

John receives instructions for the seven angels of the churches, and
then proceeds through a door that opens in heaven. Here he is addressed
by a speaking trumpet, and sees a lustrous figure on an emerald throne,
with thunder and lightning issuing from it, and a rainbow over it. Round
the throne are 24 'elders' – senior angels, perhaps – with white raiment
and crowns of gold. There is a sea of glass, and four winged beasts. An
angel is at hand to make proclamations, then after the appearance of the
Lamb, the elders fall in worship. Each one has a harp, and a golden vial
full of 'odours', which consist of the prayers of the holy. This symbolic
rendering of prayer as a sweet savour ascending to God is already
present in Old Testament writings (Hosea 14:2) and angels stand ready
to receive the prayers of the faithful in Kabbalistic poems.

While John is momentarily distracted, suddenly the place is filled with
angels – ten thousand times ten thousand, and thousands of thousands
(Revelation 5:11). Later, four angels stand at the 'four corners of the
earth', controlling the winds, while a fifth came up from the east 'with a
seal from the living God' and a message for the four (7:1-2).

After the opening of the seals, there is a silence in heaven, then
seven angels stand before God with seven trumpets, an eighth has a
golden censer of incense and prayers (8:2-3). A display of fire and light,
thunder and earthquakes follows, with great dismay in the heavens, and
falling stars. Images of destruction proliferate, with locusts, scorpions
and many torments: 'In those days shall men seek death, and shall not
find it'. Four angels of death are unleashed, and myriads of horsemen –
until a peaceable angel comes, clothed in a cloud with a rainbow on his
head, a shining face, and pillars of fire for feet. This angel requires John
to eat the book which he holds, and prophecies follow. In chapter 12,
after many dreadful portents, the famous war in heaven begins. Michael
and his angels fight against the dragon. This marks a turning point: the
angels who appear thereafter bring particular messages, guiding mankind
towards a better future, or guiding the avenging angels to harvest the
evil from the earth and remove it, pouring out the wrath of God, to
cleanse the creation. Finally, the dragon, Satan, is bound and cast into

the bottomless pit. John pays his tribute of worship to the angel who has shown him all these things, and Christ acknowledges the testimony of the angel as his own message of hope.

The angels of Revelation seem especially active, as scene after scene opens up before John. He has only to pass through that first door in heaven. In other apocalyptic writings, human beings make journeys, with angels serving as their guides. Enoch is one of these. He first appears in Genesis as the son of Jared, father of the long-lived Methuselah, and great-grandfather of Noah.[3] He is also acclaimed as the seventh of the ten patriarchs before the flood (Jude 1:14), but we learn little more about him in the Bible beyond the facts that he 'walked with God', (Genesis 5:22 and 5:24) and 'God took him' (5:24). The traditional interpretation of this, confirmed by Hebrews 11:5, is that his way of life was so pleasing to God that he was spared the experience of death.

The first *Book of Enoch* (1 Enoch), whose composition spans some 400 years from 300 BCE, contains parables, dream visions, an apocalypse, commentary on the fallen angels and the flood. Enoch becomes the repository of all knowledge on the calendar and the stars, but he is also required to act as intercessor for the fallen angels, those angels whose transgressions led to the spread of wickedness on the earth. In this book, heaven has geographical extent, but no vertical stratification.

In 2 Enoch, *The Secrets of Enoch*, which originated in the first century CE, heaven has seven layers, and different troops of angels have different functions. 3 Enoch shares similar inspiration but was written much later. Both 2 and 3 may have been intended as commentary on 1 Enoch.[4] They too are concerned with Enoch's ascent to heaven and his transformation into an angel – not just any angel, but Metatron, chief of the angels and Knower of Secrets. In 2 Enoch, he is prepared for that transformation by the Archangel Vereveil but this may be simply a corruption of Uriel.[5] Enoch also assumes a salvific role, taking away the sins of the world.

God conceived a desire to show Enoch all the wonders of his own realm, so he sent two angels to fetch him while he was asleep on his bed, having reached the significant age of 365 years. They are described as men, but they were

> exceeding big, so that I never saw such on earth; their faces were shining like the sun, their eyes too [were] like a burning light, and from their lips was fire coming forth, with clothing …

of various kinds in appearance purple, their wings [were]
brighter than gold, their hands whiter than snow.

(2 Enoch 1:6)

They bore him on their wings to the first heaven, where he saw a great
sea, and 200 angels ruling the stars. From there, he looked down to
more angels guarding the treasure houses of snow, cloud, and dew.
They led him to the second heaven, where he met dark, weeping angels:
the spirits of those who had turned away from truth. In the third heaven
they looked down on paradise with its tree of ineffable goodness, and
300 bright angels tending the garden, singing sweetly all day long. This
will be the home of the righteous 'who endure all manner of offence
from those that exasperate their souls', and who nevertheless live
according to the rule of kindness and justice. Still on the same level,
they lead him to the north, which is in every way opposite; it has its own
set of fully-armed, merciless angels, inflicting punishment on those who
lived wrongly. In the fourth heaven, that of the sun and the moon, he
observes the movements of the sun and its accompanying stars. Fifteen
myriads of six-winged angels attend it by day and a thousand by night,
while another hundred kindle the sun and set it alight (2 Enoch 11:5-
6). Other winged creatures include phoenixes and marvellous rainbow-
coloured chalkydri, with lions' tails and crocodile heads.[6] Enoch's two
angel-guides then carry him to the east to observe the seasons and the
west for the sun's setting, with another 400 angels on guard, and they
show him the details of the moon's circuits attended by spirits, six-
winged angels and elements (16:7).

In the fifth heaven, Enoch's guides show him a massive array of
soldiers who are followers of Satan, the Grigori.[7] In the sixth heaven are
seven bands of angels who are brighter than the sun, and have command
over life in heaven and on earth, even over every blade of grass. They
are named archangels, and in their midst are six more phoenixes and six
six-winged cherubim (2 Enoch 19:3). Finally, his angel-guides – though
still named 'men' – lift Enoch to the seventh heaven, full of fire, light
and archangels. From here he can see to the divine throne on the tenth
heaven. Terrified, Enoch falls down in fear and trembling, but Gabriel
flies to him, catches him up as the wind might catch a leaf, and brings
him right before the face of God. On the way he catches a glimpse of
the eighth and ninth heavens: the eighth causes the changing of seasons

on earth, while the ninth is the heavenly mirror of the eighth. In the tenth heaven, Enoch sees God's face (22:1-3),[8] and whole troops of cherubim and seraphim. The Archangel Michael comes to lift him up, the angels greet him. Michael anoints him and clothes him in garments of glory. Another archangel, Pravuil[9] is asked to bring out all the books of heavenly wisdom, together with a 'reed of quick writing', for Enoch to write. God then seats Enoch beside Gabriel on his left. What follows is a commentary on the creation story, and a renewal of moral teachings. To conclude, after 60 days in the heavenly realm, during which time he transcribed 366 books, Enoch is taken back to his home by the two 'men' and is allowed to spend 30 more days on earth to pass on all that he had learned. But just before he leaves heaven his face has to be frozen, by an aged freezing-angel, lest its radiance dazzle his family (37:1-2) – just as Moses's face was said to shine when he came down from the mountain (Exodus 34:30).

It is, however, 1 Enoch that contains the most interesting travels for it is not a simple scheme of heaven but a richly nuanced landscape of symbolic territories. Enoch's first journey is in a vision (1 Enoch 14:8–19:3). Invited by the clouds, and summoned by a mist, he is lifted by the winds and flies into heaven. Flying through crystal walls and tongues of fire he reaches a crystal house, then through fire and ice and another vision he enters a second house greater than the first, with the stars in its ceiling and more fire. Above it stands the divine throne, with cherubim and many angels. From there, Enoch is sent on a journey through the earth and the world of darkness, Sheol. He sees the mountains of darkness, uttermost depths, living waters, rivers of fire and the treasuries of the winds. There are seven mountains of precious stones: the three to the east are of coloured stone, pearl and jacinth; the three to the south are of red stone; the middle mountain is the one that reaches right up to heaven, and is of alabaster with a summit of sapphire. In the region beyond the mountains the earth comes to an end with an abyss. Beyond the abyss there is no more heaven or earth, but a wasteland, a prison for stars that have transgressed by failing to follow their appointed risings, and for the fallen angels or watchers.

Enoch's second journey is within this wasted realm, and he plies his angel guides with many questions. There seem now to be several guides, under the direction of Uriel who answers him first. Beyond the first wasteland is another, with great descending columns of fire, the place where the fallen angels will be imprisoned for ever, and here Raphael takes on the explanations. The third stage of this journey is to the western ends of the earth, with a fire that does not rest. Archangel Raguel explains how the stars are punished. Beyond all the burning, they come to seven mountains – perhaps the same as those described in the first journey – but now the emphasis is on the beautiful, fragrant tree that grows there. Archangel Michael explains the significance of the tree, which will be food for the righteous on the Day of Judgement (25). Returning to the middle of the earth he sees a blessed land with trees, and more holy mountains divided by deep dry ravines (26–27). The ravines form the Accursed Valley, and the hills a place for judging the righteous, Uriel tells him. They travel east through the wilderness to the spice groves. Further east is the tree of knowledge, and further still the portals of the stars. Raphael answers his questions here, though Zotiel is also named as presiding over the eastern reaches, which seem to include the earthly paradise of Eden.

At the eastern limit, Enoch sees how the stars rise, and Uriel helps him record their names, times, courses and positions. At the far north he sees 'a great and glorious device', namely the portals of the cold, hail, frost, snow and rain. From one portal they blow for good, but from the other two they 'blow with violence' (34). The western and the southern ends of the earth also have portals for the rain and dew, and the east a portal for the stars. Of the archangels who are named in chapter 20, which forms a short interlude between the first journey and the second, only four speak to answer Enoch's questions, but all seven have specific functions: Uriel presides over Tartarus, Raphael over the spirits of men, Raguel over the aberrant stars, Michael over both the best of mankind and over chaos. The silent ones are Saraqael, who is set over spirits and those who sin in the spirit, Gabriel, who watches over Paradise, the seraphim and cherubim, and Remiel, who is 'set over those who rise' (i.e. the stars who keep to their courses).

Enoch also figures in the book of *Jubilees*, written in the second century BCE or earlier.[10] Here, too, angels instruct him in the secrets of astronomy, chronology and history (4:17–21). He spends 294 years in their presence (six jubilees) but there are none of the colourful voyages of the *Book of Enoch*. *Jubilees* is a retelling of Genesis and Exodus, with emphasis on the law, and on the superiority of a solar calendar. However, we may note that the angels in *Jubilees* are made responsible for compiling all that Moses will learn on Mount Sinai. This includes a detailed history of the creation, in which the angels are all created on the first day and can assist in the work of creation thereafter (2:2). Here too is the division of angels into those of the Presence and those of Sanctification, while guardian angels and all those of fire, wind, cloud, darkness, snow, hail and hoar-frost all form a lesser host, together with the angels or spirits of voices, thunder, lightning, heat, cold, the seasons and the spirits of all creatures.[11]

Enoch appears again in the *Apocalypse of Abraham*, written around the end of the first century CE. This seems to be an elaborate commentary on Genesis 15, taking the familiar stories of the patriarch Abraham, embellishing them and adding a journey, with angel conversations on the way. At the heart of the text is the Bible story of the covenant God makes with Abraham. In the *Apocalypse*, animals are prepared for sacrifice on Mount Horeb under the guidance of the luminous angel Yahoel. Yahoel is none other than Enoch in his angelic form. It is not clear why the name Yahoel has been preferred to Metatron, unless perhaps because of strictures against speaking that powerful name. Abraham is instructed on no account to answer the evil angel Azazel should he appear, since that would bind him forever within Azazel's power. Azazel comes, in the form of a bird of prey (cf. Genesis 15:11), and tries to question Abraham, and to eat the sacrificial foods. Abraham follows Yahoel's instruction and speaks a formula of dismissal (which does not count as a reply) so the sacrifice is successful. This is the prelude to a journey up to the seventh heaven, travelling on the wings of two birds that were not cut up for sacrifice: the pigeon and the turtle dove, as in the illumination from the fourteenth-century Sylvester Codex (Figure 18).[12]

One of the many curious details that emerges from scholarship on this text – though not reflected in this illustration – is the observation that Yahoel lacks human features. He is described as having the body of a griffin, not a man. He is nevertheless a glorious creature, radiant because he is composed of sapphire, and his face resembles chrysolite, both gems generally associated with God's glory.[13] It is tempting to see in this portrayal a move away from peopling the heavens with angels in human form. In the same book, when Abraham reaches the divine throne, there is no vision of the divine, only an auditory manifestation in the form of a voice, coming from a stream of fire.[14] Likewise, the demon Azazel is here an 'impure bird' (*Apocalypse* 13:2-8). He is also the serpent in the Garden of Eden, having 12 wings,[15] but human hands and feet (23:7-11).

Like the third-century biblical commentary, *Genesis Rabbah*, the *Apocalypse of Abraham* has a category of angels who are born daily, from a stream of light and fire. They also die daily, or at least disappear, after uttering the hymn of praise for which they have been created. An important element of the angel's instruction in the *Apocalypse* is also on how to pray. Abraham learns the angel's own song, remarkable because we rarely find such a thing:

> Eternal, Mighty, Holy El, God only-supreme
> You who are the Self-originated, the Beginningless One,
>   Incorruptible,
> Spotless, Uncreated, Immaculate, Immortal, Self-complete,
>   Self-illuminating,
> Without father, without mother, unbegotten,
> Exalted, Fiery One! Lover of men, Benevolent One, Bountiful
>   One,
> Jealous over me, and very compassionate, Eli, My God,
> Eternal, Lord of hosts, Very Glorious El, El, El, El, Jah El!
> You are the One whom my soul has loved!
>
> (*Apocalypse of Abraham*, 19)

The song continues, praising God's power to enlighten the world and dissolve confusion, and asking especially for light to shine on the earth as well as heaven. The effect upon Abraham of singing it is to bring about a vision of the divine throne (though not of God himself), and he is lifted up to the seventh heaven, from where he looks down upon the lower heavens, the stars and the earth. God himself now takes over the task of explaining:

> Consider the expanses which are under the firmament on which you are now placed and see how on no single expanse is there any other than the One whom you have sought, even the One who loves you!'
> And while he was yet speaking, the expanses opened, and there below me were the heavens, and I saw upon the seventh firmament upon which I stood a fire widely extended, and

the light which is the treasury of life, and the dew with which
God will awaken the dead, and the spirits of the departed
righteous, and the spirits of those souls who have yet to be born,
and judgment and righteousness, peace and blessing, and an
innumerable company of angels, and the Living Ones, and the
Power of the Invisible Glory that sat above the Living Ones.

   And I looked downwards from the mountain on which I
stood to the sixth firmament, and there I saw a multitude of
angels of pure spirit, without bodies, whose duty was to carry
out the commands of the fiery angels who were upon the
seventh firmament.

(*Apocalypse of Abraham* 24–26)

Below the fiery angels of the seventh heaven and the bodiless spirit-
angels of the sixth were the stars in the fifth firmament, commanding the
elements on earth. Abraham is asked to count the stars, and cannot. He
is also puzzled how the evil Azazel can be one of God's creatures. But he
looks down and sees all the good and all the evil in the world, co-existing
as part of a single creation:

the earth and its fruits, and what moved upon it and its animate
beings, and the power of its men, and the ungodliness of some
of its souls and the righteous deeds of other souls, and I saw
the lower regions and the perdition therein, the abyss and
its torments. And I saw the sea and its islands, its monsters
and its fishes, and Leviathan and his dominion, his camping-
ground and his caves ... and the destructions of the world on
his account. And I saw there the streams and the rivers, and
the rising of their waters, and their windings in their courses
... and the Garden of Eden and its fruits ... the trees and their
blossoms, and the ones who behaved righteously ... And I saw a
great multitude, men and women and children ...

(*Apocalypse of Abraham* 24–31)

In its expressions of praise and its insistence on the unity of the creation,
the *Apocalypse of Abraham* is impressive even in translation, yet it has
suffered neglect and was known to few. It survived only in an Old
Slavonic translation, in a mere handful of manuscripts.

The books of Esdras were more widely spread, and in one of these the Archangel Uriel appears again as a principal guide. Just as the stories of Enoch and Abraham were expanded, the prophecies of Ezra here receive similar treatment. The relationship of the various Esdras books to their biblical counterpart Ezra is somewhat complicated, but 2 Esdras forms an apocryphal companion to the biblical book.[16] In it, Ezra has bewildering visions and the angel Uriel explains them. For example, while the prophet was comforting a grieving woman for the loss of her son, she suddenly vanished, and in her place stood a city. This unexpected transformation caused Ezra to swoon. Uriel comes to relate the meaning of it.

Another source describing journeys guided by angels is a set of writings ascribed to the Prophet Baruch. Baruch ben Neriah was a kinsman of the Prophet Jeremiah, staying with him in Babylon in captivity and serving as his scribe when most of the people were allowed to return home (538 BCE). There is no agreement yet on when it was written, but it is not to be confused with the Gnostic legend of Baruch we met in Chapter 2. These writings are concerned with the survival of religion after the destruction of the Temple in Jerusalem, and how the continual suffering of good people can be accounted for. Hence the significance of heavens as places of punishment and reward, and the existence of a heavenly temple tended by angels. Many legends accrue to Baruch, including a late Arabic legend that identifies him with the Chaldaean founder-prophet, Zoroaster. For the Eastern Church, perhaps because of this connection with the Magi, Baruch is a saint.

1 Baruch is accepted into the Apocrypha of the Bible by the Greeks, the Catholics and the Church of England. In its wisdom poetry we learn that the giants (children of the fallen angels) perished through their own foolishness (3:26-28). Its final chapter (sometimes considered separately as an Epistle of Jeremiah) warns the people to remain loyal and not follow the gods of Babylon, 'For mine angel is with you, and I myself caring for your souls' (6:7). God's 'angel', then, may perhaps be interpreted as the way we experience God's presence, while it is God himself who cares for our souls.

Eastern churches[17] accept three more texts of Baruch into their Apocrypha, and in these angels play a greater part. In what has come to be known as 2 Baruch, or *The Apocalypse of Baruch*, a 'strong spirit' comes and lifts Baruch aloft over the walls of the city of Jerusalem, during the invasion by the Chaldaeans (Babylonians). He sees that the city is protected by four angels standing at the corners, each with a torch in his hands, but these torches are not to be lit until the order comes, from another angel. That angel takes the holy things from within the temple, and buries them in the earth, in order that they should survive the destruction of the city. The signal is then given to the four angels to destroy the city walls. These angels convey the sense that destruction and preservation are beyond human agency, and that the human drama takes place on a much larger stage than we commonly envisage. In chapter 10, Jeremiah departs with the people into captivity, but Baruch sits down in front of the ruins of Jerusalem and laments. He calls on members of the spirit world to lament with him, not angels, this time, but *shedim*, dragons from the forest, and Lilith, the she-demon. The *shedim* are ghosts or demons, normally shunned, though they persist in folklore and superstition.[18] Baruch fasts and prays and is granted a vision of things to come. He realizes that 'the nature of man is always changeable. For what we formerly were we now no longer are, and what we now are we shall not afterwards remain' (22:15-16). Judgement will eventually come, though it passes our present understanding.

Twelve stages of destruction are forecast for the earth, from earthquakes to demon-attack, fire and oppression. But afterwards there will be resurrection and consolation. Using language reminiscent of St Paul he says,

> Whatever is now is nothing. But that which shall be is very great. For everything that is corruptible shall pass away, and everything that dies shall depart, and all the present time shall be forgotten. Nor shall there be any remembrance of the present time, which is defiled with evils … And the hour comes which abides for ever. And the new world [comes], which does not turn to corruption those who depart to its blessedness.
>
> (2 Baruch 44:8-12)[19]

In the last days, those who have lived by the law will be saved: it is their deeds that will save them. They will become like angels:

> They shall behold the world which is now invisible to them, and they shall behold the time which is now hidden from them: and

time shall no longer age them. For in the heights of that world
shall they dwell, And they shall be made like unto the angels,
And be made equal to the stars.

(2 Baruch 51:8-10)

This is the heart of the apocalypse of Baruch.

Although extracts of this book were known in the West, the full text
was preserved only by the Syriac branch of Christianity.[20] The third
Baruch text is quite another matter. Attributed to the same Baruch,
disciple of Jeremiah, it was written even later, in the second or third
century CE. Its transmission was in Greek, though Jewish in origin, with
some later Christian modifications (which can be clearly seen because
they are absent from an early Slavonic translation). 3 Baruch is also an
apocalypse, taking the form of a journey through the heavenly realms.
Baruch is weeping by the banks of the river, surveying the ruins of
Jerusalem, when an 'angel of the powers', Phamael, comes to bear him
aloft and introduce him to the mysteries of God.

This time the heavens are just five in number. They enter the first
heaven through a vast door and fly for 30 days' journey to a plain where
strange men are living – having the face of an ox, a stag's horns, the
hindquarters of a lamb and goats' feet. They had been the builders of
the Tower of Babel. In the second heaven, the journey is doubled in
length; the people there are like dogs, with feet of stags. They were the
ones who planned the tower and organized the labour teams to make
the bricks, not allowing anyone to rest from their labour, even to give
birth. In the third heaven the journey is more than trebled in length,
and on the plain a dragon eats the bodies of the wicked. Hades is here,
and a sea fed by numerous rivers, and the tree which led Adam astray.
This was no apple, but a grapevine, planted originally by the angel
Samael (the devil), against God's wishes. After the flood, when Noah
began to replant the earth, he wondered what to do about the vine,
knowing its unhappy history. He prayed many days for enlightenment,
and through the angel Sarasael he was instructed to include it. The
curse was turned to a blessing as it was to become the 'blood of God'
(this passage is clearly a Christian addition) but those who abuse it risk
eternal fire.

Baruch is then introduced to the phoenix which flies alongside the
sun, preserving humankind from the full force of its rays. The phoenix

lives on manna and dew, and excretes cinnamon. Teams of angels open 365 gates in the east, they separate light from darkness, and a heavenly bird crows to waken all the cocks on earth when the sun is about to go forth. As the sun emerges, even though the phoenix is stretching out its wings, Baruch hides in the wings of the angel. Going to the west, they see the sun return at the end of the day, the phoenix now exhausted, and the sun's crown tarnished by all it has seen on earth. Four angels carry the crown away for renewal, while the female figure of the moon goes out on a wheeled chariot, again with angels, some in the form of oxen and lambs. All this takes place in the third heaven.

In the fourth, they find huge birds round a pool where the souls of the righteous come. The water of the pool feeds the clouds, falls as rain and causes fruits to grow – over and above the earthly cycle of waters. The birds are there to sing praises. Finally his angel-guide leads him to the fifth heaven but they cannot enter until Michael comes to open the gate. Michael turns out to be the commander of Baruch's archangel-guide Phamuel, and they greet each other. The formalities of their greeting includes a silence.

They also witness the daily flow of angels bearing baskets full of flowers, which are the merits of mankind. These are poured into a large vessel held by Michael. Some come with full baskets, others partly full, but some come weeping and empty-handed, begging to be relieved of their charges, for the men they attend are all evil. Michael goes to present the offerings to God and to seek an answer for the weeping angels. He returns with offerings of oil and words of blessing for the first two groups to take back to those who had done good works. To the third group he brings the answer that they should return and provoke those who do evil, causing them to be envious and angry, and bringing pests to their crops, anger and bloodshed and demons to their children.

Some have suggested that this book is no longer complete since Baruch visits just five heavens whereas seven or ten are more usual. Yet the last chapter of what we have gives no indication of incompleteness. At the end of his journey through the five heavens Baruch is returned by the angel to the place he started from. He 'comes to himself', conscious of having received a great revelation.

4 Baruch, accepted only by the Ethiopian church, consists of passages omitted from the canonical version of Jeremiah. In it, Baruch

and Jeremiah stand on the city walls, torches in hand, waiting for angelic instruction, but little is added to our knowledge of angels.

Although works such as the ones we have cited so far were excluded from the canon of biblical literature, they retained an important place and provided rich material for imaginative speculation to later writers. One composition rooted in such texts is the *Zohar*. Here angels are mainly invisible spirits, but some become visible. Building on a tradition that Moses ascended from Mount Sinai to heaven to receive the Torah (found in the ninth-century *Pesikta Rabbati*), in the *Zohar* we see glimpses of that journey. Hadraniel, keeper of the second gate and a terrifying figure, had at first opposed Moses's presence in heaven, but was obliged to apologize to him and serve as guide:

> Moses accompanied Hadraniel until he reached the fierce fire
> of Sandalphon. It has been taught: Sandalphon transcends his
> fellows by a distance of five hundred years, and he stands behind
> the curtain of his Master, weaving His crown out of Israel's
> supplications of prayer. When that crown reaches the head of the
> Holy King, he accepts the prayer of Israel, and all the powers
> and legions tremble and shout: 'Blessed is the glory of God from
> the dwelling of His presence!'
>
> (*Zohar*, 2:58a)[21]

Moses duly receives the law and returns.

A similar journey is found in Islam: this is Muhammad's journey. On a single night, the prophet is visited by Gabriel and taken from Mecca to the 'furthest mosque' (the El-Aqsa Mosque in Jerusalem). There his angelic steed (*buraq*) is tethered, and he ascends into heaven. The first part of the journey is called *al-isra*, the second part *mi'râj*, which means ladder.[22] Muhammad and Gabriel enter the first heaven and proceed through all seven heavens, until they reach the throne of God. On the way they encounter various prophets: Adam, Abraham, Joseph, Aaron, Moses, John the Baptist and Jesus. Muhammad then appears before Allah (without Gabriel) and is instructed to recite the ritual prayers 50 times a day. Advised by Moses, Muhammad stands up for the practical needs of his people and pleads for a reduction in this obligation, which is granted. (Prayers are recited five times daily.) On his way back, Muhammad sees more of Paradise and is granted knowledge through signs, before returning to his bed in Mecca by morning.

This journey is only alluded to in the Qur'an,[23] but it enjoys a favoured place in the Hadith and later writings, and scholars still argue as to whether it was a physical or spiritual ascent, or a dream. But the footprint he left behind on the rock as he ascended is still proudly shown to visitors at the El-Aqsa Mosque. The ideal of spiritual ascent is enshrined in Sufi practices and poetry, such as that of Jalāl ad-Dīn Muhammad of Balkh, founder of the Mevlevi sect in Konya, better known to the West as Rumi (1207–73).[24]

Besides these biblical, apocryphal, Qur'anic and mystical texts, we should acknowledge other traditions whose descriptions of journeys through the world to come have sometimes influenced those we have considered. Cultures mingled and intersected in Alexandria, Jerusalem, Rome and elsewhere. Some of the oldest surviving accounts of the world to come are found in the journeys of the soul through the *Am Duat* described in the various forms of the Egyptian *Book of the Dead* (more accurately called the *Book of Going Forth by Day*).[25] In its progress through the invisible world, the soul encounters endless transformations, uttering incantations at every portal, fending off serpents and summoning ferryboats. A prayer for 'removing foolish speech from the mouth' is a useful thing to have in one's repertoire, though it is addressed to the one who 'cuts off heads and severs necks', which is less appealing (*Papyrus of Ani*, 9). This is not to dismiss Egyptian literature wholesale: its beauty and insights have much to offer,[26] but some items seem remote and strange.

In ancient Greece the task of guiding souls through the underworld was ascribed to the winged messenger god Hermes. He does not have the stately pinions of Gabriel or Michael, but neat little wings attached to his sandals and his helmet give him speed and ubiquity. His Roman equivalent was Mercury. Accounts of journeys through the underworld made by the living are few but important, exerting a deep and pervasive influence throughout the civilization of the West. The two best-known of these are the visit to the underworld described by Homer in *The Odyssey*, XI, and, modelled on it but different, a journey through the underworld in Virgil's *Aeneid*, VI. There are no angel guides, but the journeys described set important literary precedents, into which the later addition of angels by Christian writers was but a small step.

Odysseus sails to the western edge of the world, where the earth is bounded by the stream called Oceanus. In this dark and mist-filled region he makes libations and sacrifices to the dead.[27] The souls of the departed come thronging round, and he interrogates them one by one. He sees King Minos giving judgement in his infernal court, and observes the legendary punishments imposed, on Tityos (for violent rape), Tantalus (for greed, betrayal and infanticide), and Sisyphus (for arrogance and violation of the laws of hospitality). The punishments are as vile as the crimes committed, and are eternal in duration.

Reacting against this tradition, the poet Lucretius (*c.*99–55 BCE) tried to demystify such accounts. The gods are within ourselves, 'and whatsoever things are fabled to exist in deep Acheron, these all exist for us in this life'. Thus Tityos represents the torments of love, Tantalus the effects of fear, Sisyphus is an image of the life of ambition, and so on.[28]

But it was the allegory that was to prevail. Virgil (70–19 BCE), best loved of Roman poets, took up Homer's model and breathed new life into it. His hero, Aeneas, has to learn things that can only be revealed by a journey beyond death. As in the *Odyssey*, sacrifices are made, this time to the deities of the underworld, then he is led into the underworld by a priestess. A cave opens up into which they must plunge, and they stride resolutely through the 'empty halls of Dis and his phantom realms'. The hero's sword is drawn – though the threatening shapes they meet turn out to be no more substantial than shadows. In the outer vestibules of the underworld are Grief, Disease, Famine and Fear; they see the Tree of False Dreams and many monsters.[29] At the river Acheron, the pitiful souls of the unburied dead come streaming down to plead with the ferryman to take them across to their final rest. The very names of the underworld rivers indicate that allegorical interpretations were intended. Acheron is the river of sorrow, Cocytus of lamentation, Phlegethon the river of fire, Lethe of forgetfulness and Styx of hate.

Once across the river, Aeneas and his priestess-guide meet every kind of soul – those who died in infancy, those who died of love, warriors who died a death of distinction, and a kinsman mutilated in war. Then the way divides: one path leads to Tartarus, with its river of flame, to the judgement halls of Rhadamanthus, the harsh penalties meted out by the avenging Fury, and the gaping chasm where the giants lie bound in eternal punishment (reminiscent of the abyss of Enoch).[30] On the other side, the road leads to the Elysian fields, abode of the blessed, where the just enjoy bright meadows, cool groves and cushioned riverbanks.

Though no angels appear in Virgil's account, it exerted through the centuries a powerful influence on Christian interpretations of heaven and hell, and indeed Virgil himself became the guide through hell and purgatory for Dante Alighieri (1265–1321), in his *Divine Comedy*. In Dante's account angels abound: fallen angels in the *Inferno*, singing angels in *Purgatorio*, and angels of every rank and hue in *Paradiso*. When Dante emerges from Mount Purgatory into the upper realms of *Paradiso* the role of guide passes from his ancient mentor Virgil to his deceased beloved, Beatrice. The angels they meet are not the guides for the journey, but indicators of God's glory, filling the whole universe:

> A sparkling of scintillas in the spheres,
> As showers of sparks from molten metal fly.
> Tracing each fiery circle that was theirs,
> They numbered myriads more than the entire
> Progressive doubling of the chess-board square.
> I heard them sing Hosanna, choir on choir
> Unto the Point which holds them in the place
> And ever will, there where they ever were.
> (Dante, *Divine Comedy, Paradiso*, XXVIII, 89-96)[31]

In one early medieval Hebrew compilation, angels participate in deciding individuals' places in the life to come, swooping down to hear what others are saying about them at the time of burial (*Kohelet Rabbah*, 12:13). Angels also visit people in dreams, with intimations about the afterlife. One dream visit that brims with angelic light is by the poet, James Leigh Hunt (1784–1859):

> Abou Ben Adhem (may his tribe increase!)
> Awoke one night from a deep dream of peace,
> And saw, within the moonlight in his room,
> Making it rich, and like a lily in bloom,
> An angel writing in a book of gold –
> Exceeding peace had made Ben Adhem bold,
> And to the Presence in the room he said
> 'What writest thou?' – The vision raised its head,

And with a look made of all sweet accord,
Answered 'The names of those who love the Lord.'
And is mine one?' said Abou. 'Nay, not so,'
Replied the angel. Abou spoke more low,
But cheerly still, and said 'I pray thee, then,
Write me as one that loves his fellow men.'
The angel wrote, and vanished. The next night
It came again with a great wakening light,
And showed the names whom love of God had blessed,
And lo! Ben Adhem's name led all the rest.[32]

Dreams can also bring advice to change one's life in this world. Ann West recounts how the Archangel Michael watched with her as the all the sad moments of her life were replayed in a 'book of Akashic Records' (a theosophical term). Seeing again her thoughts and experiences in his presence in these dreams guided her early steps from a life of superficial glamour towards one of spiritual healing.[33]

This leads towards the subject of the next chapter, on guardian angels, but we cannot leave the imagery of journeys in the world to come, with their angelic guides and moments of insight without asking what it all means? Psychologists, historians and literary critics have all made their own interpretations, but each and every one of us should ask again. Where is the 'other world' in which such journeys may be taken? Does it intersect with the world of our everyday lives, and if so, how? Many people nowadays scoff at belief in a world to come, preferring the materialist view that life ends with the death of the body. This position is not new: it has a long-established history from Pyrrho and Epicurus in the fourth century BCE, and Axiochus in the first century CE.[34] Its revival as philosophic Scepticism in the seventeenth century led to conflicts between science and religion which are still with us, as in the writings of Richard Dawkins (*The Selfish Gene*, 1976; *The Blind Watchmaker*, 1986; *The God Delusion*, 2006) and equally impassioned responses, such as that of John Cornwell (*Darwin's Angel*, 2007). Yet even while many proclaim that there can be no God, no afterlife, and no heaven or hell – at least in the traditional sense that these things have been taught and understood – interest in the human psyche, the unconscious, dreams and higher consciousness continues apace. It is no wonder, then, that angels have not lost their power to fascinate, and continue to serve at least symbolically as our guides.

Chapter 10

ANGEL GUIDES IN THIS WORLD

I<small>F</small> the experience of angelic guides through the heavenly realm is reserved for the few, guardian angels have from the very beginning been for everyone. The idea that there are angelic beings appointed to guide and guard the way we progress through life is common to so many traditions that it is hard to escape the conclusion that we are dealing with an archetypal mode of human experience.

Guardian angels (see Figure 19) are often held to have a special connection with children, but they watch over adults too. They are to be found in Greek and Egyptian thought, as personal *daimons* or *genii*, in Judaism, Christianity and Islam as angels, and in shamanistic rites of timeless origin as guardian spirits. The shaman in his trance takes on the identity of his own guardian spirit, and knows which spirit guards each of his tribe. These spirits may be identified with animals, like the eagle, the fox or the bear, and they can be called upon to impart their own attributes of clear sight, swift-footedness, cunning or courage, in times of need.

Perhaps in Western cultures the most familiar aspect of the guardian angel is the function of guarding us from unseen dangers. This kind of a protective presence was an immensely popular subject for prints: a benign angel stands with wings extended, watching serenely over a boy and a girl who are playing perilously close to a cliff-edge, or crossing a narrow, broken bridge. For many people this is the image of angel that most readily springs to mind.

A key biblical text for this is in Psalm 91:

There shall no evil befall thee, neither shall any plague come
    nigh thy dwelling.

> For he shall give his angels charge over thee, to keep thee in all
> thy ways.
> They shall bear thee up in their hands, lest thou dash thy foot
> against a stone.
>
> (Psalm 91:10-12, echoed in Matthew 4:6)

The protection afforded by angels is exemplified, as we have seen, by Raphael's care of Tobias.[1] Although this story lost some of its authority at the Reformation, personal guardian angels were so entrenched in tradition that they persisted even in Protestant art and were certainly present in the thoughts of Anglican divines. Henry Latham, for example, doubted only whether one single guardian angel sees us through from birth to death, or whether he shares the task with others.

People have also sought specific guidance from angels on matters of practical import. John Dee, one of Queen Elizabeth I's scientific advisers, came to place great faith in angels, and sought to commune with them through a crystal ball. Some of his equipment can still be seen in the British Museum and the Wellcome Collection owns a crystal that he claimed was given to him by the angel Uriel and had powers to foretell the future and cure disease.[2] In May 1581 Dee declared 'I had sight in Chrystalla and I saw', but before long he realized that he lacked real skill and engaged an assistant, to serve as his 'scryer', gazing into the crystal and describing the angel images that Dee could not see. Dee then applied his knowledge of signs and symbols to interpret what had been seen, recording the results as 'conversations with angels'.

The first young man employed was Barnabas Saul, but they soon fell out, and Saul was proved a fraudster. From 1582, Dee employed an apothecary, Edward Kelly, who came to him under a false name, having already been punished as a forger. Nevertheless, initial results were promising. Dee records séances in which they received angelic language and directions for action. Kelly identified a spirit guide, Madini, after whom Dee named one of his daughters.

Kelly and Dee travelled together in 1583 to Poland and then to the court of the Emperor Rudolf II in Prague, in search of recognition for their discoveries. Besides crystal-gazing, they engaged in alchemy, and the emperor had high hopes of a new source of gold. These travels form a fascinating episode, though one increasingly tainted with quarrels, tensions, suspicions and even erotic charge in respect of each others' wives.[3] Yet Dee did not fall out of enchantment with Kelly until 1591, when Kelly was imprisoned for killing a court official in a duel just at the moment when the Queen was summoning them home. In all their activities, Dee was never conscious of any offence against religion since, they sought angels not demons, knowledge not power and they began every session with a prayer.

The borderline between piety and heresy in matters concerning angels was quite difficult to define. In the year 1499, a German abbot, Johannes Trithemius of Sponheim, devised a system which claimed to allow transmission of messages across large distances by angels. Although there were some disagreements with his brother monks, resulting in his resignation from Sponheim in 1506, he did not suffer any adverse consequences and was appointed to another abbey. A hundred years later, however, his work was placed on the Index of Prohibited Books, (removed again only in 1900). Rather than accepting it as some form of thought transference via angels, modern scholarship has patiently unravelled Trithemius's secrets which turn out to be a form of encryption. Because hidden, it would seem to anyone untrained in the system that the messages must indeed have been conveyed by angels, and this was no doubt part of the abbot's scheme – to put people off even looking for a code that they might then try to crack. The name he gave his work, *Steganographia*, provided a new word for the concealment of encrypted messages and steganography is still extensively used today as a tool of espionage.[4]

The examples of Dee and Trithemius serve as reminders of how often attempts at communications with angels in the early modern world were mired in deception, be it self-deception, as in Dee's case, or the deception of others for good or ill, as with Trithemius and Kelly – without even beginning to count cases of delusional angel voices heard by people under the influence of hallucination or psychosis.

Yet the idea of guardian angels has a respectable history. An early Talmudic legend tells of angels watching over babies even before birth. While the babe is still in the womb, a light is shone over its head and it looks and sees from one end of the world to the other, and receives all knowledge. But at the moment of birth, an angel comes to strike it on the lips, causing it to forget all that it has been taught (Babylonian Talmud, *Niddah* 30b). This idea may be compared to Plato's belief that all learning is a form of remembering what was known before the soul came into the body (*Meno* 81). According to Socrates, in that dialogue, disciplined effort is still required, but true knowledge is innate.

Another Talmudic source relates that each individual is always accompanied by two angels, one good, one bad, who watch over one's actions and contend with each other for influence over what will unfold next.

> Rabbi Yosi son of Rabbi Yehudah said: Two ministering angels accompany a person home on Friday night from the synagogue. One is an angel of good and one is an angel of evil. When the person arrives home to find the Sabbath candles lit, the table set and the beds made, the angel of good says, 'May it be the divine will that the next Sabbath should be the same.' And against his will, the angel of evil answers, 'Amen.'
>
> If not [if the candles are not lit and the table is not set], then the angel of evil says, 'May it be the divine will that the next Sabbath should be the same.' And against his will, the angel of good answers, 'Amen.'
>
> (Babylonian Talmud, *Shabbat* 119b)

A late Kabbalistic invocation of these two guardian angels became a Sabbath song which is still in widespread use, though the third verse, asking a blessing of these angels, raises some doctrinal issues. To some, the third stanza sounds perilously close to angel worship. But others recall Jacob, who would not let his angel go until he blessed him.

> Peace unto you, ministering angels, angels of the Most High,
> of the King above the kings of kings, the Holy One, blessed be he.
>
> Enter for peace, angels of peace, angels of the Most High,
> of the King above the kings of kings, the Holy One, blessed be he.
>
> Bless me for peace, angels of peace, angels of the Most High,
> of the King above the kings of kings, the Holy One, blessed be he.
>
> Go forth for peace, angels of peace, angels of the Most High,
> of the King above the kings of kings, the Holy One, blessed be he.
>
> (Traditional, late sixteenth or seventeenth century, Safed)

The two angels appear also in the Talmudic tract *Hagigah* (16a), where the predominant notion is that whatever a person does, even in secret, is recorded for judgement. If such angels could influence action, by a word whispered or a thought conveyed, they would be truly guardians or tempters respectively. But it implies here that they are simply recording angels – and no doubt some people prefer to interpret them as an externalized form of conscience. These two angels reappear in both Christianity and Islam. In the Qur'an they seem only to record the deeds, not to influence people (sura 82). In the *Life of Moses* by Gregory of Nyssa, a fourth-century Church Father in Cappadocia, man was perpetually between two angels, one offering him the fruits of virtue, the other offering earthly pleasures to enjoy now.[5]

What of Jacob's angel, with whom he struggled at the river Jabbok (Genesis 32)? Was he perhaps a guardian angel? In the commentary on this story provided in *Jubilees*, Isaac tells Rebecca that their two sons have guardian angels, and the angel of one is stronger than the other's. She therefore need not fear for Jacob's future (*Jubilees* 35:17). The original story of Jacob's encounter, told in Genesis, is worth examining in some detail.

Jacob was returning home, having parted angrily from his father-in-law, Laban. But leaving behind the quarrels of his midlife, he has to face again the quarrels of his youth. He learns from messengers that Esau is on his way to meet him, accompanied by 400 men. Jacob is alarmed at the news because when they last met his brother had vowed to kill him when their father died. He divides up his camp, prays to God, and sends propitiatory gifts to his brother. Then he guides his family across the river, returning by himself to be alone. The great medieval commentator Rashi tells us, in what at first sight seems a strange addition, that Jacob 'had forgotten some small jars and went back for them' and that is when the mysterious encounter occurred.[6] In the dark of the night he struggles for hours with an angel. Rabbinic tradition interprets this as a guardian angel, but as the guardian angel of Esau, with whom so much early strife had remained unresolved (*Genesis Rabbah* 77:3).[7] Rabbi Jonathan Wittenberg agrees that this fits the narrative, but offers another explanation:

Jacob is heading swiftly back to the unresolved conflict with his brother. 'Let the days of mourning for my father come and I'll

kill my brother Jacob,' were Esau's last words on the subject.
Why should his attitude have changed over the years? The fact
that the rabbis appoint him a powerful guardian angel indicates
that they, too, perceive that Esau has his rights. Jacob may have
fled his country, but he can't escape the consequences of his
conduct and now, on his return, the hour of repayment is at
hand … But I want to return to Jacob, left alone among the
almost abandoned pots and pans. Many strains of thought assail
the person who stands on the border, staring at the remnants
of the past, gazing uncomfortably into the darkness of the
future. What figures must emerge from his troubled thoughts to
confront him?

Maybe the man with whom Jacob wrestles all night is his
younger self. Who was he when he passed this place in such
a hurry twenty years ago? From what had he run away then,
which, dormant in his consciousness, returns to burn inside
him now? There were, of course, stinging moments, such as
when Laban had retorted, in justification of his own deceit in
passing off Leah as Rachel, 'It's not done in our place, giving
the younger before the older.' But now the details of his past
conduct, how he planned it, what he said, return with a louring
familiarity, just as the images of home, the pastures, the trees,
the clumps of shrub, flood back into the mind of the absentee a
moment before he turns the old corner and sees his childhood
tents.

Or Jacob struggles with the man he's since become. Those
pots and pans bear all the insignia of the last twenty years.
He'd arrived in Paddan-Aram a pauper, proposed to Rachel
with nothing to his name, then came the years of intense love,
afterwards the disappointment, the quarrels between the sisters,
the seasons of icy frost and burning sun, the disputes with
Laban, the final flight that had brought him to this lonely place:
Who was he now, in middle age, who had passed this way with a
young man's stride and his dreams of a ladder between heaven
and earth? Was this the fulfilment of all his hopes?

All night Jacob wrestles with the truth of who he has been
and the reality of who he now is.[8]

Jacob had encountered angels before. He had dreamed of them ascending and descending the ladder at Bethel (Genesis 28:11-19); he had heard in a dream the angel who righted his wrongs under Laban (Genesis 31:11) and he had met angels on first arriving at the river Jabbok (Genesis 32:1-2). On his deathbed he would also acknowledge that an angel had redeemed him (Genesis 48:16). But here his encounter is more active. Jacob fights the angel, through the night until dawn and is wounded, but will not let him go until he receives a blessing. He also asks the angel's name, but this is not given. The angel meanwhile changes Jacob's name from Jacob, 'the supplanter', to Israel, 'he who strives with God'. Jacob afterwards renames the place of the encounter Peniel, and says 'For I have seen the Divine face to face, yet my life was spared' (*Peniel* means the face of God). Related to this are the words spoken by God to Moses in Exodus 33:20, 'Thou canst not see my face: for man shall not see me, and live.' In the context of Jacob's encounter, this reminder of the face of the Almighty indicates, firstly, that we do not need the light of day to 'see', but more importantly that this story is to be perceived as an encounter with reality on a level beyond our everyday awareness. Jacob is telling us that he 'saw' God, yet Judaeo-Christian traditions of interpretation insist in spite of this, that he fought not with God but with an angel. The intention may be to maintain some distance between mankind and God – but it is clearly a distance that finds little support in the original wording.

Wittenberg then adds one more step of interpretation that opens up new possibilities:

> But what earns him [Jacob] the name of Israel, the title of one
> who struggles with God, is that he refuses to let that truth go
> and insists on turning it into blessings.
>
> (*Ibid.*)

This suggests that a dynamic encounter is possible between ourselves and our guardian angels, whatever we conceive them to be.

A wealth of commentary sprang up on why the angel refused to give his own name while significantly changing Jacob's. Rashi interprets the angel as saying, 'We have no fixed name. Our names change according to the command of the task of the mission on which we are sent.' Nachmanides (in thirteenth-century, Spain) says, 'The knowledge of my name will not help you, for power resides in God,' and Obadiah Sforno (Italy, *c*.1475–1550) said, 'In asking his name, Jacob wanted to know his essence and character. The angel answered that the spiritual essence could not be defined in human terminology.'[9]

Moving from Jewish commentary on Jacob's angel to Christian commentary on guardian angels in general, it is not surprising if confusion has held sway in theology despite popular acceptance of these beings, since Dionysius says very little on the subject. The guardian angels of individuals are held to be among angels of the lowest hierarchy, and of the lowest order in that hierarchy. His discussions are more concerned with the two orders above them, the principalities and archangels, who are guardians of whole nations, than with the simple angels.[10]

The early Church Fathers before Dionysius were not consistent on the question of whether a guardian angel attends each and every person. Some, such as St Basil (329–79) and St John Chrysostom (*c*.347–407) thought their intervention was limited to the baptized.[11] St Jerome (*c*.340–420), in opposition to this, asserts that guardian angels are for all, and he finds in that thought a celebration of the dignity of the human soul. St Bonaventure (1221–74) speculated on the personhood of guardian angels, feeling sure they must have affections and social feelings for one another. St Bernard of Clairvaux (1090–1153) felt they were individual but perfectly aligned to one another in harmony and unanimity. They were for him a model of what human behaviour might become. Bonaventure agrees, and points to the lack of jealousy between the higher and the lower, which humans would do well to follow. He also asks whether a guardian angel might experience sorrow and loss if their ward failed to find a place in heaven. Conversely, if humans failed to find joy in spiritual life or deeds of charity (apparently a common risk in monastic life), then our guardian angels were there to re-inspire us. From the eleventh century onwards there have been special prayers to guardian angels in the liturgy of the church.

Debate continued, however, over their intervention in human affairs. Theologians worried that having an angel constantly telling us what to do might in some way interfere with our free will, or diminish the merit earned through good deeds if we were simply following instructions. To resolve this dilemma, St Thomas Aquinas (1225–74) came to the conclusion that guardian angels act upon our senses and upon our imagination, but not directly upon our will.[12] The focus of their operation was to support the rational mind, especially at times of wavering and temptation. The angel, he thought, was with us from birth, to watch over the welfare of our soul.

Some Christian writers also thought we had an evil demon in attendance from birth too, matching the Jewish belief in two guardian angels, one good one bad. For many medieval Christian writers, as for example Caesarius of Heisterbach (a thirteenth-century Cistercian), the demon was of particular importance. The countless delights with which the demon could tempt the individual led him to think the angel relatively powerless against it. A person should therefore place their faith not just in his guardian angel, but in Christ and especially Mary. Above all, as many writers agreed, the angels' power is limited by humans' willingness to cooperate.

Among the questions medieval doctors never fully resolved were exactly how guardian angels operated, whether the ceremony of baptism marked a special stage in a person's relationship with them, whether one's angel could be lost or offended or whether they remained ever faithful. But perhaps the most striking feature is the enduring presence and steady rise in status of these angels who walk with us on earth.

In 1608, Pope Paul V proclaimed a special feast and office dedicated to the Holy Guardian Angels, still celebrated annually on 2 October in the Roman Catholic Church. This gave formal recognition to what was already a custom. In Bernini's Jesuit Church of S. Andrea al Quirinale in Rome, a carved angel by one of the altars was specifically described as being 'placed here to teach you that invisible angels are present and ready to combat those who bring temptations to valiant men'. It was to be, in other words, a reminder that angels serve as personal guardians. An early Jesuit teacher wrote 'Remember that you are to be guided by your angel like a blind man, who cannot see the dangers of the streets and trusts entirely to the person who leads him.' The qualities of angels were also to be imitated, so that one might come to resemble them.[13]

A Jesuit tract of 1612, reminds readers that each person's guardian angel is his or her 'most faithful friend' and 'loyal defender, who takes greater care of our affairs than we do ourselves, and when we put our salvation at risk through sin, he will work to illuminate us internally and will ask God to pardon us'. Angels can read our deeds, though they cannot know our thoughts, for these are known only to God – unless God chooses to inform the angels what we are thinking. The guardian angel is allotted to us at our birth. Before birth, in the womb, we are in the care of our mother's angel. After death, our angel accompanies us through purgatory. The many good offices they perform for us in life range from marriage guidance and cure of disease to mental illumination and moral chastisement.[14]

More recently, Pope John Paul II upheld the cult of guardian angels in his 1997 address, *Regina Caeli*, following several of his predecessors in this. Pope Pius XI (1857–1939) prayed daily to his guardian angel, and recommended that other community leaders do the same. The guardian angel, he said, will smooth out difficulties and defeat opposition. Pope John XXIII (1881–1963) described how he called upon the help of his own guardian angel:

> Whenever we have to speak with someone who is rather closed to our argument and with whom therefore the conversations needs to be very persuasive, we go to our guardian angel. We recommend the matter to him. We ask him to take it up with the guardian angel of the person we have to see. And once the two angels establish an understanding, the Pope's conversation with his visitor is much easier.[15]

In 1968, Pius XII urged his visitors to become more aware of the invisible world. When he looked out into St Peter's Square he claimed to see not just all the people gathered there, but their guardian angels too. He also encouraged parents to teach their children that they are never alone, for they have an angel at their side, and they should show them how to have a trusting conversation with this angel. Nor will the angel abandon the child when he or she becomes adult, for the angel is seen as having care of spiritual progress as well as protecting from harm. The guardian angels' love is unconditional, and their presence is constant. This is especially important for those who feel lonely or abandoned.[16]

At the Reformation, when Protestant groups swept away the cult of the saints, many sought to banish angels with them. Luther allowed some space for them, as agents of divine providence, but Calvin felt they were at best an accommodation to human weakness of understanding. Nevertheless, from the pastoral point of view, much use was made of angels by the various reformed churches of Europe and America, though people no longer expected actually to hear or see them in action and some preachers were as scathing about angelic visions as their medieval counterparts: other peoples' angelic encounters were often put down to demons in disguise.

In Massachusetts in 1676, controversy reigned over whether there was or was not an Angel of Hadley. A white-bearded figure with an ancient sword was seen protecting the people of this small settlement during a Native American raid. Some claimed it was an angel. Royalist agents suspected it was one of the regicide generals still in hiding 27 years after Charles I's execution. In 1685, Cotton Mather, later famous for the Salem witch trials, had an angelic experience of his own.[17]

In the Anglican church, though somewhat less in fashion now, guardian angels are still respected for their dual function of preventing mishap and encouraging spiritual progress and they continue to be celebrated in hymns and prayer.

Through the centuries, guardian angels were generally not known to Christians by name, though from time to time attempts were made to give them names, which one commentator has associated with vestiges of pagan magical practice.[18] There certainly are such vestiges in the *Book of Raziel*, a compendium of secret knowledge and magic dating most likely from the eleventh century, but alleged to have been written for Adam and Eve on their expulsion from the garden. Raziel is considered variously to be a cherub, one of the 'valiant ones' (*erelim* or *ishim*) or one of the *ophanim*. According to another tradition, he stands behind the curtain in heaven, listening to all the decrees of God and, with his wings, protects all the ministering angels from being burnt up by the breath of the *chayyot*.[19]

In the fifteenth century, Greek ideas on angels and daemons were revived, as we saw in Chapter 2, and soon spread. But Greeks themselves were somewhat obscure on the *daimon* that guides the life. Guardian angels were generally envisaged as winged spirits. In *Cratylus*, Plato traces guardian spirits back to the poet Hesiod's account of a golden age in former times, when men were god-like in strength and purity. When this race died out, their spirits remained on earth as beneficent guardians, or *daimons*, protecting the lesser races of mankind that followed.[20] In *Phaedo*, where the emphasis is on the individual, a spirit guide accompanies the soul in life and death. On death, it accompanies the soul to the place of judgement.[21] These guardian spirits seem different from the angel guides in the world to come discussed in the previous chapter, perhaps because, as *daimons*, they are so closely associated with the soul's life on earth too.

In the tenth book of the *Republic*, Plato relates the *Myth of Er*, who died but was revived, and recalls what he saw between death and revival. Receiving one's due, be it punishment or reward, may take thousands of years, but afterwards, souls gather in a meadow to select a new life, and with it the *daimon* who will be their new guardian spirit. Drinking from the waters of forgetfulness at the river Lethe, to wash away memory of their previous life, they then return to earth.[22]

In the *Apology*, Plato includes as a guardian spirit that *daimon* of Socrates, who restrained him from wrong action. It never prompted in a more positive way. Any positive incitement is attributed to divine inspiration, not the *daimon*. Yet in the *Timaeus*, it is the highest part of our own soul that is called *daimon* and exists to guide us, and each soul is assigned to a star.[23] Plotinus tries to resolve all these inconsistencies in Plato and makes it clear, in his treatise 'On our Allotted Guardian Spirit' (*Enneads*, III.4), that each person's guardian spirit is drawn from the level directly above that on which he or she usually lives. So one can change one's guiding spirit by changing the way one lives, and a man living the highest possible kind of life will have for his guardian spirit a god.

In the European revival of these ideas led by Ficino, the *daimon* is a guardian angel, appointed to the individual to guide him or her through life, forming character, observing choices, guarding from hidden danger, and bringing him or her to situations that need to be faced. Not constrained by ideas of language that would make of every Greek *daimon* an 'evil demon', he uses the terms 'guiding spirit', 'guardian angel', '*genius*' and '*daemon*' (Latin spelling) as if they were interchangeable. Yet he carefully distinguishes between these spirits and the ancient gods, the souls of the spheres, or the influences of the stars.

In his summary of Plato's *Apology*, Ficino tells us that *daemons* and angels are exact equivalents, and that Socrates's *daemon* is definitely not just an aspect of his individual mind, but something external, which we would call an angel. The voice of divine inspiration, however, is part of Socrates's own being: according to the *Timaeus*, it is the highest part of his intellect or soul, confusingly also called his *daemon*! Ficino explains the Greek position on guardian angels in the context of gods and daemons in general, and allocates them to various orders each under a star. All daemons work by instilling desire, and are therefore responsible for a lot of evil in the world, but they exert a guiding influence too. They may be watery, airy or fiery, governing respectively the life of pleasure, the active life and the contemplative life. The daemon of Socrates, for example, is fiery and belongs to Saturn, it is therefore able to withdraw the focus of his mind away from the body, towards rational discourse and contemplation, and to restrain him. Ficino detects in the ancient traditions a lingering possibility that some of these guiding spirits may be the souls of departed human beings:

> The ancients say that some daemons are natural, established as such from the outset, while others are wanderers, being men's souls put into airy bodies and looking after men with the same reasoning power they had accustomed themselves to in life.[24]

A curious aspect of Ficino's discussion here is that he has taken the role of guardian angel as the key feature in introducing a dialogue read by most as a meditation on justice and death.

In a letter to Callimachus, an Italian poet in exile, Ficino attempts to clarify Plato's world of guardian daemons and spirits further:

> There are as many gods, or stars, in the heavens as there are legions of dæmons around the earth, and there are exactly the same number of dæmons in any legion as there are stars in the sky. There are also twelve princes of the dæmons, just as there are twelve signs in the Zodiac. Moreover, some of these dæmons are under the influence of Saturn, others of Jupiter, Mars, or the Sun ... There are as many orders of human souls as the stars and the legions of dæmons numbered together, and souls are allotted the nature, function, and name of their respective dæmons and stars. Now they call these dæmons spirits, the innate guides of our being, each assigned to an individual soul by the law of fate, that is, by the way all the spheres are arranged and the way they influence us, when our souls descend into the embodied state. In so far as our minds are not subject to some of the lower dæmons and the senses, they may be guided every day by these spirits through an easy and hidden persuasion, just as ships are steered with a rudder by the helmsman.
>
> (Ficino, *Letters*, vol. 7, letter 5)[25]

By 'lower daemons' he means those wayward spirits we call devils or demons, tempting mankind to evil deeds or self-indulgence. But everyone has at least one good daemon, and it is possible to have more. Callimachus had written questioning the idea that more than one spirit could inhabit one place. Ficino replies jovially that Callimachus, being possessed of so many great gifts, must have many good daemons and he awards him the nickname *Polydaemon*: an Apollian daemon makes him a good poet, a Mercurial one a good speaker, a Saturnian one nurtures his interest in philosophy, a Jovian daemon gives him dignity, one from Mars magnanimity, and one from Venus refinement. Here he is blending Proclan ideas on the planetary chains with the concept of guardian spirits. Elsewhere he develops this into agreement with Plotinus that we may receive a new and worthier guiding spirit as our lives change – in other words, that there are more powerful guardian angels waiting to take care of us as we rise in personal capacity or professional service. This is partly due to the fact that we are subject to a guiding spirit for the profession we follow as well as the guiding spirit of our own nature.[26]

But more often, Ficino speaks of one guardian spirit per person, or even a shared one between two individuals who are especially close. Several times he states that people of like minds, born under the same stars, may in fact share a single guiding spirit. In the third of his *Three Books on Life* (1489), he addresses ways of finding one's own guardian spirit and bringing one's life into proper accord with it – preparing the inner being (*ingenium*) to receive the outer guiding spirit (*genius*) by finding the natural harmony between them. At other times he is more guarded: in a book on *The Sun*, published a few years after the books *On Life* (which had created something of a stir), he pointedly avoids discussion of whether the daemon of Socrates was a *genius* or an angel.[27]

Ficino was able to combine a Christian appreciation of guardian angels with ideas on guiding spirits drawn from the Platonic philosophers. Going back before these sources, and before the beginnings even of the Hebrew scriptures, how far back can we trace the individual guardian spirit? In the case of the very earliest angel-like figures found by archaeologists in the Near East, we do not have sufficient evidence to know whether they served as individual guardians. Sumerian literature is silent on the subject. In the Akkadian Gilgamesh epic, although it celebrates the power of friendship, love and the quest for immortality, angels play no part since Gilgamesh himself was two-thirds divine. In Babylon and Assyria angels are known to have been protective, but we cannot be sure of their personal guardian roles. Even on the relatively well-documented beliefs of the Chaldaeans and followers of Zoroaster, scholars hold divergent views.

Although the Chaldaeans, Assyrians and Egyptians were the subject of Iamblichus's work *On the Mysteries,* he is a late witness to the relics of their practices and beliefs, as he was writing in the late third century CE. We saw in Chapters 2 and 3 that, in his view, human aspirations depend on the help of a daemon, god or angel. But since his main interest is the contemporary debate between philosophy and religion, reports of angels and daemons found in his work reflect a Hellenistic understanding rather than a truly Egyptian, Chaldaean or Assyrian view.

In the Persian realm, guardian spirits were well established. In Avestan literature, the *fravashis* are winged beings who inhabit the upper air and have power to aid and protect those who worship them.[28] There are great hosts of them and they are to be invoked especially at times of danger, for their great force and strength. According to the mythology, these angels originally patrolled the boundaries and ramparts of heaven, but volunteered to descend to earth to stand by individuals. In this sense, each person is accompanied by a guardian angel which acts as a guide throughout life. Originally, rather like the *Pitris* of the Hindus or the *Manes* of the Latins, they seem to have been identified with the everlasting souls of the heroic dead but in the course of time they came to be regarded as related to the individual soul, providing the inner power in every being that maintains it and makes it grow and live. Whether this would be an internal function of the soul, or an external guardian angel power is harder to tell. Scholars once again are divided, and have been so since early times. One explanation offered of the relationship of *urvan* (soul) to *fravashi* (guardian spirit) is that the *urvan* dwells in the body, while the *fravashi* dwells in the presence of the supreme deity, serving as a model for behaviour and a reminder of one's task in life. At death the two are united. However even this is disputed. Nevertheless it was an established custom for Zoroastrians to choose an angel as their personal protector, and to devote themselves in prayer to that angel throughout their lives. It cannot be coincidence that the most auspicious festival of the

New Year (*Nowruz*, coincident with the spring equinox) falls, in this tradition, in the month of *Frawardin*, the month associated especially with guardian angels.

In the later religion of Mithras, the sun god, popular across the Roman Empire in the first to fourth centuries CE, some say that Mithras himself was a sort of friend-protector. But even less can be securely asserted about the cult of Mithras than Sumerian or early Zoroastrian belief. Nevertheless, it is reasonable to assume that ancient Near Eastern ideas, at least from Babylon and Persia, became at least partially intertwined with Judaism, Christianity and Islam on the concept of guardian angels, as with angels in general.

Healing Powers of Guardian Angels

We have considered the power of guardian angels to protect and guide. A natural extension of this is the power to heal, and many 'angel therapies' are promoted through books, the internet, recordings and alternative therapy centres. Some of these call for deep introspection and self-inquiry. Others are more facile, and the angels in question may be readily substituted by fairies, tree-spirits, stars or colour-visualisations, according to fashion or predilection. Of the numerous offerings, a few will stand as representative for the rest, for they have many features in common.

Linda Georgian, of the Psychic Network, came to her angel healing through a Catholic upbringing, but drew many ideas from Jewish sources.[29] One of these is Bahya ibn Pakuda's *Book of Direction to the Duties of the Heart*, written in Arabic in the eleventh century in Saragossa. It had originally been intended to provide a compendium of traditional ethical laws, but took an unexpected direction, perhaps because of its Neoplatonic underpinnings. In it Georgian finds ways of enhancing awareness of the divine in everyday things. The idea is to refine the use of the senses until a deep meditative state of union with God is attained, known as *devekut*, a state of 'clinging to God'. While recognizing that the authentic path to such union is based on many demanding steps or practices, described by her as 'gates', like many such writers she is keen to present a more manageable, 'short-cut' method. Sadly, such short-cuts often compromise the effectiveness of the approach, but the fact that they continue to sell in large numbers is perhaps indicative of a genuine need.

The original ten gates in ibn Pakuda's version include challenging tasks. One must study the divine in nature, and through this find a proper approach to worship. Fullness of trust in the divine order must follow, accepting whatever life presents and learning from one's trials to work in partnership with God; doubt and lack of sincerity must be overcome; humility, repentance, self-discipline and self-examination must all be developed. But Georgian offers a simpler way of finding contact with one's guardian angels – note they are now plural – one for each purpose to be accomplished. Her advice is to sit down comfortably, away from distractions, to choose a soothing sound or silence, take a few deep breaths, seek God first (though 'not in a solemn way'), then to list all the things in your life with which you need help and assign an angel to each. It is, she says, important to thank them in advance for all they are going to do, and to gather together some angel mementos for an 'altar'. With the more challenging elements – of avoiding distraction or seeking God – little help is offered, but some advice is practical enough: we should not expect the angels to do all the work, we must participate too; they will not act on negative attitudes, greed or rage; they should not be worshipped; and there is no point wasting breath asking them to be with you because they already are.

Communication with the angels then is more a question of becoming attuned to one's own state of mind and one's real needs. Georgian herself sees angels – though they appear not in winged glory but as 'milky white fogs'. She also reports the sobering fact that most people who report seeing angels have been in some kind of dire need, either physically or emotionally. The disappointing aspect of her work is in the angelic guides a follower can expect to encounter. Indeed, the list of angels she has appointed for herself seem a little banal: a diet angel, an exercise angel, a headache angel, one for finance and business opportunity, one for fun and laughter, a TV angel (to find her opportunities for appearing on TV) and another special one for radio and print; a city angel, a home improvement angel, and so on. Allotting the names of Saraqael or Raziel to milky white fogs in the mind seems a poor trade for the traditional tale of Tobias, or the winged being on the bridge, and a poor remedy to summon up pseudo-angels for the lonely and suggestible. Far better to find another human being and say 'Would you be an angel and go with me to the gym/hold the ladder/cheer me up today' or whatever is the task in hand.

Another approach is outlined in an Australian book by Cherie Sutherland, *In the company of Angels*.[30] Again the idea is to welcome angels into your life. This book speaks of dreams and experiences of angels, as if anecdotal evidence might strengthen one's own search. Sutherland suggests that human good deeds are needed to vitalize the chief of the angels (Metatron), though this is at variance with most other views of his place in the cosmos. Beyond such urging, and the anecdotes, she offers little to show how we might make use of angelic guidance in our lives, but she does refer to the experience of four friends in Hungary who got regular angelic visitations during the horrifically troubled years of 1943–4.

The accounts of their dialogues are worth following. They are published in translation as *Talking with Angels* by Gitta Mallasz (1907–92), who was the only one to survive the Nazi period. She kept at least a partial record of these extraordinary conversations.[31] Long after the war, while living in France, she was eventually persuaded to speak them, partly encouraged by her reading of C. G. Jung's dialogues with Philemon, his own inner guide. These conversations have much wisdom to impart on human personality, motivation and capacity for bringing change in the world. They also speak directly and indirectly of the relationship of the individual self to the divine. Yet the angels speak through human agency, through Hanna, one of the four, who had already some commitment to spiritual training.

Another practical path is offered by Claire Nahmad, in *Your Guardian Angel*.[32] Here we find forms of address to angels, prayers and meditations. Angels may be sent to help others, not just oneself, and indeed the author asserts that they should be so sent, since angels cannot act unless humans invite them in. As with Sutherland, this is in contradiction to Bible stories where angels act only on divine bidding. Furthermore her spiritual exercises, all accompanied with complicated instructions and imagery, are entering another territory far from simple awareness of the divine. She has meditations on a rose mandala, on the lake of peace, on the Garden of Delights, and more. Grounding oneself with rope-like roots from the soles of one's feet to the centre of the earth may come more naturally to some people than others, but lighting an imaginary candle can surely only spread imaginary light, and meeting with Samandriel – a female angel who will offer you three gifts, of purity, abundance and entry into a bright moonlit mirror – is surely entering into the realms of fantasy and superstition. Rituals, prayers, and meditations may indeed help attune the soul to chakra energy, and the singing, dancing and art proposed may illuminate the dark places of your soul with angelic healing and light, as claimed, but the claim is weakened when one observes that the same author has written equivalent books on fairy spells, cat spells, herbalism and folklore, together with the *Secret Teachings of Mary Magdalene* (no doubt post-Dan Brown). Indeed, as she admits, her own first experience of angelic help was muddled up with the forces of a nearby pine tree in the garden. Another prolific author, Doreen Virtue, deliberately blurs the boundary between experience and imagining. For her, angels can be bidden to attend, but summoning deceased loved ones is more difficult.

David Cooper's *Invoking Angels* bases itself on biblical and Kabbalistic texts, and provides an accompanying CD of guided meditations.[33] Although all angels come within its compass, the main emphasis is on the interplay between accuser angels and guardian angels, and on the four archangels. The *shekhinah* or presence of God is also treated as an angel. It is clearly hard to strike an effective balance between exploring the intriguing history of angels and putting one's understanding to good practical effect. Cooper's retelling of biblical and Talmudic lore is compelling. Even more so his observation that the main message angels have to tell us is just 'Be!'. But it is not so easy to impart a sense of closeness to an archangel through a pre-recorded soundtrack.

This is not to deride what we may call the imaginal world, that area of mind which lies somewhere between the symbolic and the divinely inspired. A more successful example of the genre of 'angel-healing' through suggestion may be found in a CD entitled *Angels Heal my Body*, where the voice of Jan Yoxall guides a meditation to the accompaniment of music composed for the purpose by Gabriel Currington.[34] The meditations here still use fanciful imagery of roots growing down into mother earth, uphill woodland paths, sparkling crystals and waterfalls, but responsibly led and crafted with care they are of greater value. The Archangel Raphael is here envisaged as emitting an emerald ray, but more importantly, he is invoked in soothing tones that instruct the listener to participate in a healing flow. An affirmation of wholeness in the emotional realm accompanies the healing of physical ailments.

Even at the simplest level of physical relaxation, such guidance has a part to play, for the process of relaxation has become a forgotten art in the modern world, and practitioners who can revive it play a part in helping us all to live our lives more freely and more fully. In this freedom we may even find it easier to expand our own appreciation of the unseen influences on our lives, angelic or otherwise. Healing through psychological means, with or without invoking angels, is an important field not yet fully understood.[35]

The imaginal world is an area of mind not accessed through the processes of rational, logical thinking, but it is not purely imaginary either. Rudolf Steiner speaks of it in *Guardian Angels: Connecting with our Spiritual Guides and Helpers*.[36] Steiner sought to bridge the gap between the cognitive path of Western philosophy and the inner, spiritual needs of the human being, and his teaching attracted many followers both during his period of collaboration with the Theosophical Society and afterwards. His 'anthroposophical science' describes the connection between an invisible world, in which influences from the stars connect with our bodily organs, and the visible world that we perceive with our conscious mind and senses. Steiner steers a cautious path, accepting naturalistic explanations for many things claimed by others as spiritual. Nevertheless he does believe there are spirit beings acting as guardians. One example he cites is the experience of a guardian presence who warns if an accident is about to cut short the life of a person who still has something they need to accomplish. This may be one of the commonest ways in which people experience an angelic presence, and has certainly been reported in many cases of near-death experience. Steiner embraces the theory reflected in many traditions, that in earliest times angel souls took on human bodies (e.g. Hesiod, *Works and Days*; Genesis 6). In his interpretation, rational mind has become unduly dominant over our imaginal soul, and the balance now needs to be redressed. If humans could participate in the knowledge of angels, it might help them more fully to play their part as partners in the care of the world.

The psychoanalyst Eugene G. Jussek once asked what would happen if the religious idea of a guardian angel could be examined in a clinical setting?[37] In an account of hypnotic regressions performed with one of his own patients, drawing on a combination of Jungian psychoanalysis and new age philosophy (he declares himself a follower of the Indian guru Sai Baba), he claims to have contacted a guiding spirit from beyond the world of time and space, to whom he gives the name Yan San Lu. On one level his account could be dismissed as some kind of mutual self-deception between subject and analyst, but the author attempts to bring the reader into his speculations by offering insights into the many layers within the human personality. The subject's 'spirit guide', Yan San Lu, is credited with a coherent set of teachings on topics that are of real interest, including the world at the border of living and dying. Jussek clearly intends to offer comfort, so a generous interpretation of this work, and others like it, is to see them as attempts to help individuals access inner resources of wisdom that lie deep in the subconscious. Drawing on this may guide people towards that equanimity of which angels are considered to be the guardians.

But is it justifiable to hide behind a spirit being? Jung implied that his *Seven Sermons to the Dead* (known only to a few at first but published in 1961) were the words of his spirit guide Philemon. Later he attributed them to a Basilides of Alexandria. He adopted this ruse on advice of friends, lest the work harm his reputation. The full account of his visions, the basis of all his ideas after his break with Freud, was never published, although his edited transcriptions eventually appeared in 2009.[38] Jung said, 'Philemon represented a force which was not myself ... I observed clearly that it was he who spoke, not I.'[39] However, when the teachings of a spirit guide take on the colouring of a philosophy so bound to time and place, the voice loses authority, and the author's well-meant deception becomes a barrier to any reader whose critical faculties have not been engulfed by their need for help. Many people then justifiably feel that such accounts are aimed at the gullible, at those who are desperate for a spiritual teaching that somehow bypasses the traditions and rituals of organized religion. Nevertheless, through the ages, it has been the coming together of communities in temple, synagogue, church or mosque that has provided an unending stream of real support in society. Every religious tradition extends comfort to the sick, support for the poor and renewal of hope for those in misery. Yet somehow today the institutions of religion are undervalued. Spirit angels are sought where more human angels used to bring succour.

Other Interventions

Next we should consider the accounts that often attend extraordinary escapes from danger, where people speak of a 'Third Man',[40] or at any rate a second person, whose voice instructs them in ways that seem not to be available to their conscious mind. Such benevolent presences are often reported in extreme conditions, as with Ernest Shackleton in the Antarctic in 1916, Frank Smythe on Mount Everest in 1933, and by survivors of the attack on the World Trade Center in 2001. Shackleton reported that 'during that long and racking march of thirty-six hours over the unnamed mountains and glaciers of South Georgia, it seemed to me often that we were four, not three'.[41] Frank Smythe turned to his companion to share the sustenance of his last Kendal Mint Cake, only to find there was no one there. Such phenomena are dismissed by some as 'a decay of brain function', as hallucinations caused by 'extreme cold, exhaustion and lack of oxygen' (these are the words of Dr Griffith Pugh, physiologist on Sir Edmund Hillary's 1953 successful Everest expedition), yet they ring true.

The Angels of Mons who appeared to so many soldiers and civilians in 1914 were a slightly different case. Where some people saw only a cloud formation, others were convinced they were witnessing flights of angels – and the outcome on the battlefield at Mons certainly appeared to be miraculous. Nearly a century later, many people still believe that there must have been some presence in the sky for so many people to have seen it. However the angel horseman may have been linked to a fictitious short story, *The Bowmen*, published shortly after the battle, that somehow took root in people's minds.[42]

The idea of angels intervening in daily life continues to hold power. Many novels and films draw us directly or indirectly into the world of angels and unseen powers. One of the most thoughtful of these is Wim Wenders's film depicting the angels who watch over Berlin and their fascination with human life. This meditation on materiality and spirituality appeared on screen in 1987, reaching English speaking countries as *Wings of Desire*. It found its inspiration partly in the poetry of Rainer Maria Rilke, who movingly laments the difficulty of communion with the divine in an age that has cast out devotion and belief. Wenders's interest lies in the desire of the angel to experience human life in all its direct sensory immediacy – to taste the 'now', not just eternity.

Other film forays into the world of our unseen guardians range from *Star Trek*, with its strong moral messages, and the *Star Wars* series, with their universal archetypes, to the recent *Avatar*. All these ply the border between science fiction and fantasy, but also serve as a reminder to keep the imaginal world within our vision while we continue to make good use of our rational capacities.

Among numerous authors of novels in which angels play a smaller or larger role, those who may be singled out for their wisdom and sweet humour include Jill Paton Walsh (*Knowledge of Angels*) and Salley Vickers, (*Miss Garnet's Angel*). Walsh creates an allegorical tale of innocence and wisdom both weighed in the balance against established religious belief. It is set on an island, long ago, in our pre-Reformation Mediterranean past. Vickers interweaves adventures starting from the Venetian church of the Archangel Raphael in Venice with a gradual unfolding of the story of Raphael from the Book of Tobit. Both these novels are framed by a sense of benign angelic presence, from which tranquillity can be drawn both in the tale and by the reader of the tale. They enchant, in the best possible way. By contrast, in Dan Brown's *Angels and Demons*, which might be thought to feed on a fascination with these subjects, angels actually play only a token role: Bernini's angel sculptures dotted around Rome are used as direction pointers, and the real demons are purely psychological. Philip Pullman's trilogy, and the film made of the first part (*The Golden Compass*), is of more substantial interest for its daring inversion of Milton's good and bad angels, its protective relationships and its controversial revival of interest in daemons and souls. Pullman's work provoked strong opposition, as the author no doubt intended, but he continues to write, and others surely will follow. Even in their limited and fictional roles, guardian angels still command our attention.

Chapter 11

FALLEN ANGELS

How you have fallen from heaven,
O morning star, son of the dawn!
You have been cast down to the earth,
You who once laid low the nations!

(Isaiah 14:12)

This is how we first meet Lucifer, and according to tradition, when
he fell he drew after him one third of the stars (Revelation 12:4).
Lucifer means 'bringer of light', as does his name in Greek, ἑωσφόρος
(*heōsphoros*), and the Hebrew original הֵילֵל (*heileil*) means 'shining one'.
In each language his name is identical with his original function, and he
is called the morning star. What happened to him is indeed a terrible fall
from grace:

You said in your heart,
   'I will ascend to heaven;
I will raise my throne
   above the stars of God;
I will sit enthroned on the mount of assembly,
   on the utmost heights of the sacred mountain.
I will ascend above the tops of the clouds;
   I will make myself like the Most High.'
But you are brought down to the grave,
   to the depths of the pit.
Those who see you stare at you,
   they ponder your fate:

Is this the man who shook the earth
and made kingdoms tremble …?

(Isaiah 14:13-16)[1]

The passing millennia allowed the mythical fall of Lucifer to take on great colour and detail, yet this text is full of anomalies. First, how does the morning star come to be portrayed as a male? In the astronomy of the ancients, as in modern astronomy, the morning star was Venus, the embodiment of feminine beauty. Secondly, in its context, the entire passage is not about Lucifer at all. The morning star is simply a metaphor in a diatribe against the King of Babylon. Through pride and presumption his might has been overthrown (or will be overthrown – for this is prophecy). As a result, and a third anomaly, the prince of light has turned into the prince of darkness.

The source for the more colourful accounts is probably the Christian retelling of the fall, where Lucifer is replaced by a dragon:

And there was war in heaven: Michael and his angels fought
against the dragon; and the dragon fought and his angels,
And prevailed not; neither was their place found any more in
    heaven.
And the great dragon was cast out, that old serpent, called the
Devil, and Satan, which deceiveth the whole world: he was cast
out into the earth, and his angels were cast out with him.

(Revelation 12:7-9)

Satan has become a serpent and the leader of the fallen angels. This is how the serpent in the garden who tempts Eve is taken to be Satan, at least in Christian interpretation.[2] As for the fruit, medieval preachers made much of the similarity of *malum*, 'evil' and *malus*, 'an apple tree' in Latin. The Hebrew gives no indication of what kind of fruit the tree of knowledge bears.

St Augustine sees Satan as the father of all evil, though he stops short of the Manichaean heresy that he operates independently of God.[3] He ponders whether Satan knew in advance that he was going to fall, and whether, in fact he had any choice in the matter. Augustine also expresses a wistful admiration for those who can believe in two classes of angels, supercelestial ones living in constant blessedness and a mundane class who can aspire to being blessed if they follow the bidding of their superiors, suggesting that Satan belonged to the latter group. But he can find no scriptural evidence to support such a view.[4]

Originally Satan was no more than God's agent as accuser. That is, the angel who gathers evidence of a person's misdeeds, and presents the matter before the divine court of judgement. When Balaam sets off to pronounce a curse on Israel for the Moabite king, Balak (Numbers 22) the angel he meets on the way is described as an adversary, a *satan*. This adversary angel is certainly doing God's business. In the book of Job, Satan is set to work by God to test Job's faith – or at least, he is given licence to put Job to the test. Perhaps there is from the outset an element of mischief-making on Satan's part, when he questions whether Job is really as good as God would like to believe (Job 1:9-11), and the definite article gets attached to his name, so he becomes 'the' adversary, not just one among many witness angels. In Zechariah's vision Satan is rebuked by God for accusing Joshua, and the translators of the Septuagint used *diabolos* to translate his name (Zechariah 3). Yet 'the adversary' (*ha-satan*) had been an angel and is described as appearing among the 'sons of God':

> Now there was a day when the sons of God came to present
> themselves before the Lord, and the adversary came also among
> them. And the Lord said to the adversary, 'From where dost
> thou come?' Then the adversary answered the Lord, and said,
> 'From going to and fro in the earth, and from walking up and
> down in it.'
>
> (Job 1:6-7)

Nevertheless, being described as 'also among' the sons of God, rather than simply as one of them, does allow for doubt about his angelic status. Iblis, Satan's counterpart in Islam, is described in much the same way when the angels are ordered to bow down to Adam:

> ... so they bowed themselves
> save Iblis – he was not of those
>   that bowed themselves.
> Said He [God], 'What prevented thee to
> bow thyself, when I commanded thee?'

> Said he [Iblis], 'I am better than he; Thou
> createdst me of fire, and him Thou
>   createdst of clay.'
> Said He, 'Get thee down out of it;
> it is not for thee to wax proud here,
> so go thou forth; surely thou art
>   among the humbled.
>
> (Qur'an 7:10-12)

While the first comment allows of angelic status ('he was not of those that bowed themselves'), Iblis's subsequent claim – that he is made out of fire, not light – unequivocally denies it. Iblis is classing himself as one of the *jinn*, the unseen spirits, and not an angel.[5] Yet he clearly had the run of heaven up to the point of his banishment. And even then, he bargains with God to be allowed access. God grants it, and Iblis marks out his future career:

> I shall surely sit in ambush for them
>   on thy straight path;
> Then I shall come on them from before them
> And from behind them, from the right hands
> And their left hands; Thou wilt not find
> most of them thankful.'
>
> (Qur'an 7:15-16)

This irritates God, who bids him be gone, 'despised and banished', and says he will fill hell with him and all who follow him. As translator, Arberry, uses the name Gehenna for hell (7:17), preserving closeness to the Arabic خهنم, *jehennem*, but both words come from the biblical *Ge-hinnom*, 'valley of wailing', a valley outside Jerusalem associated with fire and child sacrifice to the Phoenician deity Moloch.[6] Iblis will henceforward dwell in the fire that cannot be quenched and that consumes innocent children.

Iblis now has the self-appointed task of provoking people, whispering evil thoughts into their minds. Another Arabic name for him is *shaytan*, which is the equivalent of Satan. There are many *shaytans*, according to Islamic lore. But they are definitely *jinn*, rather than angels.

The Qur'an account makes Satan's refusal to acknowledge Adam the reason for his fall. This had its precursors in little-known Hebrew and Christian sources. It first appears in the first-century CE *Life of Adam and Eve*, (also known in its Greek version as the *Revelation of Moses*). A fourth-century Syriac 'history of the world' gives the following account:

> And when the prince of the lower order of angels saw what great
> majesty had been given unto Adam, he was jealous of him from
> that day, and he did not wish to worship him. And he said unto
> his hosts, 'Ye shall not worship him, and ye shall not praise him
> with the angels. It is meet that ye should worship me, because
> I am fire and spirit; and not that I should worship a thing of
> dust, which hath been fashioned of fine dust.' And the Rebel
> meditating these things would not render obedience to God, and
> of his own free will he asserted his independence and separated
> himself from God. But he was swept away out of heaven and
> fell, and the fall of himself and of all his company from heaven
> took place on the Sixth Day, at the second hour of the day. And
> the apparel of their glorious state was stripped off them. And his
> name was called *Sâtânâ* because he turned aside [from the right
> way], and *Shêdâ* because he was cast out, and *Daiwâ* because
> he lost the apparel of his glory. And behold, from that time until
> the present day, he and all his hosts have been stripped of their
> apparel, and they go naked and have horrible faces.
>
> (*Cave of Treasures*, fol. 5a-b)[7]

As Satan fell, so was Adam lifted up to take his place in the Garden of Eden in the third hour of the sixth day. He ascended in a chariot of fire amid much rejoicing among the angels.

Some say Adam's subsequent fall was brought about by Lucifer in revenge for his own expulsion. The Church Fathers add that Adam's fall caused great mourning among the angels, and their joy cannot be complete until mankind is restored. This is why they rejoiced at Christ's birth and participated in his Ascension which would open the way for mankind's return to the divine realm.[8]

Lucifer, or Satan, was not the only angel who fell. The Prophet Ezekiel relates a parable about a cherub who fell. Not a winged-baby cherub, but a *keruv* in the original sense of a tutelary deity. Like Lucifer, who represents the king of Babylon, the fall of this *keruv* refers to the downfall of the king of Tyre (Ezekiel 28:13 ff.). The *keruv* dwelt in Eden. Clothed in rubies and diamonds, sapphires and jade he was the 'far-covering *keruv*' – walking up and down in the midst of 'stones of fire', and perfect in his ways. His sin was overwhelming pride in his own beauty. This led him to corrupt his wisdom, forgetting God. As a punishment, he was hurled down from the holy mountain. Some later sources take this simply as a retelling of Lucifer's fall. For example, in the twelfth century encyclopedia *Hortus Deliciarum* (Garden of Delights), Satan is shown holding the text of Ezekiel 28:12 on a banner as his explusion is proclaimed. But others have seen it as a precursor for Adam and Eve's expulsion from Paradise. To demythologize the story of a powerful ancient deity, the sin and punishment of man were substituted for the sin and punishment of the cherub.

The identification of Satan with the serpent in the Garden of Eden, and hence the tempter rather than the accuser, became a cornerstone of Christian theology. The Baha'i faith offers something rather different. Satan for them is not an evil demon but the promptings of our own lower nature, the evil within. Likewise demons, jinn and fallen angels are seen as aspects of our own selves. This interpretation perhaps just makes explicit what many people read into the texts anyway. Religious myth can be interpreted on many levels. The plain meaning, the explanatory interpretation, the symbolic meaning and the inner, secret meaning all have ancient antecedents. The Church Fathers enumerated their own four methods of reading scripture: literal, moral, allegorical and anagogical (spiritual). Sir James Frazer's *The Golden Bough* (1890) extended this approach to the complexities of religious myths, their psychological underpinnings and their implications in ritual and custom for different societies, giving rise to much insight as well as to more fanciful speculations.

One such speculation links Satan with the earlier figure of Set in Ancient Egypt. Set was one of the earliest of the Egyptian gods, worshipped as a storm god and bringer of confusion. Even his form displayed confusion, being animal but like no particular kind of animal, more of a monster, with forked tail, square-tipped ears and a curved snout. Son of earth and sky, he became envious of his younger brother Osiris, who brought the blessings of civilization. It may be that their struggles reflect a history of warfare between the two kingdoms of Egypt, the prosperous north (belonging to Osiris) and the desert south (land of Set). We hear the tale mostly through the worshippers of Isis and Osiris, so it may be that some of Set's more admirable qualities have been lost in the retelling. However, one cannot help wondering whether some interaction of ideas might have helped to turn the original Jewish notion of Satan as an accuser into the fully-fledged demon king he became.

Satan's fall from heaven was much embellished in Milton's retelling. Magnificent scenes of armed and winged conflict lead up to the mighty struggle between Satan and the Archangel Michael, with sword-strokes slicing through ethereal bodies, jarring discords, grinding pain, and supporting troops numbered in their millions. The sixth book of *Paradise Lost* is largely taken up with the battle. Plans are afoot to bring that epic struggle to the screen.[9] It will be no mean task, especially as the final battle against Satan and his host is fought not by the archangel and his bands but by God in his chariot, with Christ riding on the wings of a cherub.

Among Satan's companions many are named, and some stand out as leaders, but it is futile to look for a hierarchy. Belial, whose name means worthlessness or destruction, is presented in Book I of *Paradise Lost* as the epitome of iniquity, Beelzebub, a Semitic god, as arch-tyrant,[10] and Mammon as downward-looking even before the fall. Many theologians identified such Princes of Darkness with the seven deadly sins. Thus, Lucifer is pride, Mammon greed, Asmodeus lust, Satan (here distinguished from Lucifer) wrath, Beelzebub (or Baal) gluttony, Leviathan envy and Belphegor (Baal-Peor) vanity and idleness.[11] Other fiends named by Milton include the gods Moloch (of child-sacrifice fame), Chemos(h), Baal and Astoreth (Astarte).

What is of even greater interest than Satan's fall for our enquiry into angels is the descent of angels into the world, described in Genesis 6. It is not the descent that is surprising, for after all, angels may come and go and carry out their duties, descending to earth and re-ascending whether by ladder or by wings – not forgetting that in Jacob's dream they ascend first, before descending, implying that angels naturally move about on earth as their proper domain. The surprise lies not in the descent but in its consequences:

> And it came to pass, when men began to multiply on the face of the earth, and daughters were born unto them, that the sons of

God saw the daughters of men that they were fair; and they took
them wives, whomsoever they chose. And the Lord said: 'My
spirit shall not abide in man for ever, for that he also is flesh;
therefore shall his days be a hundred and twenty years.'

The Nephilim were in the earth in those days, and also after
that, when the sons of God came in unto the daughters of men,
and they bore children to them; the same were the mighty men
that were of old, the men of renown.

And the Lord saw that the wickedness of man was great
in the earth, and that every imagination of the thoughts of his
hearts was only evil continually.

(Genesis 6:1-5)[12]

These short verses, packed with momentous happenings, form the
prelude to the great flood, from which only Noah and his family were
to be saved. The essential facts are that 'sons of God', whom we may
reasonably understand to be angels, fell in love with the young women
they encountered on earth and chose to intermarry with them. The
children who were the offspring of such unions, being heir to angelic
as well as human genes, were exceptionally tall and strong, and no
doubt also valiant warriors. But somehow evil was also magnified, and
humans are declared mortal, with 120 years being set as the maximum
span of life.

Some details are less clear. For example, how did it come about
that angelic beings, full of light and spirit, became attracted to mere
humans, whose spirit is clothed with a physical body? Secondly, how
did those angels acquire the capacity to engage in sexual relations
when traditionally angels had been considered to be without organs
of generation by virtue of belonging to the spiritual world not the
realm of 'generation and corruption'? Thirdly, what is meant by the
Nephilim? Were they, too, giants? Is this an echo of mythology like
the Titans, or are they the same angels under a different name? And
whoever they are, how do these simple facts lead on to the assertion
of wickedness?

Some medieval commentators explained the passage away, insisting
that the sons of God are really just the sons of princes, who stand in
God's stead for the community they rule. If rulers and their sons act on
their own impulses with impunity, especially in regard to their treatment

of young women, the rule of law soon collapses. Rashi was one such interpreter, and his words were influential. The Nephilim are named from *naphal*, meaning 'to fall': they fell, and caused the whole world to fall. *Naphal* is also associated with causing death, hence the prediction of doom.

However, some older interpretations took a different view, linking the passage specifically to angels. The Septuagint had translated Nephilim as giants, but a parallel tradition considered the 'falling' of Nephilim to be a description of what happened to the angels. The bare facts were then elaborated into a detailed account, furnishing the basis for much of the material in the *Book of Enoch* and the *Book of Jubilees*. There they emerge as watchers, or *Grigori*, who dwelt in the heavens, but were subsequently punished for their sins.

The *Book of Enoch* relates exactly what it was that these angels engaged in that caused their punishment: first,

> [they] took unto themselves wives, and each chose for himself
> one ... and they taught them charms and enchantments, and the
> cutting of roots, and made them acquainted with plants.
>
> (1 Enoch 7:1)

The children they bore were 3,000 ells high.[13] They consumed all the food that was available, then turned against mankind, devouring them, as well as birds, beasts, reptiles, fish and one another, until the very earth laid accusation against them. Other forms of wickedness follow:

> Azazel taught men to make swords, and knives, and shields and
> breastplates, and made known to them the metals of the earth
> and the art of working them; and bracelets and ornaments, and
> the use of antimony, and the beautifying of the eyelids, and all
> kinds of costly stones, and all colouring tinctures. And there
> arose much godlessness, and they committed fornication, and
> they were led astray and became corrupt in all their ways.
>
> Semjaza taught enchantments and root-cuttings, Armaros
> the resolving of enchantments, Baraqijal taught astrology,
> Kokabel the constellations, Ezeqeel the knowledge of the clouds,
> Araqiel the signs of the earth, Shamsiel the signs of the sun, and
> Sariel the course of the moon.

And as men perished, they cried, and their cry went up to
heaven.

(1 Enoch 8:1-4)

It was to destroy these angels who chose to fall and to rescue the earth
from the havoc they unleashed that the flood was devised. Azazel,
Semjaza and the rest were to be bound hand and foot in the desert.
The Archangel Uriel is sent to warn Noah, while Raphael is instructed
to make an opening in Dudael and cast Azazel into it, placing on him
rough and jagged rocks, and covering him with darkness: 'Let him abide
there for ever, and cover his face that he may not see light' (10:5). On the
Day of Judgement he will be cast into fire. Raphael is then to go about
healing the earth. Somehow the secrets that were disclosed have to be
covered up again. Gabriel is to destroy all the children of the watchers,
and Michael is to bind Semjaza and his fellows for 70 generations in the
lowest part of the earth, after which they will be judged, and led off to
an abyss of fire for ever (10:9-15).

Originally the watchers had been a wholly dependable class of angels,
as in Daniel 4:13-17, sent to watch over the stars and humankind, but
in the *Book of Enoch* it becomes the name for the fallen angels. Grigori
is their Greek name. After their fall they are safely trapped in an abyss.
Together with seven stars they are bound in a chaotic and horrible place
of mountains on fire. These stars are the ones that from their creation
(the 'beginning of their rising') failed to come out and shine at their
appointed time and season. They are bound for 10,000 years until their
guilt should be expiated. Those who connected themselves with women,
will stay in the abyss until the great judgement, when 'they shall be
judged till they are made an end of'. But it seems that their spirits still
wander abroad leading humans astray (1 Enoch 19).

Chapter 12

ANGELS OF RETRIBUTION
AND REDEMPTION

The troops of angels descended;
Even the stars waged war from the heavens;
At the blast of Your nostrils, the water piled up ...
The angels on high rose up
To humble the enemies of Your people;
The nations heard, they trembled.

(Elia ben Abraham)[1]

Quite distinct from the fallen angels, there is another class of
angels who cast a shadow of fear: angels of retribution. This
fourteenth-century Sabbath hymn from Macedonia, shows troops
of angels poised to execute divine judgement. Besides the angels
who record the good and evil deeds of individuals, there are angels
of retribution, whose task it is to seek out wrongs large and small
and to punish them. Christian theology speaks of the Day of
Retribution or Judgement, that end-time when the angelic trumpets
will sound and the dead will be raised to be 'judged of the deeds
done in the body'. Yet the word 'retribution' does not appear in
the Bible, and vengeance is reserved for the Almighty alone, not
for a human, nor even an angel.[2] Even then, God's vengeance is
only against those who through their lives and actions have declared
themselves enemies of the good. In medieval paintings of the Last
Judgement it is generally devils, not angels, who are casting sinners
down into furnace flames with their pitchforks. So how did angels
of retribution enter the frame?

In the last chapter, we saw archangels being sent to bind and imprison the watchers. Another clue lies in medieval fresco treatments of the scene, such as those in the Camposanto in Pisa (fourteenth century). There, in *The Last Judgement*, the Archangel Michael is shown with drawn sword, presiding over the separation of worthy souls from unworthy, while other angels, armed and unarmed, turn away the unworthy from entering heaven. On another panel, entitled *The Triumph of Death*, pairs of angels, light and dark are seen fighting over individual human beings in the skies.

It was almost certainly one single passage that gave rise to the idea of dark avenging angels as agents for the expression of God's vengeance:

> When the Lord Jesus shall be revealed from heaven with his
>   mighty angels,
> In flaming fire taking vengeance on them that know not God,
> and that obey not the gospel of our Lord Jesus Christ:
> Who shall be punished with everlasting destruction from the
> presence of the Lord and from the glory of his power.
>
> (2 Thessalonians 1:7-9)

This is far from the concept of God as redeemer or saviour, though plenty of texts remind us that vengeance is not the dominant attribute of divine justice. A very different picture is portrayed in Psalm 8:2: 'Out of the mouth of babes and sucklings hast thou ordained strength because of thine enemies, that thou mightest still the enemy and the avenger' and in Exodus 34:6-7:

> The Lord, the Lord, God, merciful and gracious, long-suffering,
> and abundant in goodness and truth; keeping mercy for
> thousands [of generations], forgiving iniquity and transgression
> and sin.

This last is traditionally known as the 'thirteen attributes of mercy'. How to derive 13, and the significance of each could occupy a whole chapter, but it is sufficient here to note the compassion for those who repent. This does not mean that misdeeds escape judgement. The next line makes it clear that the 'guilty', that is the unrepentant, will not escape punishment, and that children and grandchildren will also be affected, 'unto the third and to the fourth generation' (Exodus 34:7). Some read into it the simple recognition that wrongdoing or neglect of duty exacts its own penalty, which often falls on one's nearest and dearest in unintended ways. It has even been seen as limiting the harm done even by the worst of offenders, to 'only' three or four generations. We see in daily life that families do suffer where the parents have forgotten what society requires of them. Children and even grandchildren may well end up paying the price of parental lapses, and vice versa. But however harsh this visiting of iniquity may sound, there is still no talk of avenging angels carrying out the 'visitations'. Perhaps even the Day of Judgement should be considered, if we consider it at all, as 'the great Day wherein the Secrets of all Hearts shall be laid open' (John Locke, *Essay on Human Understanding*).[3] Indeed, Locke makes a case for a much milder form of judgement on that day than is customarily handed down by human courts. Acts we commit unconsciously could hardly be attributable to our conscious minds, since he equates our identity as a person with consciousness.

If we cannot readily find angels of retribution, what about the angel of death? These are surely present in religious tradition of every kind? In fact, the evidence is not quite as one expects. The angel of death who appears in post-biblical Jewish tradition is not named as such in the Bible. There are the 'bands of death', the 'shadow of death' and other such phrases. Seventy thousand people died of a pestilence in the second book of Samuel, before the Lord told 'the angel that destroyed the people' to stay his hand (II Samuel 24:16). In this case David actually 'saw' the angel, and went to great trouble to stop the slaying of the innocent on his account (24:17-25). A similar (or perhaps the same) story is told in Chronicles, where Satan stands up against Israel to provoke a war in which, again, King David sees the angel:

> And David lifted up his eyes and saw the angel of the Lord
> stand between the earth and the heaven, having a drawn sword
> in his hand stretched out over Jerusalem.
>
> (I Chronicles 21:16)

Once again, David is appalled to have brought so much suffering on the people. Once again he purchases a threshing floor and builds an altar, but this time, when he is chastened by the angel (tellingly called in verse 22 'a plague'), he feels unable to complete the sacrifice. He was 'afraid because of the sword of the angel of the Lord' (21:30) and decides instead to begin the task of building the temple, which will be completed by his son Solomon.

In the second book of Kings, the 'angel of the Lord' smites the Assyrians, this time slaying 185,000 men in one night. Only in the book of Proverbs do we meet the phrase *malakhe' ha-mavet,* 'angels of death', and the usual rendition takes it quite literally as 'messengers' of death: 'The wrath of a king is as messengers of death, but a wise man will pacify it.' In the book of Job, there is also a reference to 'destroyers' whose Hebrew name, in the plural, *memitim* is etymologically connected with death (Job 33:22). Yet a protective angel could still guard a person from the *memitim.*

In later rabbinic tradition there are many elaborate discussions of the angel of death. According to various midrashic explanations, he was created on the first day, he dwells in heaven, and has 12 wings.[4] He stands over the one about to die with a drawn sword, on the top of which is a drop of gall. As soon as the dying person sees him, his shock causes his mouth to open and the drop of bitter gall falls into his mouth and causes his death.[5] Amongst the tales told is one of Rabbi Hanina ben Papa who kept the angel of death at bay for 30 days while he reviewed all that he had learned. His friend, Joshua ben Levi, is said to have persuaded the angel of death to show him his place in Paradise, and to let him carry the knife, so that he would not be afraid. The angel lifted him up to see his place, and Joshua escaped – but by jumping over the wall into Paradise, not by extending his life. He was allowed to stay, but the angel's knife had to be returned, by decree of a voice from heaven.[6] It is also said that the angel of death had no power over Moses, who was taken into heaven by a divine kiss. The midrash describes how neither Michael nor Samael were able to take him.[7] In Burne-Jones's rendition of this scene, the two angels are shown supporting the body of the deceased prophet, but the accompanying text speaks only of the burial of the body, not the destination of the soul.

The New Testament does not record an angel of death either, apart perhaps from the fourth Horseman of the Apocalypse. Death is often mentioned, but not as an angel. Yet Christian literary traditions refer frequently to the Grim Reaper, a personification of death who stalks the world in a long dark robe, holding a tall scythe. In the Catholic

Church, Michael is generally viewed as carrying good souls to heaven, while Samael, identified with Satan, takes others down to hell.

In Islam the situation is clearer, as the Archangel Azra'il is recognized as angel of death, and death is seen as a return to God (Qur'an, sura 32:11). One Sufi rendition of the way the angel of death knows when a person needs to die involves a tree of life, with tiny leaves, one for each person. The leaf wilts 40 days before a person is about to die – though he himself may still feel full of life and be making plans for the future.[8] Azra'il also has the power to choose a form appropriate to the person to whom he is about to appear, and cannot be seen by anyone else at the time. It is Allah who reclaims the souls, but the angel of death who goes, with his helpers, to release the soul from the body. These helpers are described as angels of mercy and angels of torment.

Given the comparative lack of clarity in biblical sources, set against the rich elaborations of later traditions, one cannot help wondering whether these later ideas about the angel of death have been imported from elsewhere. In Hindu mythology, death is a god, Yama – from whom concessions might be won, such as knowledge about life and how to live it, as in the tale of the determined young Nachiketas (*Katha Upanishad*). To the ancient Greeks, Death (*Thanatos*) was a young man with large wings and a sword, who looks like many depictions of the Archangel Michael (see Figure 20).

He is the twin brother of Sleep. Just and gentle, he escorts the dying soul to the underworld, handing him over to the boatman Charon, for now the soul must cross the river Acheron that separates the world of the living from the world of the dead. Souls whose bodies lacked proper burial or funeral rites were thought to be stranded upon the shore. In Virgil's *Aeneid*, at the moment of Dido's death, the rainbow-goddess Iris comes on saffron wings to bear her spirit away.[9] Iris and Thanatos are not angels, but they are winged figures associated with the moment of death. The god with winged sandals, Hermes, or Mercury, was also responsible for guiding the souls of the deceased to their place in the underworld.[10] For Zoroastrians, Vohu Manah, the spirit of wisdom, has particular association with guiding the soul at death. But it is perhaps above all the ancient folklore of the Middle East that has shaped our picture of the angel of death. The *Arabian Nights* contains many tales from Persia, India and Arabia, some long predating Islam. A cluster of three tales concern the angel of death, one of which presents two different types of man. Though the outcome is the same, in that both die, the manner of death is the product of their own attitudes:

> It is related that one of the olden monarchs was once minded to ride out in state with the officers of his realm and the grandees of his retinue and display to the folk the marvels of his magnificence. So he ordered his lords and emirs to equip themselves and commanded his keeper of the wardrobe to bring him of the richest of raiment, such as befitted the King in his state, and steeds of the finest pedigrees ...
>
> And Iblis came to him and, laying his hand upon his nose, blew into his nostrils the breath of hauteur and conceit, so that he magnified and glorified himself and said in his heart, 'Who among men is like unto me?' And he became so puffed up with arrogance and self-sufficiency, and so taken up with the thought of his own splendour and magnificence, that he would not vouchsafe a glance to any man.
>
> Presently there stood before him one clad in tattered clothes and saluted him, but he returned not his salaam, whereupon the stranger laid hold of his horse's bridle. 'Lift thy hand!' cried the King. 'Thou knowest not whose bridle rein it is whereof thou takest hold.' Quoth the other, 'I have a need of thee.' Quoth the King, 'Wait till I alight, and then name thy need.' Rejoined the stranger, 'It is a secret and I will not tell it but in thine ear.' So the King bowed his head to him and he said, 'I am the Angel of Death and I purpose to take thy soul.' Replied the King, 'Have patience with me a little, whilst I return to my house and take leave of my people and children and neighbours and wife.' 'By no means so,' answered the Angel. 'Thou shalt never return nor look on them again, for the fated term of thy life is past.' So saying, he took the soul of the King, who fell off his horse's back dead, and departed thence.
>
> Presently the Death Angel met a devout man, and saluted him. He returned the salute, and the Angel said to him, 'O pious man, I have a need of thee which must be kept secret.' 'Tell it in my ear,' quoth the devotee, and quoth the other, 'I am the Angel of Death.' Replied the man: 'Welcome to thee! And praised be Allah for thy coming! I am aweary of awaiting thine

arrival ...' Said the Angel, 'If thou have any business, make an
end of it,' but the other answered, saying, 'There is nothing so
urgent to me as the meeting with my Lord, to whom be honour
and glory!' And the Angel said, 'How wouldst thou fain have
me take thy soul? I am bidden to take it as thou willest and
choosest.' He replied, 'Tarry till I make the *wuzu* ablution and
pray, and when I prostrate myself, then take my soul while my
body is on the ground.' Quoth the Angel, 'Verily, my Lord (be
He extolled and exalted!) commanded me not to take thy soul
but with thy consent and as thou shouldst wish, so I will do thy
will.' Then the devout man made the minor ablution and prayed,
and the Angel of Death took his soul in the act of prostration
and Almighty Allah transported it to the place of mercy and
acceptance and forgiveness.

(*The Angel of Death with the Proud King and the Devout Man*)[11]

Certainly the angel of death holds a place in our imagination, and when
that title was accorded to Dr Joseph Mengele, who conducted notorious
genetic experiments at Auschwitz from 1943–5, everyone understood
what was meant by the name.

Returning to the aspect of punishment, the angels who separate the
worthy from the unworthy in medieval paintings might be regarded as
agents of retribution, just like the *daemon* described by Hermes: when
the soul leaves the body, it passes to the jurisdiction of the chief daemon.
If he finds it faithful and upright, he lets it stay in an appropriate place,

But if he sees it covered with the stains of crime, and oblivious
of its vices, he hurls it from the heights to the depths, delivering
it to storms and whirlwinds, to the ever contending elements of
air, fire and water so that it is caught between heaven and earth,
continually buffeted in different directions by the turbulence of
the world.

(Hermes, *Asclepius*, 28, tr. Salaman)

But in all the traditions we have considered, retribution takes place only
under divine decree.

Redemption

Linked with retribution is its opposite twin, redemption, of great interest
to the early Church Fathers. For them, the Angels of Redemption are
those who come to gather in the souls on the Day of Judgement. The
gospel of Matthew says that after the days of tribulation, 'He shall send
his angels with a great sound of a trumpet and they shall gather together
his elect from the four winds, from one end of heaven to the other'
(Matthew 24:31; Mark 13:27). The angels will separate the faithful from
the workers of iniquity, and will assist at the last judgement. In the great
drama of the end of days, the angels play an active role trumpeting,
gathering and separating. But they also rejoice at the entry of the faithful
into heaven. According to St Hilary, after the second coming of Christ,
'the entire creation of angels is freed from the great burdens of its
ministry'.[12] In Judaism and Islam, the Day of Reckoning is generally
seen as a more personal affair, and the angels' ministry may therefore
have no set term. But in all three Abrahamic faiths one can find traces
of the idea that in the last days, mankind will at last join with the angels,
to the great rejoicing of all.

But redemption also has a more immediate aspect that does not have
to wait for the 'end of days'. Redemption in its Christian theological sense
means deliverance from sin and the consequences of sin. More broadly,
it means deliverance from being bound. What constitutes bondage is a
limited way of life, be it sin, self-absorption, pride in our own powers or
simply failure to appreciate the wonder of our surroundings. These are
among the fetters that bind. Release from these may be attained through
atonement and grace, and the form that atonement takes varies from one
religion to the next. If we are Muslims or Jews, we must rely on our own
atonement and the grace of God. If we are Christian, we may rely on the
atonement and grace of Christ. Buddhists, Hindus, Sikhs, Jains, Baha'is
and Zoroastrians all have rituals of reverence and appreciation. Even if
we follow no religion at all we may still engage reverently with the forces
of nature, the magic of the cosmos or our own ethical conscience.[13]
All of these have redemptive power. Yet there seems to be little room
for angels in this process. But was it always so? Does a guardian angel
or an angel of instruction play a part? Certainly guardian angels are
supposed to bring their charges safely through life to a happy conclusion
in heaven, but this is not quite redemption. An angel of instruction may

have a more redemptive role. In many tales of Islamic origin, such an angel appears at the end of the story, to convey some apprehension of general wisdom that releases the soul from its fetters. Thus at the end of John Hawkesworth's *Almoran and Hamet* (1761):

> that which passed in secret was revealed by the Angel of
> instruction, that the world might know, that, to the wicked,
> increase of power is increase of wretchedness.

The angel of instruction is also invoked in Robert Forsyth's *Principles of Moral Science* (1805) to convey secret knowledge of a system that provides both wisdom and redemption. It does so in a vision sequence, called the 'Vision of Hystaspes'.[14] It also teaches how such knowledge should be hidden from public gaze. A sour-tongued contemporary reviewer wished the author had followed his own hint and hidden it all from public gaze![15] A less frivolous response would be to ask what part an angel of instruction or a guardian angel may play in personal liberation from bondage.

The English divines, Saunders, Hamond and Latham, all urged us to consider the angels as we go about our normal business in the world. Through remembrance of their presence, we would inflict harm on none. Perhaps such mindful action can remove the obstacles to liberation. But for liberation itself, rather than appealing to any winged beings, we should surely turn to that universal 'Angel' of Avicenna and Ficino,[16] the constant presence of divine mind expressed as Angel. To this we may turn, and we may be absorbed into it as soon as we are willing to give up what separates us from it. This Angel pours out light, but the light has come from beyond the realm of angels. It is the light of divine love. We may therefore fittingly conclude that it is divine love that both judges and redeems, but if we honour the idea of angelic influence, it may help that love to flow, in both directions.

EPILOGUE

In *Paradise Lost*, when Adam is deep in contemplation of the heavens above, the Archangel Raphael reminds him of the limitations of his capacity:

> Heav'n is for thee too high
> To know what passes there; be lowly wise;
> Think only what concerns thee and thy being;
> Dream not of other worlds, what creatures there
> Live, in what state, condition, or degree ...
>
> (*Paradise Lost*, VIII, 172-76)

In this book we have tried to look more closely at the creatures of those other worlds. Together, we have surveyed a long history of three or even four millennia, tracing the thread right down to the present day. I have tried to avoid both excessive credulity and dismissive doubt, and to remain mindful of Raphael's warning of presumption. Our conclusions can only ever be of a tentative nature, drawing on scripture, myth, philosophy and such experience as we ourselves, or others known to us, recount. If you have come to the conclusion that talk of angels is vain talk, you will be in the company of many distinguished philosophers and rationalists through the ages, both religious and secular. But if the discussion here has called forth a way of understanding angels that has any depth and validity of meaning, it will have made the writing of this book worth the labour.

For my own part, I have been amazed at how rich and expansive the literature is on all things angelic. I found myself fascinated by questions I had at first wished to exclude, such as the demons and fallen angels. I have equally felt nourished and enriched by contemplating representations of angels in art, reference to angels in poetry and music, stories and sermons, and by the whole range of philosophical and theological debate. My growing interest also led to many wonderful conversations, with family, friends and new acquaintances. This short account can only be considered as an introduction to a field that has many treasures still in store.

People often ask whether I believe in angels, but this is a question that needs to be broken into several parts. Without doubt, I have respect for the views of those who wrote of angels in a scriptural setting, reflecting their deeply-held beliefs about the operation of unseen numinous powers. I have also been moved by the encounters of those who found solace through angels, or who trembled with awe, as in Rilke's encounter at Duino, where 'every angel is terrifying'. Writing this book has been an exploration, and, during the course of it, more than once my answer to questions of belief was 'I will know what I think when I have finished.' As I now reach that point, the words Paul Tillich used about myth seem particularly appropriate: he spoke of it offering a kind of truth which cannot conflict with scientific, historical or philosophical truth because it is of a different order.[1] I feel angels enjoy a similar status.

Along the way I have met people who were happy to share with me their experiences. One friend spoke of an angelic being who could be plainly sensed in the room, and who brought with him or her (it was not clear which) the presence of a recently deceased person with an important message to impart. One distinguished professor of neurology fondly remembered as an angel the man who had suddenly appeared in a small Italian street to help mend his car, and then promptly disappeared – in an area better known for tricks played on motorists to rob them of their luggage. No tale was more moving than that of our friend, Shlomo Fischl, who survived terrible events in Bohemia during the Nazi occupation thanks to a very human angel, his own stepmother, Mlada, whom he still, 70 years later, always takes care to name as 'Angel Mlada'.

My own personal encounters with angels have been limited. Just three episodes might possibly qualify. Like many people, I feel a certain reluctance to talk about them, but having just set out my views in the foregoing chapters, I accept a certain obligation to declare them. One of them is undeniably relevant. During the birth of my third child, which took place at home, things were not going smoothly, and I was beginning to drift in and out of consciousness. Two midwives were in attendance and two doctors, as some problems were foreseen because the baby was three weeks overdue. Things were becoming increasingly slow and difficult, and I was encouraged to get out of bed and move about for a bit. My memory is of being on my feet at the end of the bed (this part at least was confirmed by others), and of moving forwards into a space (that was in fact very restricted) where I was met by a small but powerful figure, whom I could only dimly perceive, and who seemed to be insisting that I go back. Some sort of moral and physical struggle ensued. My overwhelming desire was to go forward, into oblivion, but I seemed to be being forced back, and certainly I returned somehow to the bed. Not long afterwards, the baby was born. I did not talk about the experience at the time, except with my husband, as it seemed such a strange event. One of the doctors did confirm, about a week later, that they had at that stage feared for my life and had been debating whether to send for an ambulance, but concluded that it was safer to proceed with an assisted delivery there and then. I was left with the impression of having struggled with an angel. Unlike Jacob, there was no clear sense that I had prevailed. From my point of view, it felt like being forced back against my will, or at least forced to face things that seemed beyond my strength to endure – though, of course, with hindsight, I am extremely grateful that it was so!

A second sense in which angels became a reality for me was in a hot and crowded underground train shortly before a broadcast on angels in which I participated and which, ultimately, gave rise to this book.[2] I had a seat and was reading a book on medieval angels. Looking up, I suddenly became aware that any or all of the people in the carriage crowding above the seated passengers were potentially angels, each with a message to convey either to some particular human being, or even for any who might have ears to hear.

A third episode took place long before either of these, back in November 1972, and can best be described as a sense of some unseen watchful presence. My husband and I were travelling in the Punjab towards the foothills of the Himalayas. At three particular points in the day, disasters were averted by the most unexpected and inexplicable means. We were to set off at dawn from Amritsar in the plains, to travel through the Kangra valley to the small village of Dharamsala, now famous as the home in exile of the Dalai Lama. But it was then little known. The journey had to be planned in advance, as there were few buses that went there, and even fewer that made the journey to the upper village, where we were to ask for a particular man, of whom we knew only the name.[3] A bus would leave Amritsar early, reaching the railhead, Pathankot, around noon, and from there another bus would take us to Dharamsala by nightfall.

To reach the bus station in Amritsar we had to begin with a half-hour ride in a bicycle-rickshaw which was duly summoned for us, and we left as a soft grey light began to herald the dawn. The lad at the pedals was thin, undernourished, maybe even a little lazy, and our progress was very slow. Mounting concern and irritation was of no avail: we missed the bus, and had to take a later one that we knew would fail to make the midday connection. However some distance along the way, the bus we were on passed some dazed and injured people, sitting by the side of the road, while at the foot of a steep bank on the left lay the bus we should have been on.

The journey continued, with the heat rising. The crowded bus continued on its way, the passengers all drowsing now in the midday heat. As the flies droned and the motor strained, it was impossible to stay awake. Yet as we neared Pathankot, a sudden jolt of a pothole caused my eyes to open just as we passed a sign in front of the army barracks warning all personnel to eat and drink nothing in Pathankot as hepatitis was raging. This had been our planned refreshment stop, the only place we might find a meal, but this now was out of the question. Another obstacle in our path, but again the sense that someone, some angel perhaps, was clearly protecting us. Why had I been jolted awake just then, and not before or after? There were plenty of other potholes.

Thirdly, at the end of the day, as the bus neared its destination we fell to wondering how we would find somewhere to stay in the wrong village, after dark, with no knowledge of the local language. At that moment, two young people came back from the front of the bus, to introduce themselves in perfect English and see if they could help us. Were they angels? Not by their account! Were they moved by angels? Who knows? They took us to a monastery that night, then by mountain paths the next day they led us straight to the man we had to find. This chance meeting also led to a collaboration that had its angelic side for some. By ways unimaginable in advance, we undertook a project that brought tangible, physical relief to the elderly and frail members of the Dalai Lama's immediate entourage, the ones who had administered the international aid, and therefore could take no benefit from it themselves. The fulfilment relied upon the energetic help of at least one more 'angel' on the way, who deserves to be named, the late Miriam Dean, of blessed memory.

Finally, I am always happy to join with angels, be they real or imagined, in that invocation of holiness in public prayer that uses the words of Isaiah's seraphim: *Kadosh, kadosh, kadosh, adonai tzevaot, melo kol ha-aretz kevodo*, 'Holy, holy, holy, Lord God of hosts. The whole earth is full of Thy Glory.'[4]

But three possible experiences and a susceptibility to the language of prayer do not add up to proof of any kind. Besides, personal anecdotes and reminiscences generally do not convince others. Indeed, my own reaction to angel anecdotes in the work of eighteenth-century divines was definitely one of scepticism. However, in a more general way, I subscribe to the view that our individuality is not entirely bound by bodily form, and that many influences are at work in the world, in forms unseen.

In the *Advaita* (non-dualist) tradition of India, it is taught that the individual soul is eternal, pure and free, and has only a light connection with the body and its ever-changing needs, beyond the fact of enlivening it. The soul, they say, is nourished by the pure sounds of mantra and prayer. This puts it in the same league as the Judaeo-Christian-Islamic angels, who neither eat nor drink. Yet if the soul is breathed into this body – as Judaism and Christianity certainly agree – and other bodies are all enlivened in exactly the same way, why might soul not also be poured out through the whole universe in non-bodily form? Are we, in our most essential form of soul, perhaps no different from what Marsilio Ficino called Angel?

It is easy enough to understand belief in Angel and in angels. We can see how these have operated, and how they have enjoyed a persistence not granted to certain other beliefs. But here and now, what choices are really open to us? We may stake out a firm belief in angelic beings, we may entertain a respectable degree of doubt about them, or we may deny them altogether. Too ardent a belief may indicate a degree of suggestibility, or manipulation at the hands of others. Too firm a denial sweeps away a powerful symbol of divine goodness working in the world. Somewhere in between those extremes, there is a middle ground.

For some, like Cecil Collins, angels are with us every day and may be perceived through simple courtesy.[5] For others, angels are more other-worldly. Some can associate the idea of angel with a sense of unity among all beings, even if they do so without any religious or other-worldly labelling. If we are not entirely the product of a particular time, place and circumstance, if there is kinship across a wider human family, who are all lit by the same essential spark of life, then it is reasonable to accept the possibility of something more universal finding expression through individual lives, and through the cosmos. Attempts to see and hear this universal 'something' may be what gives life to angels and accounts for their extraordinary endurance into the modern age. Listening to one another, perhaps we may still catch angels' voices – but we ourselves would be among the angels. So let Dante's words conclude this tour of angelic realms:

Consider well the breadth, behold the height
Of his eternal goodness, seeing that o'er
So many mirrors It doth shed Its light,
Yet the One abideth as It was before.
(*The Divine Comedy, Paradise*, canto 29, 142-6)

For we are the mirrors.

NOTES

Introduction

1 By some strange psychology – or perhaps just colour-coding – an angel-on-horseback consists of an oyster wrapped in bacon, while a devil-on-horseback is a bacon-wrapped prune. 'Angel cake' is as pale and as light as can be, while 'devil's food' is a chocolate sensation.

Chapter 1

1 F. Brown, S. R. Driver, C. A. Briggs, *Hebrew and English Lexicon of the Old Testament with an Appendix of Biblical Aramaic* (Oxford: Clarendon Press 1907, revised 1951 and 2000), p.521.
2 *Pesikta Rabbati*, 8, *Vayikra Rabbah*, 32:2 and other medieval Rabbinic sources.
3 Discussed in Chapter 10.
4 I refer especially to the eruption of Eyjafjallajökull in Iceland, in 2010.
5 Aquinas, *Summa Theologica*, q. 52, art. 3. D'Israeli (1766–1848, the father of Prime Minister Benjamin Disraeli) referred back to Martin Scriblerus, a fictitious writer Alexander Pope had invented for his satirical attack on the misuses of learning, *The Dunciad* (1728). Peter Marshall and Alexandra Walsham, in *Angels in the Early Modern World* (Cambridge: Cambridge University Press, 2006), p.1, attribute an earlier remark of similar tenor to William Chillingsworth in 1628, asking 'whether a million angels might not sit upon a needle's point'.
6 Swedenborg, *A Disclosure of Secrets of Heaven contained in Sacred Scripture*, Author's Introduction, and Chapter 1, sections 50 and 59. This book forms part of the *Arcana Coelestia*, 8 vols, published in Latin 1749–56; English translation (London: Swedenborg Society, 1934), and as *Secrets of Heaven*, tr. Lisa Hyatt Cooper (West Chester, PA: Swedenborg Foundation, 2007).
7 I omit for now interpretations of Genesis 3:1-19 that see the serpent who tempts Eve as a fallen angel. For a magnificent version of this, see John Milton, *Paradise Lost*, book IX.
8 In Psalm 104:3 the clouds form the chariot, and he walks upon the wings of the wind. Such variations illustrate the difficulty of interpreting poetic detail.

9   *Elohim* may refer to God, but is sometimes understood as angels. The most accurate translation here may well be 'the sons of the gods'. Some biblical commentators have proposed that we see relics in the early books of the Bible of a gradual transition from early concern with many gods to a monotheistic belief in which only one God has divine power, and any other divine beings are powerless, except as his agents.

10 Rashi is Rabbi Solomon ben Isaac who lived in Troyes in Provence at the time of the first crusade. His commentaries on the Bible and on the Talmud had, and still have, immense influence.

11 Babylonian Talmud, *Bava Metzia* 86b.

12 The English Standard Version and New International Version offer both readings.

13 Seymour Rossel, *Bible Dreams: The Spiritual Quest* (New York: SPI Books, 2003), p.93.

14 He calls the place *Machanayim*, meaning two camps, human and angelic.

15 The Greeks, too, loved paradoxes as a means of probing philosophically difficult points, e.g. Zeno of Elea whose famous puzzle about Achilles and the Tortoise is preserved in Aristotle's *Physics*. See also the book of *Problemata* attributed to Aristotle.

16 RSV translation (see Bibliography).

17 *Vayikra Rabbah,* 27:3. A *midrash* is a Jewish commentary, ancient or modern, in which a biblical text is expounded with free use of allegorical interpretation or legend. *Vayikra Rabbah* contains material from the third to tenth centuries CE.

18 KJB translation (see Bibliography).

19 'Colour of an emerald' in KJB. Other versions here have beryl, chrysolite or other variants (Ezekiel 1:16).

20 Translated as 'sapphire stone' in most versions, modern scholars consider lapis lazuli a better rendering. See also Chapter 5.

21 1 Enoch survived through use in the Ethiopic church. Its authenticity was also confirmed through finds among the Dead Sea Scrolls at Qumran. The English translation of R. H. Charles (Oxford: Oxford University Press, 1912) is widely available. 2 Enoch was probably composed in the first century CE by a Hellenized Jewish author in Alexandria or possibly Palestine. It survived in both a long and a short form, not in its original language but through a seventh-century translation into Old Slavonic. 3 Enoch probably belongs to the fifth century CE, though it purports to describe the experiences of Rabbi Ishmael ben Elisha, who flourished in the second century (90–135). Its language is Hebrew.

22 For a summary of the little that is known of Zechariah's background, see W. Gunther Plaut, *The Haftarah Commentary*, translated by Chaim Stern (New York, 1996), pp.xliv–xlv.

23 The *Haggadah* is the recitation of the Exodus, with commentary, that forms part of the Passover ritual celebrated in the home each year.

24 Named here as an angel, not an archangel.

25 Angels speak, for example, in Acts 5:20, 7:38, 8:26, 10:3, and 12:7. St Paul refers to the 'tongues of angels' in I Corinthians 13:1, and Revelation 8:13 refers specifically to the angel's 'loud voice'. Medieval discussions of angelic speech recognize the possibility that angels may implant ideas in the mind without

needing the use of the tongue or speech, though achieving the sound of angel song was the highest aspiration of some Renaissance musicians.

26 The Taino throne is among the 100 objects from the British Museum selected by its Director, Neil MacGregor, *A History of the World in 100 Objects* (London: Allen Lane, 2010), also broadcast on BBC Radio 4 during 2010. Object no. 65.

27 Some medieval mystics used visualization without such disturbances, as, for example, Richard of St Victor (d. 1173) in his *Mystical Ark* and his illustrated *Commentary on Ezekiel*. See Steven Chase, *Angelic Wisdom: the Cherubim and the Grace of Contemplation in Richard of St. Victor* (Notre Dame & London: University of Notre Dame Press, 1995). On the other hand, in some cases visual disturbances have been authenticated. For example, the paintings of El Greco (1541–1614), with their elongated luminous figures, have been ascribed to sensory disturbances after prolonged fasting. Likewise, the Kabbalistic mysticism of Abraham Abulafia (1240–91) combined breathing techniques of a kind liable to induce trance with intensely focused concentration on mantra-like names of God.

28 These include John Allegro, *The Sacred Mushroom and the Cross: A Study of the Nature and Origins of Christianity within the Fertility Cults of the Ancient Near East* (London: Hodder & Stoughton, 1970) and more recently Benny Shanon, 'Biblical Entheogens, a Speculative Hypothesis', *Time and Mind*, 2008, 1/1, pp.51–74.

29 The core of the *Rig Veda*, a collection of hymns, is thought to date from the Bronze Age (second millennium BCE). This would make it one of the world's oldest extant sacred texts, although it was not written down until later.

30 The epic poems include the *Ramayana* and the *Mahabharata*. The *Ramayana* in its original form is thought to date from the fourth or fifth century BCE; the *Mahabharata* is much harder to date. Both have many layers of composition.

31 *Vishnu Purana*, 5:114. For a full list of references, see Monier Monier-Williams, *A Sanskrit-English Dictionary* (Oxford: Clarendon Press, 1899 and many reprints), p.346.

32 According to the *Ramayana*, Apsarasas are the wives of Gandharvas. Their name suggests they are the very embodiment of mist.

33 Normally, being supreme among the gods, Zeus does nothing: he simply hears the views of all the other gods and goddesses, and then nods or withholds assent from what they propose. The Ganymede story has a precursor in Akkadian myth, where a hero-king ascends into heaven on eagles' wings. Cf. Isaiah 40:31.

Chapter 2

1 Hamond's *A Modest Enquiry into the Opinion concerning a Guardian Angel* (London: 1702) will be discussed further in Chapter 3.

2 *Paradise Lost* was first published in ten books 1667, and then expanded to twelve in 1674. Though little read nowadays, it is still considered one of the greatest works of English literature, and rightly so.

3 *Midrash Rabbah Bereishit*, 10:6. The original form of this saying, ascribed to Rabbi Simon, is 'Every single blade of grass has a *mazal* [lit. constellation] in the

heavenly firmament which strikes it and says, 'Grow!' but angels are considered to have charge of the stars and their constellations.

4	On the history and content of the Dead Sea Scrolls, see John Allegro, *The Dead Sea Scrolls* (London: Penguin Books, 1956) and Geza Vermes, *The Complete Dead Sea Scrolls in English* (London: Penguin Books, 1962, and subsequent editions). High quality digital reproductions of the material are now being been made available online by the Israel Museum. *The Songs of the Sabbath Sacrifice: a Critical Edition* was prepared by Carol Newsom and published as Harvard Semitic Studies 27 (Atlanta, GA: Scholars Press, 1985). The War Scroll is in *Discoveries in the Judaean Desert*, vol. 7, ed. by M. Baillet (Oxford: Clarendon Press, 1982) pp.12–72.

5	The Maccabean revolt against the invasion of Antiochus Epiphanes (167 BCE) is described in I and II Maccabees, which are generally included in the Apocrypha. Like other biblical books, they cannot be taken as purely factual accounts, but are nevertheless highly illuminating. For a recent account of the mix of myth and history, see Tessa Rajak, *Translation and Survival. The Greek Bible of the Ancient Jewish Diaspora* (Oxford: Oxford University Press, 2009, and 2011), esp. pp.47–50.

6	Controversy over the nature of the Qumran community continues. The original consensus, proposed Roland de Vaux, was that it was an Essene group living in the desert. This has been challenged in three ways. Some believe that the scrolls were produced by the priesthood and other mainstream groups in Jerusalem, who then carried the scrolls to the desert and buried them during the Roman war. Some have seen the Qumran community as an early Christian group. Lawrence H. Schiffman and Rachel Elior have championed the idea of a Zadokite priesthood living in exile or hiding in the desert. See Schiffman, *Qumran and Jerusalem. Studies in the Dead Sea Scrolls and the History of Judaism* (Grand Rapids, Michigan: Eerdmans, 2010). Elior in particular has linked the angelic liturgy of the *Songs of the Sabbath Sacrifice* with the calendrical concerns of the banished priesthood. See Elior, *The Three Temples: On the Emergence of Jewish Mysticism* (Oxford: Littman Library of Jewish Civilization, 2004). For a contrary view, see Peter Schäfer, 'Communion with the Angels. Qumran and the Origins of Jewish Mysticism', in *Wege mystischer Gotteserfahrung: Judentum, Christentum und Islam (Mystical Approaches to God in Judaism, Christianity and Islam)*, (Munich: Oldenbourg Wissenschaftsverlag, 2006), pp.37–66, and *The Origins of Jewish Mysticism*, 2009 (Tübingen: Mohr-Siebeck, 2009; Princeton and Oxford: Princeton University Press, 2011).

7	Nine copies of the *Songs of the Sabbath Sacrifice* were found at Qumran. Studies of its language and imagery suggest it was not just a sectarian text but enjoyed a wider use. This was confirmed when a copy was also found at Masada.

8	Difficulties in tracing the origins of the *Kedusha* prayer are discussed by Ismar Elbogen, *Jewish Liturgy a Comprehensive History*, translated by Raymond P. Scheindlin (Philadelphia: The Jewish Publication Society, revised edition, 1993), pp.54–7.

9	Newsom, *Songs*, pp.306–7. 4Q405, fragments 20-22: cols 2, 7-9 and 12-14. Brackets indicate lost or damaged text.

10 Only one set of 13 songs has so far been found, though in several copies, so either they were repeated each quarter, or the finds are incomplete.

11 Newsom, *Songs*, pp.211–12. I have adapted the layout of Newsom's text for ease of reading.

12 Newsom, *Songs*. Their angelology is discussed on pp.23–38.

13 See Peter Schäfer, *The Origins of Jewish Mysticism*; Moshe Idel, *Absorbing Perfections* (New Haven & London: Yale University Press, 2002).

14 In *The Gnostic Bible*, ed. by Willis Barnstone and Marvin Meyer (Boston & London: Shambhala, 2003), pp.414–37. Select passages are reprinted in *Essential Gnostic Scriptures* (Boston: Shambhala Publications, 2011), pp.90–8.

15 On the various traditions, see Roelof van den Broek, *The Myth of the Phoenix according to Classical and Early Christian Traditions* (Leiden: Brill 1971). On the phoenix in 2 Enoch and Baruch, see Chapter 9.

16 *The Gnostic Bible*, pp.138–65.

17 Cf. the creation of human beings partly by God and partly by the 'gods' and the 'young gods' in Plato, *Timaeus*, 41–2.

18 *The Gnostic Bible*, p.147.

19 *The Testimony of Truth*, IX, 3, 41-42, late second- or early third-century Alexandrian, in *The Nag Hammadi Library in English*, translated by members of the Coptic Gnostic Library Project of the Institute for Antiquity and Christianity, Claremont California (3rd edn, San Francisco: Harper Collins, 1990) pp.448–59.

20 *The Book of Baruch*, in *The Gnostic Bible*, pp.119–33 is quite different in both style and content from those books also called Baruch, which will be discussed in connection with journeys in the afterlife, in Chapter 9. It does, however, share with them a preoccupation with the eternal conflict of good and evil.

21 F. H. Colson & G. H. Whitaker, *Philo*, Loeb Classical Library (Cambridge MA: Harvard University Press, 1929) vol. 2, p.449.

22 Plato's *Parmenides* dialogue is essentially about the One and its relation to relative states of Being.

23 See Plotinus *Enneads*, III.8, 'On Nature and Contemplation'.

24 In its purest form, as propounded by Plotinus, the theory of emanation had only four levels. Expanded by Proclus, the system continued to grow, so that emanationist philosophers of the later Middle Ages could envisage a highly elaborate system, with each being occupying their own place and 'degree'.

25 I use the spelling daemon in English as it reflects the Greek δαιμων (*daimōn*).

26 *Tempest*, I, ii. 'O, a cherubin thou wast, that did preserve me!'

27 Ficino published a Latin translation of the complete works of Plato in 1484, of Plotinus in 1492, and of several other Neoplatonists in 1497, which appeared under the title of its first item: Iamblichus, *On the Egyptian Mysteries*. This contains works on daemons by Porphyry and Psellus, extracts from Proclus, Synesius, Priscian, other Platonists and Pythagoras. Although many have maintained that Shakespeare read no Latin and therefore had no access to Ficino's works, his ideas soon spread through French translations and other English writers. See my article 'Ficinian Ideas in the Poetry of Edmund Spenser', *Spenser Studies*, XXIV (2009), pp.73–134.

28 Porphyry, *On Abstinence from Killing Animals* edited by Gillian Clark, Ancient Commentators on Aristotle Series (London: Duckworth, 2000), II, 37. Translation modified. See also *The Letters of Marsilio Ficino*, vol. 7, letter 29.

29 For the text of this hymn, see Chapter 10.

30 Rabbi David ibn abi Zimra, Responsa, III, no. 848, cited in H. J. Zimmels, *Magicians, Theologians and Doctors. Studies in folk-medicine and folk-lore as reflected in the Rabbinical Responsa, 12th-19th centuries* (London: Edward Golston & Son, 1952), p.83. Several authorities agreed that fumigations were permitted, to drive away demons.

31 Porphyry's Greek is ambiguous here, at least in the understanding of his translator, Ficino.

32 The word used for spirit is *pneuma*. According to fully developed Neoplatonic thought as expressed later by Proclus, every being has a starry body, which is totally immaterial, a chariot (*ochema*), which allows it to move, and a spirit-body (*pneuma*) or 'breath'. Human beings also receive a fourth body, the physical body, which the daemons lack. As the human soul descends to take up residence in a body in the mother's womb, it passes down through the heavenly regions, receiving influences from whichever heavenly bodies are powerful at the time of its descent.

33 Porphyry, *On Abstinence*, II, 39-40.

34 Origen (185–254 AD) was the last theologian of antiquity who tried to harmonize Platonism and Christianity. His views on the pre-existence of the soul were branded as heretical in the fourth century, but he is now accepted as a Church Father.

35 Origen, *De principiis*, II, 1.

36 Plotinus, *Enneads*, 4, 3, *On difficulties about the Soul*, is a key text, especially section 11.

37 Modern translations have rendered these texts more accessible: Brian P. Copenhaver, *Hermetica: the Greek Corpus Hermeticum and the Latin Asclepius* (Cambridge: Cambridge University Press, 1992 and reprints); Clement Salaman, Dorine van Oyen and William Wharton, *The Way of Hermes*, (London: Duckworth, 1999); *Asclepius*, tr. Clement Salaman (London: Duckworth, 2007). For an introduction to their history, see Garth Fowden, *The Egyptian Hermes* (Cambridge: Cambridge University Press, 1986, reprinted Princeton, 1993).

38 Iamblichus (*c.*250–325), *On the Mysteries*, translated by Emma Clarke, John M. Dillon, and Jackson P. Hershbell (Atlanta: Society of Biblical Literature, 2003; Leiden: Brill, 2004) III, 18. Though born in Syria, Iamblichus probably studied under Porphyry in Rome.

39 Proclus, *Elements of Theology*, tr. E. R. Dodds, (Oxford: Clarendon Press, 1932, 1962 and reprints), propositions 7, 11, 14, 15, 32, 33 etc.

40 Constantine the African (1017–87) brought many Arabic texts to Salerno in Latin translation.

41 In Spain, cross-fertilization of ideas between cultures was a feature of intellectual life from the eighth century onwards. Forgotten works of Greek philosophy and science were revived through Hebrew and Arabic translations, inspiring Maimonides (1135–1204) and many others. In the thirteenth century, through a circle of translators assembled in Toledo by King Alfonso X of Castile, a

flow of Latin translations spread their influence more widely. Thomas Aquinas (1225–74) benefited from these. For more on Maimonides and Aquinas, see Chapter 3.

42 The author of this system was Claudius Ptolemy (90–168 CE). Before it was finally overthrown, many attempts were made to reconcile his theory with increasingly discordant observations, including the invention of complex 'epicycles'. The precise order of Mercury, Venus and the Sun also presented a difficulty, as the true nature of their orbits was not accounted for by the Ptolemaic system.

43 Maimonides appears to make this identification in his *Guide for the Perplexed*, and it became commonly accepted.

44 Lenn E. Goodman, *Avicenna* (London: Routledge, 1992). See also Henry Corbin, *Avicenna and the Visionary Recitals*, tr. by Willard Trask (New York: Pantheon Books, 1960, reprinted Dallas, 1980); Soheil M. Afnan, *Avicenna: His Life and Works*, (London: Allen & Unwin, 1958); Peter Heath, *Allegory and Philosophy in Avicenna* (Philadelphia: University of Pennsylvania Press, 1992); Shams Inati, *Ibn Sina and Mysticism* (London & New York: Kegan Paul International, 1996).

45 Dionysius, because of the erroneous identification with St Paul's convert, is sometimes known as Pseudo-Dionysius – though it might be more correct to call him Dionysius the Pseudo-Areopagite. It is also now thought that he may have been a Monophysite, believing in the single nature of Christ, his humanity being not separate but subsumed in his divinity. This was one of many competing doctrines that caused rifts within the church and it came to be regarded as a heretical position. Dionysius's reputation remained untarnished by this, because of the mistaken identity.

46 To the original group of angels, archangels, cherubim and seraphim found in Hebrew scripture, Dionysius finds in St Paul thrones, dominions, principalities, powers and virtues. See Romans 8:38, Ephesians 1:21 and Colossians 1:16-17.

47 *Celestial Hierarchy*, chapters 6-9. The most accessible edition of this work is by Colm Luibheid, *Pseudo-Dionysius, The Complete Works* (New York: Paulist Press, 1987) pp.143–91. The French edition by Maurice de Gandhillac has useful notes (Paris: Aubier, 1943).

48 Individual terms are sometimes hotly debated. Wesley Carr, *Angels and Principalities* (Cambridge: Cambridge University Press, 1981) devotes an entire monograph to the meaning of St Paul's terms, 'principalities and powers' (*hai archai kai hai exousiai*) in Colossians 2:15.

49 Dante Alighieri, *The Divine Comedy, Paradiso*, canto 28, lines 97-139.

50 See the commentary of Dorothy L. Sayers and Barbara Reynolds on Dante's *Divine Comedy, Paradiso* (London: Penguin Books, 1962; 2nd edn 1964).

51 Augustine, *City of God* and Eusebius, *Preparation for the Gospel* preserve many philosophical viewpoints by quotation, even if only to censure them.

52 The *Divine Comedy* was written during the years 1308 to 1321. It circulated widely in manuscript and was among the earliest books printed (Foligno, 1472). A major commentary by Cristoforo Landino was printed with it in Florence, 1481. For an English translation, the Penguin edition of Sayers and Reynolds is among the best. Parallel Italian-English editions include one by Israel Gollancz, Temple Classics (London: J.M.Dent & Sons, 1896) and online versions, such as the Princeton Dante Project.

53 The literature on Ficino is now vast, but the best introduction to his thought is through his own letters of which there are twelve books. Eight of these are translated so far, and the remaining four in preparation: *The Letters of Marsilio Ficino,* translated by Members of the Language Department of the School of Economic Science (London: Shepheard-Walwyn, 1975–).

54 Marsilio Ficino, *Commentary on St Paul's Epistles,* in his Latin *Opera Omnia* (Basel, 1576, reprinted several times in facsimile), p.425; an English translation is in preparation for I Tatti Renaissance Library, Harvard University Press. This passage, which appears to be quite radical, nevertheless has its roots in the work of Dionysius, and reflects the practice of some monastic communities, e.g. Franciscan and Camaldolensian. Cf. Dionysius, *De mystica theologia,* I, 1 (which Ficino translated) and Bonaventure, *The Soul's Journey into God,* 7.5.

55 Ficino, *Commentary on St Paul's Epistles,* p.425.

56 *Commentary,* p.430. Cf. Ficino, *Platonic Theology,* translated and edited by Michael J. B. Allen and James Hankins, I Tatti Renaissance Library, 6 vols (Cambridge MA and London: Harvard University Press: 2001–06), 3.1.13-16.

57 *Platonic Theology,* 1.1.1-3, and throughout the first book.

58 For motionless angels, see *Platonic Theology,* 1.5.2-5; for multiplication of angels, 1.5.10-11. Cf. Avicenna, *Metaphysics,* 9.3.

59 Ficino, *Philebus Commentary,* tr. M. J. B. Allen (Los Angeles: University of California Press, 1975; repr. Tempe: MRTS, 2000), ch. 26; Dionysius, *Divine Names,* IV.8.

60 His surviving sermons will also be published with the St Paul Commentary, see note 54 above.

61 Ficino, *De Christiana religione,* 14. An English translation of this work is still awaited. It can be found in Latin in Ficino's *Opera omnia,* pp.1–77, or in a modern Italian edition by Roberto Zanzarri (Rome: Città Nuova, 2005). Ficino's own Tuscan version was printed in 1474. In 1578, Guy Le Fèvre de la Boderie published a French translation in Paris.

62 Ficino, *Letters,* vol. 7, letter 5, entitled 'How each person has a guardian angel'. The daemons have 12 princes, and are also under planetary influence. Human souls are even more numerous than the daemons. See also Chapter 10 (p.184).

63 Cf. *Platonic Theology,* 18.8.12.

64 *Platonic Theology,* 18.2.2. Plato had made much of the two 'means', arithmetic and harmonic, which Ficino also explores in his commentary on Plato's *Timaeus,* especially in chapter 28. See *All Things Natural. Ficino on Plato's Timaeus,* translated by Arthur Farndell (London: Shepheard-Walwyn, 2010), pp.47–53.

65 *On the Sun* (1492). In the biblical account of creation, Ficino notes that when God creates heaven and earth conceptually, in Genesis 1:1, angelic light is already present in that conception. It comes into being when he says 'Let there be light' (Genesis 1:3). The Sun is created on the fourth day (Genesis 1:14-18). St Augustine had already equated angels with light (*City of God,* XI, 9) and similar discussions are found in the work of Jewish and Islamic philosophers with Platonic leanings.

66 According to St Jerome each person has from birth an angel commissioned to guard him or her. The idea was widely accepted, although not an article of faith.

67 Ficino, *Letters*, vol. 7, letter 5.

68 Ficino, *On the Sun*, ch. 12.

69 Ficino strenuously opposed the idea of a collective soul being proposed by followers of Averroes (1126–98) in the University of Padua. Despite sharing a strong sense of the unity of creation, and supporting the idea of a universal world soul or angelic mind, Ficino defends immortality of the individual soul.

70 Traherne's reading notes on Ficino are in the British Library, MS Burney 126 f.1, *Platonis speculations practicae, a Ficino breviter digestae*.

71 Traherne, *Wonder*, see Chapter 5 below.

72 Alcott, *How Like an Angel Came I Down* (Boston: James Monroe & Co, 1836; abridged edition Lindisfarne Books, 1991). Alcott was the close friend of Ralph Waldo Emerson, and father of Louisa May Alcott, author of *Little Women*.

73 Kevin P. Sullivan's *Wrestling with Angels* (Leiden: Brill, 2004) analyses ancient Jewish and Christian literature on the relationship between humans and angels. For a survey of angelic interpretations of Christ, see Charles A. Gieschen, *Angelomorphic Christology. Antecedents and Early Evidence* (Leiden: Brill, 1998).

74 The word for angels here is *elohim*. Some Hebrew commentators have therefore taken *elohim* in its other sense, giving the meaning 'scarcely lower than God'.

75 *Sanhedrin* 93a, and repeated in *Midrash Tanhuma, Vayikra*, 1. Since the Talmudic passage is in Hebrew, not Aramaic, it is probably very early (first to third centuries CE).

76 *Authorised Daily Prayer Book* with Commentary (London: 1946 edition) p.432. Hertz comes down firmly on Maimonides's side in the debate about whether angels are purely allegorical. See Chapter 3.

77 Adin Steinsaltz, *The Thirteen Petalled Rose. A Discourse on the Essence of Jewish Existence and Belief*, translated by Yehuda Hanegbi (New York: Basic Books, 2006) pp.7–8. Steinsaltz proposes a modified form of Neoplatonic emanationist thinking, based on the *Zohar*, a key text in Jewish mystical thinking.

78 See Gregory of Nyssa, *Homily on Psalm 2* and Daniélou, *The Angels and their Mission*, pp.48 and 113.

79 Reported by Thietmar of Merseburg, and related by Henry Mayr-Harting in *Perceptions of Angels in History*, his Inaugural Lecture as Regius Professor of Ecclesiastical History in Oxford (Oxford: Clarendon Press, 1998) p.8.

80 For the angels in *Paradiso*, see especially cantos 28 and 29.

81 Brown, Driver and Briggs, *Lexicon*, p.521.

82 Swedenborg, *Secrets of Heaven*, Introduction.

83 The reply of the oracle to a delegation from Oenoanda is quoted in Copenhaver, *Hermetica*, p.xxv. Apollo is described in monotheistic terms as 'self-born, without a name, has many names, and dwells in fire'. For a full account of the Oracle at Claros, see Robin Lane Fox, *Pagans and Christians in the Mediterranean World from the Second Century CE to the Conversion of Constantine*, (London: Viking, 1986; Penguin, 2006), pp.168–77.

Chapter 3

1   Steven Pinker, *The Better Angels of Our Nature: The Decline of Violence in History and its Causes* (London: Allen Lane, 2011).

2   As a devotional practice this probably dates back to the eleventh century, but gradually the role of the angelus bell increased, and came to mark three sets of prayer at 6 am, noon and 6 pm.

3   Matthew Fox and Rupert Sheldrake, *The Physics of Angels. Exploring the Realm where Science and Spirit Meet* (San Francisco: Harper Collins, 1996).

4   Other interpretations of the plural form include a deliberative (Abravanel), an Aramaic grammatical idiosyncrasy (Luzzatto); as God and Earth acting together (Nachmanides) or God addressing the Torah (*Pirke de R. Eliezer*, 11). In the *Epistle of Barnabas* 5:5 and 6:12 (first or second century) God is represented as consulting Christ. In other Christian commentators the plural is simply considered the natural form for a triune deity to use. Similar considerations apply to the moment when God first speaks, at Genesis 1:3. To whom is God speaking?

5   Although Rabbi Eliezer lived during the first and second centuries BCE, the work ascribed to his name dates from the eighth century CE.

6   Rashi considered that man was like God in having discernment; Maimonides, like God in having reason; ibn Ezra, in having a soul that is immortal and completely fills its body.

7   Reported by Ficino, *Platonic Theology*, 4.1.11. The souls are themselves then instrumental in forming matter.

8   Maimonides, *Guide for the Perplexed*, tr. M. Friedländer (London: Society of Hebrew Literature, 1881; revised Routledge, 1904; New York: Dover, 1956 and London: Kegan Paul, 2006), II, 8. For the spheres themselves, see II, 4. See also the edition of S. Pines (Chicago: University of Chicago Press, 1963 and 1974). The *Guide*, written in Arabic, was translated into Hebrew by Maimonides' pupil Samuel ibn Tibbon.

9   *Guide for the Perplexed*, II, 4. His discussion of the spheres at the beginning of Book II wrestles with the discrepancies between Aristotle's *De caelo*, Ptolemaic astronomy and the subsequent observations of Arab astronomers, all of which are also to be set against religious teachings. Astronomy itself was in a state of perplexity, and of course it was not yet appreciated that stars themselves undergo changes in form.

10   *Hilchot Yesodei ha Torah* forms part of Book I of the *Code of Law*. Unlike the *Guide*, this work was written in Hebrew. The English edition from Yale University Press does not yet include Book I. I have therefore used the translation of Immanuel M. O'Levy (1993, available online at Jewish Virtual Library, Fordham University and several other host sites), with corrections and additions of my own, with the patient and generous assistance of Rabbi Yuval Keren.

11   This can also be translated as 'he makes his angels like the winds' and Maimonides is insisting that again this is only analogy. An angel cannot be turned into a wind, or vice versa.

12   Sometimes rendered *chayyot* or *hayyot*.

13   See Chapter 7.

14   See Chapter 5.

15 I have found no commentary on this.

16 In his discussion of these passages, Menachem Kellner takes the angels' total number as ten, not ten ranks, suggesting that Maimonides was challenging those who think angels innumerable. However this last paragraph seems clearly to suggest plurality in each of the ten levels. Kellner, *Maimonides' Confrontation with Mysticism* (Oxford: Littman Library, 2006), pp.274–6.

17 Nachmanides *Commentary on the Torah*, at Genesis 18:1. Nachmanides is also known as Ramban, and Maimonides as Rambam. Their different viewpoints form a counterpoint that was highly fruitful for successive generations of students, and their underlying differences of interpretation persist.

18 'Blessings of the Shema', *Daily Prayer Book of the United Hebrew Congregations of the Commonwealth*, fourth edition, with new commentary and translations by Rabbi Lord Sacks (London: Collins, 2007), pp.63–5. The recitation here of the triple 'Holy' formula is in addition to that of the *Kedusha* prayer (see Chapter 6).

19 Maimonides, *Guide for the Perplexed*, III, 28 and II, 34.

20 Citing *Bereshit Rabbah*, 10.

21 All these arguments are in *Guide for the Perplexed*, II, 10.

22 *Guide for the Perplexed*, II, 6.

23 *Ibid.*, and see above.

24 The title 'Doctor of the Catholic Church' is granted posthumously, and only after canonization. There are 33 in all. Thomas was declared a saint in 1323, Bonaventure rather later, in 1484. Both were declared Doctors of the church in the sixteenth century.

25 This had been proved at Questions 14:8 and 19:4.

26 *Summa Theologica*, Ia, 51, 2 ad 1.

27 Bonaventure, *The Life of St Francis*, Prologue. 'Angel of peace', Isaiah 33:7, although the Hebrew *mal'akhei* and the Greek *angeloi* have been lost in most English translations, transformed into 'ambassadors of peace'. For angels' food (manna), Psalm 78:25.

28 St Augustine devotes several chapters to angels in his *City of God*, especially XI, 9 to XII, 9. See also *The Literal Meaning of Genesis*, especially VIII, 24-5 and XI, 17-27.

29 Giorgio Benigno Salviati (Juraj Dragišić) from Srebrenica, Bosnia, came to Italy from Ragusa (Dubrovnik) in 1463. He defended both Ficino and Savonarola at Rome in the 1490s, and later Reuchlin (1518). His first writing on angels was in 1488–9, a short unpublished *Summa de angelis* written for Lorenzo di Pierfrancesco de' Medici. During the late 1490s he wrote a longer work of nine books, usually listed by its incipit 'de natura caelestium spiritum quos angelos uocarnus' (Florence, 1499). This is the *De natura angelica* referred to here.

30 Ficino, *Platonic Theology*, 13.2.10.

31 Sandfurt was born near Antwerp and educated partly by the Dutch humanist Murmellius, but he served most of his active life in Germany. He was a vigorous anti-Catholic polemicist. His *De angelis quaestiones ex sacra scriptura XX* is held by the British Library, shelfmark 4371.aaaa.49 (Guglielmus Santphurdius). It can also be read online at the website of the Bavarian State Library, http://nbn-resolving.de/urn:nbn:de:bvb:12-bsb00029786-8.

32 Ten volumes seem to have been planned, but only six, or possibly seven appeared.

33 Rosselli, *Pymander Mercurii Trismegisti*, vol. 2 (1585), *De spiritu sanctu et angelis*, pp.323–5.

34 *Ibid.*, p.401.

35 The meaning of *Pymander* has been much debated, and modern scholarship has moved away from a Greek etymology, based on 'shepherd' and 'man', to an Egyptian origin meaning 'understanding of Ra'.

36 C. Scheibler, *Theologia naturalis et Angelographia, hoc est, summaria repetitio totius doctrinæ metaphysicæ de Deo et Angelis*, Marburg, 1632.

37 Citing the commentary of Langius on Justin Martyr, he claims that Hermes calls them 'angels', making him one of the Christians rather than one of the Ethnics. The Ethnics would then be Aristotle, Maimonides and Avicenna. However it reveals that he has not been reading Hermes in the original, since they are mainly called daemons there, not angels.

38 Jacob Musselius of Pomerania, *Disputatio Pneumatica de Angelographia*, 3 June 1625 (Wittenberg: Thamm, 1625).

39 His thesis was printed by the house of Caspar Chemlin. The Academy of Marburg re-merged with its breakaway academy of Giessen for a while. The teachers of Giessen remained Lutheran when those of Marburg turned Calvinist in 1606. However in 1625 they were operating jointly again.

40 The argument that they are simply movements in the human mind is attributed here to the Sadducees in Acts 23:8, where the Sadducees are said to deny resurrection, angel and spirit. Since Sadducee writings do not deny angels or spirit, it has been argued by some that the denial intended was probably related to resurrection through angels or spirit. Discussions on this are summarized in Sullivan, *Wrestling with Angels*, pp.21–2.

41 Mogius's definitions, thesis 31. This meaning of Belial follows *Sanhedrin* 111b and Rashi, who derive the word from *b'li-ol*. More widely recognized nowadays is the derivation from *b'li-ya'al*, without worth (BDB, p.116). Belial is a name for one of the princes of hell, the embodiment of wickedness. *Poneroi* is a Greek word meaning 'good-for-nothings'.

42 *Synopsis purioris theologiæ, disputationibus quinquaginta duabus comprehensa ac conscripta* per J. Polyandrum, A. Rivetum, A. Walæum, A. Thysium (Leiden: 1625). These four were closely involved in the Synod of Dort that shaped Dutch Calvinism during the long struggle against Spanish rule. For this reason the Academy at Leiden is often considered a bastion of progressive religious thought.

43 Clemens Brancasius, *De angelis* (Naples: 1646), p.613. Maimonides understood Aristotle to have said fifty, of which he, Maimonides, admitted only ten as real Intelligences.

44 Hamond, *A Modest Enquiry* (London: 1702), p.7. Origen, *Contra Celsum*, 1.8.

45 *Ibid.*, p.8.

46 *Ibid.*, p.24, quoting Philolaus (fifth century BCE) and St Bernard.

47 After a few years, Hamond became a non-conformist minister and set up a boarding school of his own.

48 The title *Angelographia* (angel treatise) was a popular one, used also by Otto Casmann (1597), Jacob Musselius (1625), Christoph Scheibler (1632), and the

American Puritan minister, Increase Mather (1696). Mather was famous for his part in the Salem witch trials and as president of Harvard. His *Angelographia* is a collection of sermons on angels.

49 R. Saunders, ed. G. Hamond, *Angelographia*, 1.1.3, p.8.

50 *Angelographia*, 1.1.7, pp.10–11.

51 *Ibid.*, ch. 9, pp.182–203.

52 *Ibid.*, ch. 12, pp.236–53. Saunders grants one exception: Joseph was angelically instructed to marry Mary, although the fact that she was already with child made such marriage unlawful.

53 *The Seraphick World or Celestial Hierarchy* etc. Being an account of the Nature and Ministry, the different employments, Ranks and Stations of Angels and Archangels etc. with some Remarks in favour of our late erected Charity Schools or Orphans, the Charge of Angels (London: J. Baker of Paternoster Row, 1714).

54 *Seraphick World*, pp.11–12.

55 *Ibid.*, p.16

56 *Ibid.*, p.18.

57 Isaac Ambrose, *Ministration of, and Communion with Angels*, (Berwick, 1797 edn), pp.39 and 55. This seems to be the first separate printing, but it had already been published six times with other works of his.

58 *A Service of Angels* saw three editions but then lay largely forgotten (Cambridge: Deighton & Co, 1894, 1896; Deighton Bell, 1903). However a reprint is now available (Charleston, SC: Bibliobazaar, 2010).

59 Latham cites it as the view of Frederick Denison Maurice (1805–72) a leading educationalist and a friend. Maurice was a theologian, Christian Socialist and Professor of History, Literature, and then Theology at King's College, London. Latham quotes from Maurice's theological works. Latham himself was Senior Tutor at Trinity Hall, Cambridge from 1855, and Master from 1888 until his death in 1902. He introduced many successful reforms.

60 Alfred Edersheim published his *Life and Times of Jesus the Messiah* in 1890.

61 *A Service of Angels*, p.60.

62 *Ibid.*, p.145.

63 *Ibid.*, p.122.

64 *Ibid.*, p.168.

65 Alfred, Lord Tennyson, *Wages*, 1868.

66 Latham, *A Service of Angels*, p.174.

67 *Ibid.*, p.170.

68 It certainly kept Latham in vigour to the age of 81 as Master of Trinity Hall.

69 It uses a story written by Annie Collins for *The Temperance Mirror* (the penny monthly of the National Temperance League), in which whispering angels inhabit two trees by a brook where a young girl, Madeline, seeks solace from the suffering caused by her father's drunkenness. Burnham interwove with the story a selection of existing hymns and it was published for use in churches, Sunday Schools and temperance meetings (London: Weekes & Co, no date). Burnham compiled a number of such services.

70 The Compton cemetery chapel was built and decorated by local workers under Mary Watts's guidance. They had been trained in the clay-modelling classes she

had begun in her home, as part of the Home Arts and Industries Association within the Arts and Crafts movement promoted by John Ruskin.

71 Notable stained-glass angels by Burne-Jones (1833–98) and William Morris (1834–96) from the early period of their association with John Ruskin (1819–1900) can be found in several Cumbrian churches, including St James at Staveley (1873), Troutbeck (1873), St Martin's, Brampton (1878–80); he made angels for the lancet windows at St Margaret's, Rottingdean in Sussex (1893), and the series reached its glorious conclusion in the Gladstone memorial chapel of St Deiniol's Church in Hawarden in Flintshire, North Wales (1898). His designs continued to be used after his death, as at Lanercost Priory (1912).

72 *The Zohar*, Pritzker edition, 6 vols to date (Stanford, CA: Stanford University Press, 2004–), translated by Daniel C. Matt, vol. 3, pp.246–7. Authorship of the *Zohar* (Book of Splendour), a foundational text of Kabbalah, is deliberately concealed behind the fiction that it was written by Simon bar Yochai in the second century CE, under Roman persecution. It is now generally accepted to be the work of Moses de Leon (*c*.1250–1350) in Spain. It represents a reaction against the scientific rationality and allegorical readings promoted by followers of Maimonides.

73 Nāṣir-I Khusraw, from the introduction to *Kitāb Jāmiʿ al-ḥikmatayn* (Book joining the Two Wisdoms), translated by Latimah Parvin Peerwani, in *An Anthology of Philosophy in Persia*, ed. by Seyyed Hossien Nasr with Mehdi Aminrazavi, 3 vols (London: I.B. Tauris, 2008), vol. 2, pp.318–23. Khusraw was an outstanding philosopher and poet. After his conversion to the Ismaili form of Islam, he lived and taught first in Cairo, then in Afghanistan.

74 See Chapter 11.

75 Henry Corbin translated this in *Avicenna and the Visionary Recital*, 3 vols (Teheran, 1952–4; English translation by Willard R. Trask, New York: Routledge & Kegan Paul, 1960; reprinted Princeton University Press, 1990), pp.137–59 in the 1990 edition. Corbin's version, with minor corrections, is now reprinted in *An Anthology of Philosophy in Persia*, vol. 1, pp.312–20. Another version of Avicenna's tale gained immense popularity, written as a philosophical novel under the same title, by Abu Bakr Muhammad Ibn Tufail (1105–85) better known to the west as Abubacer, in Andalusia. This version was translated into Latin (1671) and English (1708). It inspired many Enlightenment philosophers, and prompted Daniel Defoe to write *Robinson Crusoe*. A recent edition is by Lenn E. Goodman, *Ibn Tufayl's Hayy Ibn Yaqzān: A Philosophical Tale* (London: Octagon Press, 1982 and reprints).

76 Tr. Salaman.

77 Tr. Salaman.

78 Tr. Copenhaver.

79 *Corpus Hermeticum*, 16:15. Tr. Salaman.

80 *Corpus Hermeticum*, 1:26. Copenhaver notes the rarity of the term *angelos* in the *Hermetica*. Here they are called 'powers'.

81 Porphyry's great opponent Iamblichus, says that the 'anger of the gods' is a metaphor for the effects of our turning away from them. *De Mysteriis*, I, 13.

82 *On Abstinence*, II, 42.

83 The various versions of the Egyptian *Book of the Dead* are replete with similar creatures in the realm between earth and heaven. See Chapter 9.

84 The King James Version translates *se'irim* here as satyrs; other versions have wild goats capering. But I am indebted for this translation and discussion of other passages in this section to the generosity and scholarship of Rabbi Dr Naphtali Brawer.

85 Lilith is sometimes understood as a primordial being who broke away from the divine plan, or as one of the *shedim* (see below). In medieval folklore she was regarded as Adam's first wife, who later mated with the fallen Archangel Samael. Babies were to be protected from Lilith by amulets.

86 Mishnah, *Avot* 5:6.

87 An alternative derivation from Akkadian *šedu* suggests protective powers. This is not a contradiction if they were seen as foreign gods, protecting only their own.

88 Nachmanides, *Commentary on Leviticus*, 17:7.

89 Babylonian Talmud, *Berachot* 6a.

90 Joseph Caro, *Shulchan Aruch* (The Set Table), *Orach Chayim*, 90:6. Written in Safed in 1563, this book rapidly became an authoritative source on Jewish law.

91 Not all agree whether the goat was supposed to remain alive, but our interest lies in the tradition of Azazel, not the fate of the goat. The term 'scapegoat' was coined by William Tyndale in 1530 for the first English translation of the Bible. In its original context it means the recipient of the acknowledged guilt of the whole community. It is more commonly used today to indicate someone who can be blamed for misfortune.

92 *Torah with Rashi*, Sapirstein edition (New York: Mesorah Publications, 1994), Leviticus, p.196.

93 *Ibid.*

94 Ibn Ezra (1089–1167) biblical commentator, poet and philosopher. Born in Spain, he travelled to France, Italy, England and possibly the Holy Land.

95 This story is ascribed to Rabbi Horowitz of Dzikov and is quoted in *Forms of Prayer: Machzor*, Reform Synagogues of Great Britain (1985 edn), p.830.

96 Apulieus (*c.*123–180 CE), *On the God of Socrates*; Plotinus, *Enneads*, III, 4, 'On tutelary spirits'; Iamblichus, *On the Mysteries*.

97 Iamblichus, *On the Mysteries*, I, 5; II, 2-3; IV; 2-3; IX, 6-10.

98 *Isis the Prophetess to her son Horus*, cited in Copenhaver, *Hermetica*, p.xxxvi.

99 This tale is related in Paphnutius, *Histories of the Monks of Upper Egypt*, an early fifth-century text, translated by Tim Vivian (Kalamazoo: Cistercian Publications, 1993), pp.85–97. The same work also relates numerous encounters with angels, as does the *Life of Onophrius* published with it. See also Helen Waddell, *The Desert Fathers* (London: Constable, 1936 and several reprints).

100 It is thought that the form 'genie' came into English through French. The translators of the *Thousand and One Nights* adapted an existing French word, *genie* (derived from *genius*) to render the Arabic *jinn*, since there were obvious similarities of meaning. *Djinn* is sometimes found as an alternative spelling for *jinn*.

101 The difficulty is sometimes explained away with reference to Arabic grammar. But in pursuing this question I also came across an undercurrent of popular belief

102 Witelo's mother was Polish, his father Thuringian. He studied at Padua from 1260, and became a close friend of William of Moerbecke, famous for his translations of Greek philosophy and science. Witelo's *Perspectiva* was printed in 1535 and again in 1572 together with Al-Haytham's work.

in the presence and power of jinn including a claim of photographic evidence for these invisible beings. For more on Iblis, see Chapter 11.

103 This manuscript, a sole survivor, was published in facsimile by E. and G. S. Battisti, *Le macchine cifrate di Giovanni Fontana* (Milan: Arcadia Edizioni, 1984).

104 John Dee, *The Mathematicall Praeface to the Elements of Geometrie of Euclid of Megara*, (London: 1570), fol. B.j verso. This and other such devices are discussed by Sven Dupré, 'Optical Games, Magic and Imagination', in *Spirits Unseen. The Representation of Subtle Bodies in Early Modern European Culture* ed. by Christine Göttler and Wolfgang Neuber (Leiden: Brill, 2008), pp.71–90.

105 *The Disoverie of Witchraft* (London: 1584, reprinted 1886), VII, 15 (p.122). Spelling modified. Scot claimed to have consulted no less than 212 works in Latin and 23 in English in compiling his work, which was intended to expose the practice of witchcraft as deception or illusion.

106 It was Rilke who said of Klee in 1921, 'Even if you hadn't told me he plays the violin, I would have guessed that on many occasions his drawings were transcriptions of music.'

107 Walter Benjamin, *Theses on the Philosophy of History*, section 9, in *Illuminations* (1940).

108 The full text of this poem shows that it was written specifically for the *Angelus Novus* painting, which Benjamin had bought from Klee. See *The Correspondence of Walter Benjamin and Gershom Scholem*, 1932–1940, ed. by Gary Smith (Harvard University Press, 1992), p.79.

109 Angel paintings by Collins include a crystalline, light-filled *Angel of Resurrection* (1953), a lithograph of three *Angels* (1960), the *Angel of Flowing Light* (1968), and an angel of love flying over a hilly landscape (*Divine Land*, 1979). One of his last canvases, *The Music of Dawn* (1988) shows a priestess against a background suggestive of angel wings. Several of these works are held by The Tate Gallery in London.

110 John Allitt, *The Magic Mirror. Thoughts and Reflections on Cecil Collins* (London: Temenos Academy, 2010), pp.55–8. Twenty-three of his angel paintings are reproduced in Judith Collins, *Cecil Collins: a retrospective exhibition* (London: Tate Gallery, 1989).

111 Maxwell, *Seven Angels* (London: Oberon Books, 2011). Other operas concerning angels include Sergei Prokofiev's *Fiery Angel* completed in 1927 (Opus 37). This full length opera based on a novel of the same title by Valery Bryusov (1908) also met with unfavourable reactions at the time but has since been revived. It is more concerned with alchemy and the summoning of spirits than with angels themselves, being an adaptation of events in sixteenth-century Germany based on the life of philosopher-alchemist Agrippa of Nettesheim.

Chapter 4

1 A hymn, for the last day of Passover, composed in Italy, quoted in Leon J. Weinberger, *Jewish Hymnography*, London, 2010, p.153.

2 For more on the divine throne, see the second half of Chapter 7.

3 On Rublev's icon, see Paul Evdokimov, *The Art of the Icon: a theology of beauty*, translated by Fr. Steven Bigham (Redondo Beach, Calif: Oakwood Press, 1990); Leonid Ouspensky and Vladimir Lossky, *The Meaning of Icons* translated by G. E. H. Palmer and E. Kadloubovsky (Boston, 1956); Mikhail V. Alpatov, *Andrey Rublev* (Moscow: Iskusstvo, 1972).

4 See, for example, Bogdan Gabriel Bucur, *Angelomorphic Pneumatology. Clement of Alexandria and other Early Christian Witnesses*, (Leiden: Brill, 2009).

5 St Jerome, in his *Preface to the Commentary on Matthew*, links each animal with the starting point of each gospel – the manhood of Christ, the lion in the wilderness, the calf of Zacharias's sacrifice, and the eagle's wings for John. Other identifications were advanced by St Augustine and St Irenaus, but St Jerome's is more widely adopted.

6 *De consensu evangelistarum*, 1.6.9.

7 Pliny, *Natural History*, X, 3. The analogy with Christ is not perfect: in Pliny, any chick whose eyes began to water or blink was rejected from the nest.

8 The large number of surviving manuscripts indicates the great popularity of Le Clerc's Norman-French *Bestiary*. It drew on many ancient and medieval sources. St Augustine, also citing Pliny, thought the eagle's beak grew so large it prevented the eagle from eating in old age; it then struck its beak on a rock to break off the overgrown part, and could then eat and be reinvigorated (*Exposition on Psalm 103*).

9 Dionysius, *Celestial Hierarchy*, XV, 337a.

10 See, for example, the Noh play *Hagoromo*.

11 Sandalphon is the name given to the Prophet Elijah on his assumption into heaven. Some derive the name from the Greek *syn* and *adelphon*, meaning mean co-brother (to Metatron). A Kabbalistic derivation from *sandal* and *fon* means 'matter in process of becoming a face'.

12 According to Kabbalistic interpretation, and St Jerome (repeated by Dante), the creation of angels predates the rest of the creation. As regards reproduction, I am here discounting the disputed episode of the Nephilim (see Chapter 11), even though it is the foundation for much apocalyptic literature and for Danielle Trussoni's recent novel, *Angelology* (London: Michael Joseph, 2010).

13 John Chrysostom 'Ad eos qui scandalizati sunt', III, *Patrologia Graeca*, 52:184.

14 Chrysostom, 'Homily on Isaiah', 6:1, *Patrologia Graeca*, 56:137.

15 The famous classical winged-victory sculpture, the *Nike of Samothrace* (*c*.190 BCE) also inspired many paintings, sculptures and monuments in the nineteenth and twentieth centuries, with angelic overtones, from Abbott Handerson Thayer's *The Virgin* of 1892–3 to decorative elements by Frank Lloyd Wright.

16 Henry Mayr-Harting, *Perceptions of Angels in History* (Oxford: Clarendon Press, 1998), p.16.

17 Recorded by Caesarius of Heisterbach, whose *Dialogus magnus visionum ac miraculorum* was a favourite sourcebook for medieval preachers. Quoted in

Mayr-Harting, p.18. Lorenzo Monaco and Sandro Botticelli paint numerous female angels, often as musicians.

18   Aquinas, *Summa Theologiae*, Part I, Q 51, Article 2, reply to Objection 3. In a sermon on *Star of the Magi*, Ficino describes how the angel Gabriel was able to form a comet by condensing light and air around his own body. Ficino, *Letters*, vol. 6, Appendix, p.64.

19   Gregory, *Moralia*, II, 3. This observation is also drawn from Mayr-Harting's short but profound work cited above.

20   See Chapter 1, note 20.

21   Moses and Elijah were talking with him, both of whom had been raised to heaven without experience of death.

22   By birth Persian, Al-Qazwīnī travelled widely, settling eventually in Baghdad. He wrote in Arabic, and his works were popular, and frequently translated. Several beautiful manuscripts have survived, and deserve to be better known.

23   Donne (1573–1631), *Air and Angels*.

Chapter 5

1   *Zohar*, tr. Daniel Matt, vol. 3, p.397: *Va-yhi*, 1:231b. 'In this place', means Standing beneath the *shekhinah*, God's presence.

2   *Zohar*, vol. I, p.142, *Be-Reshit* 1:18b.

3   See Alice Wood, *Of Wings and Wheels. A Synthetic Study of the Biblical Cherubim* (Berlin & New York: Walter de Gruyter, 2008).

4   Brown, Driver and Briggs, *Hebrew and English Lexicon*.

5   *Garuda* is generally depicted with a man's body, a white face, red wings, an eagle's beak and a crown. He is described as massive and strong, large enough to block out the sun.

6   Babylonian Talmud, *Sukkah* 5b; and *Chagigah* 13b. Maimonides also takes up this explanation in Part III of *The Guide for the Perplexed*.

7   Driver, Regius Professor of Hebrew and Canon of Christ Church at Oxford from 1883 to 1914, was a major contributor to the *Lexicon*.

8   Confusingly, the chief architect of Solomon's temple sent by King Hiram was also called Hiram, but was the son of a Hebrew woman by a Tyrian father. A surviving sarcophagus shows the winged sphinxes of King Hiram's throne. Egyptian sphinxes do not have wings.

9   Described and illustrated in, *Of Wings and Wheels,* pp.177 and 237, this figure has been variously interpreted. Other similar figures have been found in Samaria, probably belonging to the followers of Baal.

10   Josephus, *Antiquities of the Jews*, VIII, 3.3.

11   JPS translation.

12   That God dwells between, or sits enthroned upon, the cherubim is mentioned repeatedly, e.g. I Samuel 4:4; II Samuel 6:2; II Kings 19:15; Isaiah 37:16; Psalms 80:2 and 99:1.

13   There are of course many other interpretations of the event.

14   Philo, *On the Cherubim*, VII-IX.

15 The length of the cubit varied from place to place, and at different times, but the biblical cubit is thought to have been approx. 52 cm (20 inches). It was based upon the length of a man's forearm, including the hand.

16 'Thou shalt not make unto thee a graven image, nor any likeness of any thing that is in the heavens above, or that is on the earth beneath, or that is in the waters under the earth. Thou shalt not bow down to them, nor serve them ...' Exodus 20:4-5. For the almond and pomegranate as decoration, see Exodus 25:33, 28:34, 37:19 and 39:26. Palm trees and flowers are in I Kings 6:29-35, with the addition of lions as an afterthought in v.36. For the oxen, lions and cherubim on the water features in front of the temple, see I Kings 7 and II Chronicles 4.

17 For a view of the calf as a footstool for God, rather than an idolatrous substitute, see W. Gunther Plaut, *The Torah: A Modern Commentary* (New York, 1981), p.650. The brazen serpent was originally prescribed and beneficial (Numbers 21:9).

18 Cf. Jeremiah 3:16-17.

19 F. N. Lindsay, *Kerubim in Semitic Religion and Art* (Columbia, 1912, repr. 2008) from illustrations of E. B. Tylor, 'The winged figures of the Assyrian and other ancient monuments', *Proceedings of the Society of Biblical Archeology* 12 (1890) pp.383–93. For another interpretation, see George Sarton, 'The Artifical Fertilization of Date-Palms in the Time of Ashur-Nasir-Pal B.C. 885-860', *Isis*, Vol. 21, No. 1 (Apr., 1934), pp.8–13.

20 The rabbis puzzled over this too. How does a cherub's face differ from the face of a man, if a cherub is 'like a child' (*ke-ruv*). They resolved it by referring to a large face and a small face. Babylonian Talmud, *Chagigah* 13b. The Kabbalists then extended the notion to being like father and son. *Zohar*, 1:18b, p.143.

21 This name *Kevar* means 'joining'; it is generally now taken to refer to a great canal cut by Nebuchadnezzar between a minor river and the Euphrates, where he held the captives from Jerusalem. The consonants of the river's name *k-v-r* happen to be an inversion of those of the word *keruv*, but any connection drawn from this would be pure conjecture.

22 Daniel I. Block, *The Book of Ezekiel. Chapters 1-24* (Grand Rapids: Eerdmans, 1997), p.102.

23 JPS translation. KJV has 'the anointed cherub'. See also p.200 above.

24 Alice Wood, *Of Wings and Wheels*.

25 Yuval Keren, *Exploring chapter 1 of Ezekiel in relation to Gudea's Dream as a Text supporting the building of the Temple*, unpublished thesis, Leo Baeck College, 2005.

26 Quoted in Newsom, *Songs of the Sabbath Sacrifice*, p.30.

27 Bonaventure, *The Soul's Journey into God*, ch. 5.

28 This abbey was founded in the twelfth century by Abelard's adversary, William of Champeaux.

29 For a detailed account of these developments, with illustrations, see Charles Dempsey, *Inventing the Renaissance Putto* (Chapel Hill: University of North Carolina Press, 2001).

30 The use of *putti* in funerary art is studied in Jeannie Łabno, *Commemorating the Polish Renaissance Child: Funeral Monuments and Their European Context* (Farnham: Ashgate, 2011).

Chapter 6

1   Benjamin Disraeli (1804–81): his best known novels were *Sibyl* (1845) and *Endymion* (1880). He served as Prime Minister in 1868 and 1874–80.
2   Herodotus, *Histories*, II, 75 and III, 107-9.
3   Aelian, *On Animals,* 2, 3.
4   D. Woetzel, 'The Fiery Flying Serpent', *Creation Research Society Quarterly*, 42, (March 2006), pp.241–51.
5   R. P. Millett and J. P. Pratt, 'What Fiery Flying Serpent Symbolized Christ?', *Meridian Magazine*, (9 June, 2000). Other possible explanations for winged snakes include the posture adopted by a snake in agitation, or the wing-like appearance of a snakeskin in process of being shed.
6   On a copper snake found at Timna mines and the use of bronze, see J. Milgrom, *JPS Torah Commentary: Numbers* (Philadelphia: Jewish Publication Society, 1990), p.175.
7   Brown, Driver and Briggs, *Lexicon*, pp.976–7.
8   It should be noted, however, that the root of *Sharrabu* is *sh-r-v* rather than *s-r-f*.
9   Precise dating is difficult, but opinions range between 740 and 733 BCE.
10 As the translation variant used in the Roman rite makes clear, the 'whole earth' includes heaven.
11 *Paradise Lost*, VII, 198, though he uses a singular form for both cherub and seraph.
12 In accordance with the idea of a single straight leg, it is traditional to rise on tiptoe with legs tightly together.
13 Paul Woodruff, *Reverence: Renewing a Forgotten Virtue* (Oxford University Press, 2002), p.8.
14 See Chapter 7.
15 Tr. R. H. Charles, who dates this section to the early first century BCE.
16 For more on Lucifer, see Chapter 11.
17 Liturgical poem, translated by Raphael Loewe, *Ibn Gabirol* (London: Peter Halban, 1989), p.99. Gabirol follows the Aramaic rendering of *Psalms Targum* in making angels the singers of glory in Psalm 29:1-2.
18 Naomi Shemer, *Jerusalem of Gold*, 1967. This song achieved instant and lasting popularity, in Israel and beyond.

Chapter 7

1   The definite date does not stop scholars from arguing about the meaning of 'in the thirtieth year'. The most convincing explanation of this is that it occurred in the thirtieth year of a jubilee, a 50-year cycle, rather than in Ezekiel's thirtieth year, or any other thirtieth.
2   Babylonian Talmud, *Hagigah* 13b.
3   Other translations have beryl, chrysolite or topaz. I have mostly followed JPS here, but 'emerald' is from KJB, see Bibliography.
4   JPS translation.

5   One interpretation sees the whole vision in the context of authenticating Ezekiel as a prophet, through contact with the divine, like Isaiah. Wood, *Of Wings and Wheels*, p.134f.

6   Jewish mysticism became a subject of analytical study with Gershom Scholem's *Major Trends in Jewish Mysticism* (New York: Schocken Books, 1946). Moshe Idel noted two main branches, ecstatic and theosophical, with angels, of course, appearing in both. He explores a wide range of Kabbalistic texts, many brought to light for the first time. Among his many works, see *Absorbing Perfections: Kabbalah and Interpretation* (New Haven & London: Yale University Press, 2002). Rachel Elior notes the proliferation of names for God and angels and interprets it as a shift in belief from a single divine entity to a whole complex of divine forces: 'Mysticism, Magic and Angelology', *Jewish Studies Quarterly*, 1 (1993), pp.3–53, esp. p.34; see also Elior, *The Three Temples*. Elliot R. Wolfson, *Through a Speculum that Shines* (Princeton: Princeton University Press, 1994), examines the visual and imaginative elements of mysticism. For a clear review of current research, see Schäfer, *The Origins of Jewish Mysticism*. The most important early mystical texts are *Heikhalot Rabbati, Heikhalot Zutarti, Ma'aseh Merkavah, Merkavah Rabbah* and 3 Enoch.

7   Quoted in Schäfer, *Origins of Jewish Mysticism*, pp.265–6. This is at the time of the afternoon *Kedusha*. By contrast, at the morning *Kedusha* the angels cover their faces, and God's countenance is unveiled.

8   *Tosefta Hagigah* 2:3 (second century CE) and Babylonian Talmud, *Hagigah* 14b. For a thoughtful retelling of this tale, see Milton Steinberg, *As a Driven Leaf* (Indianapolis: Bobbs-Merrill Co, 1939; reprinted Aronson, 1987; Behrman House, 1996).

9   *Baal Shem Tov* means 'Master of the Good Name' or, more correctly, 'Good Master of the [Divine] Name', conferred as a title on the Ukrainian Rabbi Israel ben Eliezer, founder of the Hasidic movement.

10 Louis Jacobs, *Their Heads in Heaven* (Portland: Valentine Mitchell, 2005), p.60.

11 See John R. Martin, *The illustration of the Heavenly Ladder of John Climacus* (Princeton: Princeton University Press, 1954).

12 The Camaldolese hermits, founded in 1012, were a reformed branch of the Benedictine Order. For their presence in Florence, see Dennis F. Lackner, 'The Camaldolese Academy: Ambrogio Traversari, Marsilio Ficino and the Christian Platonic Tradition', in *Marsilio Ficino: his Theology his Philosophy, his Legacy*, ed. by M. J. B Allen and V. Rees (Leiden: Brill 2002), pp.15–44.

Chapter 8

1   Rossetti (1830–94) wrote this Christmas poem for *Scribner's Monthly* around 1870. It was set to music by both Gustav Holst (1906) and Harold Darke (1911) and adopted as a carol into the *English Hymnal*.

2   Thornton Wilder, *The Angel That Troubled the Waters, and Other Plays* (New York: Coward-McCann, 1928) p.147 ff.

3   *Ibid.*, p.149.

4   The memorial prayer *El molé rachamim* asks for shelter in the shadow of God's wings.

5   *Jubilees* 2:2. Other authorities ascribe the creation of angels to the second day of creation (*Pirke de Rabbi Eliezer* 2; *Zohar, Be-Reshit* 1:18b), or the fifth with other winged things (*Genesis Rabbah* 1:5). Augustine supports the first day, as does Ficino, who places their creation before time, but 'time' is a dimension introduced with the heavenly bodies, on day four.

6   Marshall, and Walsham, *Angels in the Early Modern World*, pp.27–8.

7   1 Enoch was compiled over a long period. The list of seven archangels dates from the earliest section (third century BCE) while the four-archangel list is from the part written last (first century BCE).

8   Jerusalem Talmud, *Rosh Hashana*, Ch. 1, p.56, col. 4, *halacha* 2. The names of the months were also from Babylon. Before becoming a scholar, Resh Lakish (*c.*200–75) was a notorious bandit. He is a great example for the principle that it is never too late to change one's ways, or to begin to study.

9   Vohu Mana, Asha Vahishta, Kshathra Vairyar, Spenta Armaiti, Haurvatat and Ameretat.

10   G. H. Dix, 'The Seven Archangels and the Seven Spirits: A Study in the Origin, Development and Messianic Associations of the Two Themes', *Journal of Theological Studies*, 28 (1926–7), pp.233–50.

11   2 Enoch 22. Dix uses the name Uriel here, although some versions have Pravuil or Vereveil, names that do not occur elsewhere.

12   *A Dictionary of Angels* (New York: Free Press, 1967, 1971; Simon & Shuster 1994).

13   In the Catholic and Eastern Orthodox traditions, both Gabriel and Raphael have at times also enjoyed the title of saint. All three have feast days appointed to them.

14   Its French predecessor, from around 1340, was the *angelot*, a word also used for 'cherub'. (This supports those who see Michael as guardian cherub of Eden.) The value of an English angel under Edward IV in 1465 was six shillings and eightpence (one third of a pound), but it rose later to eleven shillings.

15   JPS translation.

16   *Bava Metzia* 86b, and the Bible commentaries of Rashi and Rabbi Eleazar of Worms (*c.*1165–1230.)

17   *Pirke de R. Eliezer* 27.

18   Midrash, *Genesis Rabbah* 44:16; Talmud, *Bava Metzia* 86b; *Pirke de Rabbi Eliezer* 37; Targum ps.-Jonathan, on Genesis 32:25; Midrash, *Deuteronomy Rabbah* 11:6.

19   A twelfth-century icon of this episode at the Monastery of St Catherine at Sinai is illustrated in Glenn Peers, *Subtle Bodies. Representing Angels in Byzantium* (Berkeley: University of California Press, 2001), p.57.

20   For other Byzantine icons, there are two excellent exhibition catalogues: *Byzantium 330-1453*, ed. by Robin Cormack and Maria Vassilaki (London, Royal Academy of Arts, 2008) and *Byzantium. Faith and Power (1261-1557)*, ed. by Helen C. Evans (New Haven and London: Yale University Press, 2004).

21   In an intended parallel, it is the Angel Moroni who is said to have led Joseph Smith in 1823 to the Golden Plates on which his Book of Mormon was founded.

22 *Sahih al-Bukhari* (816–878 AD), 4:54:455.

23 See Konrad Eisenbichler, *The Boys of the Archangel Raphael: A Youth Confraternity in Florence, 1411-1785* (Toronto: University of Toronto Press, 1998).

24 S. Vickers, *Miss Garnet's Angel* (London: Fourth Estate, 2000; Harper Perennial 2008).

25 In a note to his poem *Israfel*, Poe claimed this was a Qur'an quotation, but it has not been found there. See Gustav Davidson, 'Poe's *Israfel*', *Literary Review* (Fairleigh Dickinson University), XII (1968), pp.86–91. The *Liber Israfel* compiled by the notorious Aleister Crowley is an occultist ritual handbook composed *c.*1912 and has no authority other than his own.

Chapter 9

1 Tylor (1832–1917) published seminal work on ancient and modern societies between 1861 and 1889; Frazer (1854–1941) wrote *The Golden Bough*, on mythology and religion, in 1890. Durkheim (1858–1917) wrote on many aspects of society including religion; Eliade (1907–86) and Couliano (1950–91) were both historians of culture and religion. See especially Couliano, *Out of this World: Otherworldly Journeys from Gilgamesh to Albert Einstein* (Boston: Shambhala, 1991).

2 NIV translation.

3 An earlier Enoch was the son of Cain (Genesis 4:17).

4 On the history and survival of the three versions, see Chapter 1, note 20.

5 Perhaps influenced by Slavonic e.g. *vera-v-el* 'belief in God'. Different recensions also record Pravuil, or Vretil in this role.

6 The Phoenix is usually considered singular, renewing itself in fire. See Chapter 2. There are some etymological grounds for relating the phoenix back to the ancient griffin. Chalkydri are thought to be bronze hydras or crocodiles, whose name may have been corrupted in transmission.

7 See Chapter 11.

8 Few writers have dared to describe a vision of the divine countenance. Enoch says: 'I saw the appearance of the Lord's face, like iron made to glow in fire and brought out, emitting sparks, and it burns. Thus (in a moment of eternity) I saw the Lord's face, but the Lord's face is ineffable, marvellous and very awful, and very, very terrible' (2 Enoch 22:1-2), translated by W. R. Morfill (1896).

9 See note 5 above.

10 *Jubilees* survived in Ethiopic, but then many Hebrew copies were found at Qumran.

11 In *Jubilees* 15:27, the two privileged classes of angels also share with humans the honour of circumcision, a claim which must sit awkwardly with those who claim that angels have no organs of generation.

12 This remarkable manuscript has been made available online at the Holy Russia site of the Ministry of Cultural Affairs of the Russian Federation: http://www.svyatayarus.ru/data/manuscripts/87_silvestrovskiy_sbornik. See p.351.

13 Cf. the angel Gabriel in Daniel 10:6.

14   See Andrei A. Orlov, 'The Pteromorphic angelology of the Apocalypse of Abraham', *Catholic Biblical Quarterly*, 71 (2009): 830–42 and reprinted in *Divine Manifestations in the Slavonic Pseudepigrapha* (Gorgias Press, 2009) pp.203–15. There are English translations of the *Apocalypse*, by Canon G. H. Box (1919), in *Old Testament Pseudepigrapha*, ed. J. H. Charlesworth (New York: 1983) vol. 1, pp.681–705, and by Alexander Kulik (2004).

15   Or six, in another recension.

16   The biblical book of Ezra recounts the return from Babylon and the re-establishment of religious life after the long exile. It is linked historically to the book of Nehemiah. The first book of Esdras is an expanded version of Ezra; books 2, 3, 4, 5 and 6 Esdras are all counted as pseudepigrapha, but bear some relation to the biblical texts of Ezra, Nehemiah and Chronicles. On 4 Ezra, see James R. Davila, *The Provenance of the Pseudepigrapha. Jewish, Christian or Other?* (Leiden: Brill, 2005) pp.137–41.

17   This includes the Eastern Orthodox, Armenian, Georgian, Syriac and Ethiopian churches.

18   *Shedim* are the 'devils' of Deuteronomy 32:17 and Psalm 106:37. The etymology of their name has been linked either to *shadad* (destruction) or to the Akkadian protective divinities (*shedu*). What protected an Akkadian was deemed hostile to an Israelite – though the name *El Shaddai*, 'God Almighty', may possibly come from a similar root. Scholars are not yet agreed. It is, however, agreed that provisions were made in traditional building regulations to allow an escape route for any *shedim* attached to the deceased owners of a house: in blocking up former window openings a small space should be left. See also pp.85–6 above.

19   Cf. 1 Corinthians 15:50-55. St Paul was writing not long before the probable date of 2 Baruch.

20   In 1886, a full text was discovered among papers in the Biblioteca Ambrosiana in Milan but this too was in Syriac (a form of Aramaic). It is thought that 2 Baruch was translated into Syriac through Greek, from a Hebrew original.

21   Tr. Daniel Matt, with minor adjustments.

22   In the original version of the *Mi'râj*, the prophet is first purified by Jibra'il and Mikha'il, then directly transported by Jibra'il to the lowest heaven. But early in Muslim history the ascenscion became associated with Muhammad's night journey and the two separate incidents were combined.

23   Sura al-Isra, 1: 'Glory be to (Allah) who took His servant on a night journey from the Sacred place of prayer to the Furthest place of prayer, the precincts of which We did bless, so that We may show him some of Our signs. Surely (Allah) is the All-Hearing, All-Seeing.'

24   His mystical poems have been translated many times. Especially sensitive are the versions of Robert Bly, for example, in *The Winged Energy of Delight* (New York: Harper Collins, 2004). See also the mystical poetry of Hafez and Kabir: Bly and Lewisohn, *The Angels Knocking at the Tavern Door: Thirty Poems of Hafez* (New York: Harper Perennial reprint, 2009); Bly, *Kabir: Ecstatic Poems* (Beacon Press; revised edn, 2004); Rabindranath Tagore's translation, *Songs of Kabîr* (New York: Macmillan, 1915) can be read on www.sacredtexts.com.

25   See especially the British Museum's *Papyrus of Ani* (*c.*1250 BCE), translated by Raymond Faulkner, with facsimile reproductions of illustrations originally

produced by Sir E. A. Wallis Budge (1890): *The Egyptian Book of the Dead*, ed. by James Wasserman (San Francisco: Chronicle Books, 1994).

26 A personal favourite is the 'Dialogue of a Man and his Soul' in *The Tale of Sinuhe and Other Ancient Egyptian Poems, 1940-1640 BCE*, edited by R. B. Parkinson (Oxford: OUP, 1997).

27 Homer, *Odyssey*, XI, 1-36.

28 Lucretius, *On the Nature of Things*, III, 978-1052.

29 Virgil, *Aeneid*, VI, 236-678. Virgil's Latin poetry is of incomparable beauty. English translations include those of W. F. Jackson Knight (Penguin, 1956), David West (Penguin, 1990) and C. Day Lewis (Oxford, 1966). H. R. Fairclough's version (Loeb Classical Library, 1916) still has value as it stays closer to the Latin text.

30 E.g. 1 Enoch 10:4-5.

31 Tr. Sayers and Reynolds.

32 First published in *The Book of Gems: the Poets and Artists of Great Britain*, edited by Samuel Carter Hall (London, 1836–8). The original for Abou ben Adhem is thought to be an eighth-century Persian prince who responded to repeated inner (angelic?) promptings and gave up his royal life to become a mystic.

33 Ann West, *Truth from the Source* (Hawaii: self-published, 2003), pp.114–24.

34 Pyrrho and Epicurus are known mainly through Sextus Empiricus and Lucretius. Axiochus's dialogue *On Death*, long thought to be a work of Plato, was translated by the poet Edmund Spenser (1592) and more recently by Jackson P. Hershbell (Chico, CA: Scholars Press, 1981).

Chapter 10

1 See Chapter 8.

2 This silver-mounted crystal, looks more like a viewing glass than a crystal ball. It is no longer on public display, after a theft from which it was eventually recovered. Marek Kohn, 'The Wellcome at 75', *Financial Times Magazine*, 24 September 2011. The crystal ball held by the British Museum may or may not have been Dee's, but the supports, inscribed discs, and obsidian mirror were.

3 Julian Roberts and Andrew Watson, *John Dee's Library Catalogue* (London: Bibliographical Society, 1990); Deborah Harkness, *John Dee's Conversations with Angels* (Cambridge: Cambridge University Press, 1999).

4 Part of Trithemius's system was understood by 1606, when the book appeared in print. But the last section resisted all efforts until recently. See Jim Reeds, 'Solved: The Ciphers in Book III of Trithemius's *Steganographia*', *Cryptologia*, 22/4 (1998), pp.291–317. Reeds acknowledges the parallel work of Thomas Ernst, 'Schwarzweiße Magie. Der Schlüssel zum dritten Buch der *Steganographia* des Trithemius', *Daphnis* 25 (1996), pp.1–205.

5 *Patrologia Graeca*, 337d-340a, discussed in Daniélou, *The Angels and their Mission according to the Fathers of the Church* translated by David Heimann (Notre Dame: Christian Classics, 1957; 1982), p.81.

6 Rashi, commentary on Genesis 32:25.

7 A midrash collection of the fifth or sixth century CE.

8   Quoted with kind permission of Rabbi Jonathan Wittenberg, from a commentary on *Vayishlach* (Genesis 32–36) written for *A Taste of Limmud*, 2006.

9   See the respective *Commentaries on the Torah* of Rashi, Nachmanides and Sforno, which are also cited at Genesis 32:30 in *The Soncino Chumash*, ed. by A. Cohen (London: Soncino Press, 1947, 1983).

10   For more on Dionysius see Chapter 2.

11   St Basil, *Homily* on Psalm 43; St John Chrysostom, *Homily* 3 on Colossians.

12   *Summa Theologica*, I.3.3-4, I.106:2, I.111:2 and I.108:7. Also 1.13.5.

13   St Aloysius Gonzaga, *Meditations*, quoted by Trevor Johnson in his study of 'Guardian angels and the Society of Jesus' in *Angels in the Early Modern World*, pp.195-7. Aloysius died young in 1591.

14   Francesco Albertini (1542–1619), *Trattato dell'Angelo Custode*, Rome and Naples, 1612, quoted by Johnson *ibid.*, pp.199–200.

15   Reported in Georges Huber, *My Angel will go before you*, tr. by Michael Adams (Dublin: Four Courts Press, 1983), p.18.

16   Huber, *My Angel will go before you*, pp.23 and 114.

17   David Levin, 'When Did Cotton Mather See the Angel?', *Early American Literature*, 15/3 (1980/1981), pp.271-5.

18   David Keck, *Angels and Angelology in the Middle Ages* (New York: Oxford University Press, 1998), p.164.

19   *Revelation of Moses*, B, 6-7. This pseudepigraphic text was previously thought to predate Christianity, but is now considered to contain many medieval elements.

20   Plato, *Cratylus*, 397-98; Hesiod, *Works and Days*, 121-26.

21   Plato, *Phaedo*, 107D.

22   Plato, *Republic*, X, 614-18. See also the less detailed account in Virgil's *Aeneid*, VI, 730-51.

23   Plato, *Timaeus*, 89 and 41. In 41-43, the lesser gods (whom later commentators would regard as angels) weave together the physical form of created beings, into whom God alone then breathes the living spirit.

24   Ficino, 'In Apologiam Socratis Epitome', *Opera Omnia*, p.1387.

25   Undated, but between 1484 and 1488.

26   Marsilio Ficino *Three Books on Life*, translated and edited by Carol V. Kaske and John R. Clark (Binghamton, NY: Medieval & Renaissance Texts & Studies) III, 23, esp. p.375. Ficino also discusses daemons in his commentary on *On Love*, VI, 4, *Platonic Theology* X, 2; *Letters*, vols 6, 9 and 10; vols 7, 29; his commentary on Plotinus, *Enneads*, III, 4-5 (not yet translated) and in many other places.

27   *On the Sun*, chapter 13. This chapter was originally written as a letter to Count Eberhard of Württemberg, around 1492 (*Letters*, Book XII, 2).

28   The sacred texts of the Zoroastrian tradition are thought to have been passed down orally from earliest times, taking written form in the third to fourth centuries CE, but there may have been an older written collection. There is a specific hymn to the guardian angels (*Frawardin Yasht*) in the ancient *Khorda Avesta* (Book of Common Prayer), as well as hymns to angels and archangels. A change in role may have developed in response to contact with Western religions. The term *fravahar* is usually taken to mean the symbol of a winged disc with a figure of wisdom, representing a *fravaši*, but it may be simply a Middle Persian variant of the older pre-Avestan term *fravaši*.

29 Linda Georgian, *Your Guardian Angels* (New York: Simon & Shuster, 1994). Her access to ibn Pakuda seems to be through Perle Epstein, *Kabbalah: The Way of the Jewish Mystic*. Ibn Pakuda is generally considered to be a rationalist philosopher rather than a Kabbalist. See Ibn Pakuda, *The Book of Direction to the Duties of the Heart* translated by Menahem Mansoor (Oxford: Littman Library, 1973 and 2004).

30 Sutherland, *In the Company of Angels* (Milson's Point, NSW: Random House, 2000; Dublin: Gateway, 2001).

31 Mallasz, *Talking with Angels*, Eisideln: Daimon Verlag, 1988 with further editions in 1992, 1998 and 2006.

32 Nahmad, *Your Guardian Angel: How to connect, communicate and heal with your own divine companion* (London: Watkins, 2007).

33 Cooper, *Invoking Angels for Blessings, Protection and Healing* (Boulder CO: Sounds True, 2006).

34 Yoxall and Currington, *Angels Heal my Body* (Aylesford, Kent: Diviniti Publishing, 2007).

35 For a substantial study of spiritual healing alongside the use of powerful herbs see, for example, Stanley Krippner and Patrick Welch, *Spiritual Dimensions of Healing: From Tribal Shamanism to Contemporary Health Care* (New York: Irvington Publishers, 1992).

36 A transcription of lectures by Steiner from 1908 to 1923, compiled by Margaret Jonas and translated by Pauline Wehrle (London: Rudolf Steiner Press, 2000).

37 Eugene G. Jussek, *Reaching for the Oversoul* (York Beach, ME: Nicholas-Hays, 1994), p.55.

38 C. G. Jung, *The Red Book: Liber Novus*, ed. Sonu Shamdasani (New York: Norton, 2009).

39 C. G. Jung, *Memories, Dreams, Reflections*, recorded and edited by Aneila Jaffé, translated by R. and C. Winston (New York: Pantheon, 1961), p.183.

40 John Geiger, *The Third Man Factor: Surviving the Impossible* (Edinburgh: Canongate, 2009). Geiger also co-authored *Frozen In Time: The Fate of the Franklin Expedition* with Owen Beattie (London: Bloomsbury, 1987) and, 'The Sensed Presence as a Coping Resource in Extreme Environments', with Peter Suedfeld, in Harold J. Ellens (ed.), *Miracles: God, Science, and Psychology in the Paranormal* (Westport CT & London: Praeger, 2008), vol. 3, pp.1–15.

41 Ernest Henry Shackleton, *South: The Endurance Expedition*, London: Heinemann and Penguin, 1919 and 1999), p.204.

42 See especially the account by the author himself, Arthur Machen, *The Angels of Mons. The Bowmen and Other Legends of the War* (London: Simpkin, Marshall & Co, 1915).

Chapter 11

1 NIV translation

2 In the Hebrew version, this serpent is clearly of the reptile variety: the word used is שָׁחָנ (*nahash*). Although some medieval Hebrew commentators identify the serpent with 'the tempter', others insist on the literal meaning.

3   St Augustine, *The Literal Meaning of Genesis*, XI, 13.

4   *Ibid.*, XI, 19.

5   The creation of men from mud and *jinn* from fire, and the refusal of Iblis to bow down like the angels, is also related in suras 15:26-34, 18:50 and 38:71-79.

6   Roman writers and archaeological finds confirm the practice of child sacrifice, though interpretation of the evidence varies. Eighteenth-century Bible illustrations of Moloch are explicit, but scholars still debate whether Moloch was a deity, a ritual or a terrible misunderstanding of language. To Milton, Moloch was chief of Satan's angels (*Paradise Lost*, I, 392-96).

7   This text was attributed to a Christian writer, Ephraim the Syrian (306–73). Translation by Sir E. A. Wallis Budge (London: Religious Tract Society, 1927).

8   See Jean Daniélou, *The Angels and Their Mission*, chapter 4.

9   A film adaptation of *Paradise Lost* has been announced by Alex Proyas. The suspense thriller made in 2007 under the same title is not an adaptation.

10   Beelzebub (more properly Beelzebul) was worshipped by the ancient Philistines. His name means 'Lord of the Flies'.

11   Leviathan, one of God's own creatures, is no more than a great sea-beast in the psalms but becomes the gatekeeper of hell in later literature. The most extensive description of Leviathan is in Job 41:1-34, where pride is his main characteristic. See also Isaiah 27:1 and Psalms 74:14 and 104:26.

12   JPS translation.

13   The length of an ell has varied from place to place, but a giant of 3,000 ells would probably be the size of a mountain.

Chapter 12

1   Quoted in Weinberger, *Jewish Hymnography*, p.310.

2   'Vengeance is mine, and recompense', Deuteronomy 32:35. See also Psalm 94:1-2; Micah 5:15; Romans 12:19.

3   Locke, *An Essay Concerning Human Understanding* (London: 1690), II, xxvii, 22.

4   *Midrash Tanhuma*; *Berakhot* 4b; *Pirke de Rabbi Eliezer* 13.

5   Talmud, *Avodah Zarah* 20b.

6   Both these tales are in Talmud tractate *Kethuvoth* 77b.

7   Midrash, *Petirat Moshe*, from the seventh century. See also Chapter 8 above. Talmud, *Bava Batra* 17a names not only Moses as being taken from life by a kiss but also Abraham, Isaac and Jacob, and Moses's siblings, Aaron and Miriam.

8   From the Naqshbandi order of Sufism.

9   Virgil, *Aeneid*, IV, 693-705.

10   The Greek god Hermes was adopted by the Romans as identical with their own god Mercury. Aspects of the Egyptian Toth were later added to his attributes.

11   Sir Richard Burton, *The Book of the Thousand Nights and one Night* (London: The Burton Society 1885–8), slightly abbreviated. The core parts of this compilation date back to the eighth century, supplemented with a continual stream of later additions. Many of the tales are Persian or Indian in origin, but were transmitted in Arabic translation.

12 *Patrologia Latina* 9, 879c, Commentary on Psalm 148. Quoted in Daniélou, *The Angels and their Mission*, pp.112–13.

13 This would also apply to religious traditions which focus primarily on ethical considerations rather than redemption, such as Taoism, Confucianism and Shinto.

14 Hystaspes was the name of an early follower of Zoroaster.

15 Robert Forsyth (1766–1846) was a would-be minister in the Church of Scotland, and an advocate. His *Principles of Moral Science* (Edinburgh: Longmans, 1805) was the subject of an unfavourable essay in the influential *Eclectic Review* in 1807. The review carries no author's name, but the editor at the time was the non-conformist Daniel Parken.

16 Discussed in Chapter 2.

Epilogue

1 P. Tillich, *Dynamics of Faith* (London: Allen & Unwin, 1957).

2 The transcript of that programme is published in Melvyn Bragg, *In Our Time* (London: Hodder & Stoughton, 2009), pp.489–509. It can also be heard on the BBC website, http://www.bbc.co.uk/programmes/p003k9gf.

3 The friend who had urged us to go and find him told us no more than his name, and that he would look after us. As it turned out, he was a bodyguard of the Dalai Lama and our friend had sponsored the daughter's education – but we knew none of this beforehand.

4 Isaiah 6:3.

5 John Allitt, *The Magic Mirror*, p.58, quoting Cecil Collins.

BIBLIOGRAPHY

Many general and specialist works were consulted in the making of this book and the most important have already been included either in the text or in the notes. This section therefore offers only some information on versions of particular works, and a short list of suggested further reading accessible to the general reader.

For quotations from the Bible, I have in general followed the King James Version (KJV) out of affection for its magnificent language and rhythm, but where later versions were more helpful in clarifying the meaning I have used those instead, and have indicated where I have done so. JPS is the 1917 translation of the Jewish Publication Society. RSV is the Revised Standard Version of 1952. NIV is the New International Version (1978). KJB is The Koren Jerusalem Bible of 1998. I have also consulted the Anchor Bible and other modern versions, especially for their commentaries. Occasionally verse numbers vary between versions, especially in the Psalms. In simple references I give the KJV number.

The Vulgate is the Latin Bible, originally translated by Jerome, though it has been amended at various times. The Septuagint was the first Greek translation carried out between the third and first centuries BCE). According to legend, 72 Jewish translators were enlisted in Alexandria, and were kept apart from one another but each produced an identical translation (Babylonian Talmud, *Megillah* 9).

For the Apocrypha, Pseudepigrapha and Talmudic sources, quotations have been taken from English translations old or new, as available.

For the Qur'an I have generally used Arthur J. Arberry's version, *The Koran Interpreted* (London: Allen & Unwin, 1955; Oxford: Oxford University Press, 1964 and several later reprints). Verse numbers in this edition sometimes vary from other Qur'an texts.

One valuable resource which has not yet been referred to is a collection of recent research, *Angels. The Concept of Celestial Beings – Origins, Development and Reception* (Deuterocanonical and Cognate Literature Yearbook) edited by Friedrich V. Reiterer, Tobias Nicklas, Karin Schöpflin (Berlin: Walter de Gruyter, 2007).

Selected Further Reading

Original sources

Original texts are by far the best place to start. Besides the Bible and Qur'an, pre-eminent among these are:

The Book of Tobit (Apocrypha).

The Book of Enoch (1 Enoch, or *The Ethiopic Book of Enoch*), translated by R. H. Charles, with an introduction by W. O. E. Oesterley (London: SPCK, 1917) and reprints.

The Hebrew Book of Enoch (3 Enoch) edited and translated by Hugo Odeberg (Cambridge: Cambridge University Press, 1928).

The Book of Jubilees, translated by R. H. Charles (London: SPCK, 1917), reprinted with new material (San Diego: The Book Tree, 2003).

The Gnostic Bible, edited by Willis Barnstone and Marvin Myer (Boston & London: Shambhala, 2003).

Much Talmudic and Midrashic literature is now available in translation, as, for example in the multi-volume series of the Soncino editions of the *Babylonian Talmud*, the *Midrash Tanhuma* and *Midrash Rabbah* (New York: Soncino Press).

Plotinus, *Enneads*, translated by Stephen MacKenna, revised by B. S. Page, 4th edition (London: Faber, 1969).

Augustine, *City of God*, translated by Henry Bettenson (London: Penguin 1984).

Dionysius, *The Celestial Hierarchy* in *The Complete Works of Pseudo-Dionysius* translated by Colm Luibheid (New York: Paulist Press, 1987).

Maimonides, *The Guide for the Perplexed*, translated by M. Friedländer (London: George Routledge, 1904; New York: Dover Publications, 1972; Kegan Paul, 2006).

——*The Guide of the Perplexed*, translated by Shlomo Pines with Introduction by Leo Strauss, 2 volumes (Chicago: University of Chicago Press; 1963 and 1974).

Aquinas, *Selected Writings*, translated by Ralph McInerny (London: Penguin, 1998).

The Zohar is hard to read without some expert guidance, but is available in two versions:

——*The Wisdom of the Zohar, an Anthology of Texts*, edited by Fischel Lachower and Isaiah Tishby, translated by David Goldstein (Oxford: The Littman Library of Jewish Civilization, 1989 and reprints).

——*The Zohar*, translation and commentary by Daniel C. Matt (Stanford: Stanford University Press, 2004–).

Marsilio Ficino, *Platonic Theology*, translated by Michael J. B. Allen and edited by James Hankins, 6 volumes, I Tatti Renaissance Library (Cambridge MA: Harvard University Press, 2001–06).

——*The Letters of Marsilio Ficino*, translated by members of the Language Department of the School of Economic Science, 8 volumes to date (London: Shepheard-Walwyn, 1975–2009, continuing).

Theology and Church History

Peter Brown, *The World of Late Antiquity: AD 150-750* (London: Thames & Hudson, 1989).
——*The Rise of Western Christendom: triumph and diversity, 200-1000 A.D.* (Oxford: Wiley-Blackwell; 2nd edition, 2002).
Henry Chadwick, *The Penguin History of the Church: The Early Church* (London: Penguin, 1967).
Jean Daniélou, S. J. *The Angels and their Mission According to the Fathers of the Church*, translated by David Heimann (Notre Dame: Christian Classics, 1957).
Robin Lane Fox, *Pagans and Christians in the Mediterranean World* (London: Viking, 1986; Penguin, 2006).
Louis Jacobs, *Jewish Mystical Testimonies* (New York: Schocken Books, 1977).
David Keck, *Angels and Angelology in the Middle Ages* (New York & Oxford: Oxford University Press, 1998).

Literary sources

Dante Alighieri, *The Divine Comedy*, 3, *Paradise*, translated by Dorothy L. Sayers and Barbara Reynolds (London: Penguin, 1962 and reprints).
John Milton, *Paradise Lost*, 1667 (London: Penguin Popular Classics, 1996).

Angel Art

Charles Dempsey, *Inventing the Renaissance Putto* (Chapel Hill: University of North Carolina Press, 2001).
Erika Langmuir: *Angels* (London: National Gallery, 1999 and reprints).
Gilles Nérert, *Angels* (Cologne: Taschen, 2004).
Glenn Peers, *Subtle Bodies. Representing Angels in Byzantium* (Berkeley & Los Angeles: University of California Press, 2001).
Linda Proud, *Angels* (Andover: Pitkin, 2006).

General

Gustav Davidson, *Dictionary of Angels*, New York, 1967.
George J. Marshall, *Angels. An Indexed and Partially Annotated Biblio-graphy of Over 4300 Scholarly Books and Articles since the 7ʰ Century BC* (Jefferson NC: McFarland, 1999).
Larry Richards, *Every Angel in the Bible* (Nashville: Thomas Nelson, 1997).

INDEX

References in **bold** indicate major points in the text